Fu@k Fibro

One Woman's Two-finger Salute to Chronic Illness

Marie Paddington-Chivers

ISBN 978-1-9162230-0-4

Disclaimer.

This publication contains the opinions and ideas of the author. It is intended to provide helpful and informative material on the subjects within the publication. It is sold with the understanding that the author and publisher are not engaged in rendering medical, health, psychological, or any other kind of personal professional services. If the reader requires personal medical, health, or other assistance or advice, a competent professional should be consulted.

The author and publisher specifically disclaim all responsibility for any liability, loss, or risk, personal or otherwise that is incurred as a consequence, directly or indirectly of the use or application of any of the content within this book.

For Ian

In it together

Contents

INTRODUCTION

Firstly, if you're on the sensitive side and the title of this book offends you in some way then sorry, not sorry. Why? Because Fibromyalgia is a complete fuck, it 100% fucks with your Mind, your Body, and your Soul. It's a sneaky, brutal, and seemingly unrelenting condition. It does its damnedest to steal your life and the drain the very essence of you – I think it thoroughly deserves to be shown the door with a two- finger salute!

Before we go any further let's address some expectations you might be having when opening this book. Let me start by telling you what this book is not. If you're expecting to read this and unearth some kind of quick-fix magic wonder cure, then this is not the book for you. This is not a "copy me and you'll be free from fibro" kind of thing. I know, disappointing huh? - sorry about that, but bear with me for a moment.

The reason that I won't be making such promises or giving you a "get out of fibro jail free" card is that I have a strong belief that as individuals we are unique in our fibro/illness experiences. This is exactly why it makes it so hard for me to tell you that doing things the exact way I did them will 100% make you better. However, evidence points to the fact that with this diagnosis we share many commonalities, and because of that there is a very good chance that stuff written here in this book will be a good fit for you too.

Within these pages, there is also some basic foundational things that I know will improve anyone's health regardless. Therefore, there will be certain things that I will suggest you give a go or challenge you to consider. There will be times where I write in a more directive way because I know from my previous life as a counsellor and my research into healing that a lot of this is shit that works.

This book has been written because I honestly believe that given the right set of conditions and with the right amount of work, the vast majority of people can experience healing of some sort and start to reclaim their life. To what degree that will be is always going to be uncertain; again, it depends on the individual and the variables of their life. There's no doubt that healing yourself will take commitment and some tweaking to find what works just right for you, but I am confident you can find it and you can begin to heal.

What you'll find in these pages is my story of how after getting nowhere with standard fibromyalgia treatments, I decided to ditch conventional medicine and heal myself through a natural holistic approach. It's an honest account of how I believe I came to find myself slapped with the fibro label (my route to illness), and a compilation of everything I have done to date to overcome symptoms and get myself back on track.

Everything that I write about in this book is what I have learned on my journey: all the stuff that enabled me to heal and what helps me to maintain my health. I have been encouraged to write this book by those around me who have witnessed my recovery from a debilitating and bizarre spectrum of health issues. A journey that has seen me go from a pained, brain fogged, too-fatigued-to-get-dressed kind of gal to road tripping around the US and more – something I never thought would be possible.

This book is for others who currently find themselves wearily trudging along the fibro path and who are at their wit's end. I wrote it because it saddens me to know that there are so many people out there who have been given this diagnosis and have been led to believe that there is no hope of recovery.

I know what it's like to feel that level of hopelessness, to think that your life is a write-off, but I also know that is not entirely true. Today, I live a good life, free from the constant pain and the crazy symptoms. I am once again able to embrace the spontaneity that seems to vanish from life when a long-term illness strikes. I am defying the diagnosis day by day, year by year and I truly believe others can too. This book is something that I wished I'd had access to when I was trying to figure out how the hell I was going to get myself out of the mess illness had made of my life.

Sometimes this book pulls no punches. I'm a straight talker, a bit of a curser, therefore there will the odd contentious moment in this book that may challenge you or piss you off. Feel free to feel it! At the end of the day, this is just my opinion and my experiences, you are free to get on board with them or dismiss them - that is your prerogative, but I truly hope you get something useful from these pages.

My main aim throughout this book is to get you to think, perhaps consider a different perspective, look at your thought patterns, habits, and behaviours so that you can identify the areas of your life where making changes could help you to move forward into better health.

By writing this book and sharing my journey, I hope to inspire and encourage you to take responsibility for your own health. To explore healing naturally using a holistic approach or to consider using it in combination with the conventional. I want you to gain trust that your body, when treated as a whole, has an amazing natural ability to heal. I hope this book will help guide you, provide you with some ideas, and with luck, plant a seed of determination within you that will spark a desire to help yourself overcome illness.

I am aware that in comparison to the length of time that I was sick, it could be argued that this healthier state that I am now in is relatively in its infancy. That may lead some people to question its sustainability; is it just a temporary reprieve? I'm not going to lie to you, I can't answer that question, simply because I can't foresee the future or how my health will be from here on in - who can? But for now, I am content for my progress to be described as a reversal of symptoms and more than happy to be enjoying my new healthier life.

While I'm not making any noises about being fully cured, I am going to shout from the rooftops about a holistic approach to health because the path I have chosen to follow has, so far, hands down beaten the conventional methods. I believe my results speak for themselves. I have been able to turn things around and enjoy a better quality of life and for me, that is good enough.

I am content in my belief that I am defying a chronic illness diagnosis. I know that I can still increase my level of health (who can't), but judging by the progress I have made so far and the level at which I am able to live my life, I am in no doubt that a natural approach is a sound option. Even though on a day-to-day basis I feel good, I know that I still have layers to peel away, there are still areas I can improve on, and I think there will always be. Life In general is in a constant state of flux and I don't think health is an exception to that rule. There will be other health concerns and challenges that arise through different stages of my life and I accept that, however, I feel confident that I can get past them too.

Healing is not a linear process; it can be a backward and forward kind of thing and sometimes more than a bit messy. There is always room for more exploration and improvements. As we peel back the layers, at times we may feel worse before we feel better, but isn't that how it goes for a lot of things in life? Life is a work in progress, challenges will arise, there is always room for more or something different. In terms of healing, there will always be a greater level of health to be achieved. Healing and then remaining in that state is like a relationship, it requires maintenance and work in order to be able to fully to reap the benefits.

In the holistic world, there is no set timescale for healing. It's different for everyone, but the general consensus is that it takes years for you to become unhealthy, so it's going to take months or maybe years to get you out of that state. If you take into consideration that many people in today's world inherit imbalances and a less than stellar nutritional status from their parents pretty much from the point of conception, then the journey to regain health is not going to be a quick fix. It's a sad fact, but a person's health clock can be set ticking from birth before manifesting as illness later in life.

I know, I know, that's probably not what you want to hear, but healing holistically is a reversal of the process that caused us to become ill in the first place; healing that involves the total reintegration of all our parts so that they can begin to work in synergy.

When healing holistically, we are asking our body to realign and reverse many things that have probably been out of kilter for years alongside addressing other areas of our lives to create a healthy state of being, and that takes time. As the quote goes, "What comes easy won't last long and what lasts long won't come easy."

It may seem more than a little daunting to think that you potentially have years of healing ahead of you, but believe me, it's a damn sight better than treading water with a bunch of crazy symptoms for the rest of your days. It's better than sitting around waiting for someone to fix this thing. Being proactive is empowering and inspiring, it will bring purpose, focus, and hope back into your life. It will help you to feel more in control. Something that you have more than likely discovered for yourself is that illness takes a lot of control away from you. Once you start on this journey you will be surprised that sometimes just making the smallest of adjustments can have powerful results.

I know that when you've been diagnosed as suffering from this condition you dream that someone will have the answer, will tell you exactly what you need to do to fix things or give you some kind of secret formula that will magically restore you to your former glory. Wouldn't that be amazing! But here's the thing - it totally sucks, but as I stated earlier, I'm not going to be that person. I won't be making the claim that what I share with you within these pages about my own healing journey will be your holy grail.

The bottom line is a condition can have many different causes that manifest in the same symptoms and receive the same diagnosis. The reason I don't have the answers to your individual health issues is because we all have different biochemistry and I am not you. We may well have many things in common but may also have different causative factors/root causes of illness. Simply put, if I claim to be able to heal you, I would be a big fat pants-on-fire liar who is taking advantage of you. So, I'm going to stick with giving you a helping hand and telling you that you can heal too.

The fact that we are all unique in our experiences is why I believe conventional fibro treatment doesn't work too well for a lot of people. It is simply just too standardised. A one-size approach is never going to work because we need to be treated as individuals with unique systems and we need treatment plans that are tailored to meet our specific needs. Yes, there will be many modalities that will work well for a lot of us and there will, of course, be people who can help us to explore different options, but ultimately we need to discover for ourselves what works best for us - believe it or not, you are your own expert, you just need to give yourself the chance to step into that role.

So, I guess, having just read the above, you may be wondering if there are any merits to what's on offer here. You might be having some growing doubts about picking up this book. Perhaps you're thinking, "Wtf is the point of reading this if it's not going to tell me what to do?" Well, let me ask you this...

Would it not be worth taking the leap? If I'm right, you've already lost a whole heap of things from your life, things are already more than a bit fucked up for you, so why not try something different? Why not give taking responsibility for your own health a go?

I may not be able to give you the exact answers to your individual health puzzle, but what I can give you is a starting point, some suggestions, things to get you thinking, some avenues to consider exploring, and encouragement to seek your own path back to health. I can help you to help yourself to try and kick your illness to the curb and regain a zest for life.

During the last few years, one thing I have learned in this healing game is that it only takes one phrase, one pointer, one idea, to set you on the right path, to inspire and encourage you enough to look into something deeper, and from that point you can begin to take steps forward. Surely that must be better than continuing to live in a fibro limbo?

One thing that I am confident in saying to you is that should you choose to pursue the holistic approach to improve your health, you will be taking a proactive step towards putting yourself firmly back in the driver's seat of your life. This one step alone will empower you. It will help you to set yourself onto the path of start trusting in yourself and your body again and to know what is right for you. Taking the Mind, Body, and Soul approach to your health WILL without a doubt lead you to some kind of positive change and progress.

One reason I have written this book is that when I set out to heal myself, most of the time, I felt like I was shooting in the dark. It was a very lonely, rocky road of trial and error - a lot of error! If I'd had a book like this to use as a rough guide, I think I could have cut down on the vast amount of time I spent going around in circles trying to figure out my next step. This book is intended to be that rough guide, a guide for others wanting to take their healing into their own hands. It is something that I hope will plant a seed of curiosity in you, something you can run with that will inspire you to go on to discover what exactly what works for you.

In part 1 of this book, I write about all the factors that came into play which pushed me to the point of ill health, alongside the process I went through before and after diagnosis before turning to a holistic approach. I have included it in my writing because I want to convey how important I feel it is to fully understand all the contributory factors that are involved in a route to illness. Discovering your personal route will help you to identify what you need to work on.

I also want what's written in these pages to demonstrate that you don't always have to take the things that you're told at face value, that you have the right to question your treatment, the management of this condition, and most certainly the prognosis. You have the right to take your healing into your own hands. In fact, that is pretty much the premise of this entire book!

Reflecting on my personal history has helped me to gain awareness of how my own life experiences and consequently my reactions to them were instrumental in my ending up with a fibromyalgia diagnosis. Exploring my past has enabled me to uncover patterns in my life and to understand exactly how I reached a crisis point.

More importantly, it has taught me how to free myself from the habits and unhelpful patterns of behaviour that were continuing to drive illness. By writing about my earlier life, I want to encourage you to reflect on your own route to illness and discover the signposts and patterns that will help you to make useful connections between the past and your current situation. Understanding our past helps us to make sense of our present and helps us to create a healthier future.

Through this journey of mine, I have come to learn that when we understand all the elements aside from just the physical that are involved in the development of an illness, it is far easier to identify the areas that we need to work on. Be it our relationships, our reactions, or behaviours; awareness of these aspects helps us to avoid the same pitfalls in the future. Simply put - if we don't understand both the external and internal factors of how we got to be where we are with an illness, then how can we know to make the necessary changes to get ourselves out of it? The same goes for questioning. If we never question ourselves or what others are telling us, how will we know for sure something is the right path for us?

I'm not going to judge anyone who is currently on the conventional path, but if this is you, two questions I would like you to ask yourself are: are you willing to follow one method of treatment and management just because it's the only option that has been offered to you? And what could you gain from trying something different?

I encourage you to ask yourself these questions because questioning and researching have been my saviours and the things that have enabled me to start to take back control of my health. I believe that questioning our past and current situations, exploring alternative methods, can lead to more insight and potential options and that can only be a good thing.

It is also my belief that understanding ourselves on a deeper level enables us to build a stronger foundational pillar. This helps to underpin any work we do and can lead us to a greater level of health and progress. We all have our own life puzzle made up of variously shaped pieces. Some are of own making, others we may have inherited, some are a good fit, others not so much. Sometimes we're not aware of how we even got to have some of our pieces. Identifying what pieces are useful to us and what would be better for us to disregard or work on letting go of can go a long way in helping us heal.

Of course, my story, my route to illness won't be yours. As you read this book you may think, "My life was/is nothing like that." Then again, you just might recognise a little of yourself in my experiences, who knows! But what I hope you will gain from reading it is a desire to investigate your own life story, to put together the pieces that will help you to look at your bigger picture and make the connections that may have contributed or are still contributing to your own health challenges. I hope it will give you the courage to start questioning where you're at and where you could get to, by taking on the responsibility for your own healing.

Please note that although I haven't referenced this book page to page, there are articles, research papers, and the like in the "Resources & Notes" section at the back of the book that support what's written in this book. Feel free to check them out if you wish to do your own research, or just use them to check out that I'm not talking complete BS.

PART 1: CHAPTER 1

WHERE IT ALL BEGAN

I don't see my route to ill health as starting with the onset of symptoms. Of course, that was the point where I started to sit up and take notice, but it wasn't the start. No. The symptoms were just my body's way of frantically signalling that I was fast reaching the end of the road of life as I knew it.

To go back to its conception, I needed to look back much further to pinpoint where things started out, where the seeds of ill health were first sown. From the work and research I have done in trying to regain my health, it is now my belief that those seeds came from a combination of inherited imbalances coupled with emotional stress and trauma that were years in the making. It was this deadly combination that formed the foundations of illness which led me to develop other conditions that eventually resulted in a fibromyalgia diagnosis.

It was a combination that went unnoticed and unchecked for a long period of time, way before my body started to raise red flags to draw attention to the fact that my whole being was in trouble. Looking back through the years, I can see my susceptibility to chronic illness first had its roots planted back in my childhood. My diagnosis at the age of 37 years old was just the final confirmation that I had passed the tipping point. That the wheels had well and truly come off my health wagon. The official diagnosis might have been the point where I received confirmation of illness, but it certainly wasn't where it all began.

Rewinding back to my early years, I wasn't an unhappy child. In fact, if you were to ask those who knew me at a young age, they would more than likely describe me as a mix of boisterousness, funny, and cheeky - definitely cheeky! And a lot of the time, I was a genuinely a happy little person. However, it wasn't until I was an adult that I realised that I had often used my bubbliness and sense of humour as a mask to hide behind and a coping mechanism to diffuse some of the angry tense moments in my life that inwardly caused me to feel unstable, anxious, and upset.

As a child, I took on the responsibility of making uncomfortable situations feel okay again by using humour as a deflection - making jokes and acting the fool to lighten the mood. Later on in life it became a form of protection, using those aspects of my personality to minimise and deflect from the enormity of the traumatic events that I was threatened by.

As physical illness goes, I didn't suffer from anything particularly out of the norm for your average child, but I have been told and can recall that common childhood illness hit me hard. Also, from as early as I can remember right up until the age of 30, I struggled with regular bouts of tonsillitis - Anyone who has read Louise Hay's book, You Can Heal Your Life, and understands her principles behind the manifestation of physical ailments will know that it wasn't a coincidence that these recurrences stopped when I finally found my voice and felt confident to able to speak freely.

I know that at an early age, I outwardly came across as a confident and an extroverted child, but the reality was this blasé, cheery nature was a cover-up for an inner oversensitivity and an ever-growing feeling of not being good enough. I was an extremely sensitive child, an over-thinker who took everything to heart and didn't cope at all well with the expressions of anger. The combination of my sensitivities and the short fuse of a fiery parent was at times a recipe for emotional overload, which would often leave me feeling wobbly, tense, and uncertain of how to be or act.

From this, I developed a habit of internalising a lot of my emotions, never speaking out how I really felt inside; a habit that I would carry through into my adult life and one that would over the years build layers and layers of frustration, resentment, anger, and hurt. I am convinced that these layers of what I see as "stuck" emotions were contributory factors in my developing an illness. In hindsight, after tracking back how I came to be ill, it's now obvious how years of chronic emotional stress can lead to a diagnosis of a chronic illness. They are as connected as if they were family; if you like, emotional stress can be a parent of illness.

As a young person, my emotional stressors came from my internal responses and reactions to angry confrontations. My sense of dread surrounding emotionally charged situations meant that I spent a lot of time inwardly on edge. I became watchful, tuned in, and on high alert for any changes in mood or flashes of anger that the wrong word or behaviour might cause. There were many times when I would feel confused as to what part I could have played in the onset of an angry outburst. I often had the feeling that I was walking on eggshells, afraid that somehow, I might be responsible for "rocking the boat" if I said what I was thinking or expressed how I truly felt. I began to sit on the things I really wanted to say, the things I wanted to do, squashing them down in case they caused problems.

I don't know if it's because I held a lot of inner tension, but I can recall that when I was younger I often felt very tired, far more tired than someone of my age should be feeling. As a teenager I struggled to stay awake longer than 9 p.m. - It wasn't until I had teens of my own that I realised how atypical of teenage behaviour this was! From the time of puberty I also use to experience daily headaches and sore, tender muscles.

As I grew older, developed and formed my own opinions of my world and the people around me, the feeling of not being able to be free to speak out began to intensify, leaving me with more than the average teenage angst and frustrations. By sitting on my thoughts and suppressing my emotions I felt trapped within myself. I can recall filling up with intense anger and hurt at feeling as if I didn't have a voice. Because my opinions and thoughts were often different than my parent, I knew that if I took the risk to express my point of view it would more than likely be met with anger or dismissal - leaving me feeling like I didn't have anywhere to go with my thoughts or opinions.

At the times when it just became impossible to keep my thoughts or feelings to myself any longer, it would invariably lead to raised voices and arguments. By this stage of my life, I had also experienced bullying because of the way I looked (ginger hair), which over a period of a couple of years had slowly ground me down and placed me under continual emotional stress. Again it was something I internalised and never spoke to anyone about.

It is these experiences from my earlier years that I feel were the first steppingstones to building an illness pathway. When the emotional issues I developed in my childhood converged with the prolonged emotional trauma I experienced later in my life, it eventually led to the manifestation of physical illness.

Now, before I go any further, I want to make it clear that I don't sign up to the "my parents fucked up my life" way of thinking. Any experience we have in life, good or bad, has the power to shape and influence our lives in so many ways. My own experience, my perception of my earlier years is what it is, and I am certainly not laying blame at anyone's door. I have many, many happy memories and experiences from my childhood. My drawing of conclusions and mapping out of what I see as the connections between my emotional experiences as a child with sickness later in my life are simply that - a connection.

By making this connection I have been able to understand how being the type of person I was and my internal reactions to certain situations throughout my childhood created emotional stressors that stuck with me and shaped my self-image. It is a recognition that the sensitivities I was born with meant I was less emotionally robust than some and therefore more deeply affected on an emotional level than maybe the next person.

A combination of my sensitive personality and the, at times, volitile home environment led me to develop a fragile sense of self, a lack of worth and low self-esteem; all of which would later influence my personal relationships and lead me to enter a prolonged and far more damaging period in my life.

In my late teens, events were set in motion that would cause deep and lasting damage to my emotional wellbeing. When 16 years old, I made the terrible decision to hitch my wagon to the very first train that promised to spirit me away from the angry clashes at home. Unfortunately for me, that ill-fated decision meant that my ticket out led me into a long-term relationship with a partner who was an abusive alcoholic; a true case of "out of the frying pan and into the fire."

As you can probably imagine, this relationship was anything but plain sailing, and throughout this time the emotional stress ramped up exponentially. Like many millions of other abused women, I stayed because I couldn't see a way out. I coped day to day. I hid behind a mask of denial, deflection, and even sometimes humour, internalising my feelings to the point that I became desensitised to all the awful things happening to and around me.

Over the years that I was in that relationship, I developed an incredible amount of resilience and adaptive behaviour. I learned to think on my feet and to adapt almost instantaneously to the slightest changes in behaviour. I became hyper-vigilant and chameleon-like, constantly changing my views, expressions, outer personality, and behaviour to fit whatever situation arose. I didn't know from one situation to the next who I was supposed to be. It was a physically and mentally exhausting period of my life. I existed in such a constant state of flight or fight mode that it is no wonder that as time went on my body struggled to maintain balance.

The sheer amount of energy required to stay alert, to second-guess situations, and to invent plausible excuses to keep the humiliating truth from people meant that it felt like I was constantly running on empty. Most of the time my own needs didn't enter the equation, as just getting through one crisis to the next took precedent, and later the need to shield my children from my experiences became paramount.

In a period of life (from teens to twenties) that is typically meant to be formative, confidence-building, and filled with self-exploration, I was just surviving. There was simply no space for self-love or positive personal growth. Time passed in a whirl of believing the okay times might just last and surviving the fallout when my partner's triggers inevitably shattered the peace.

During this part of my life, I very much felt like a nonperson. I did what I had to do to stay safe whether I wanted to or not, and this took me further and further away from who I really was. I had become so conditioned into believing that what I had in life was as good as I could get that it didn't cross my mind to think I could do better or develop enough self-care to realise that my future health was in jeopardy from all the stress.

When I look back on this time, I can see how the repeated stressful events and constant underlying unhappiness developed into physical illness. It wasn't until nearly 10 years had passed, when I was 25 years old, that something finally ignited a spark, creating a pivotal moment in my life where I finally drew a line in the sand.

During one particularly awful incident I heard a voice in my head (that wasn't my own) telling me (well actually, shouting at me) that if I didn't get out of this relationship, I was literally putting my life at risk. Call it instinct, divine intervention, or whatever, but I had finally reached my saturation point. I had a moment of clarity where I realised that by staying in this relationship, I was constantly de-valuing myself and creating a relationship "blueprint" for my children that was dysfunctional and damaging. From that moment on our future security and wellbeing became my priority and the catalyst for change, finally giving me the courage to say, "Enough is enough," and make my escape.

As anyone who has been through a difficult relationship break-up knows, the subsequent stress can be immense. You will know that although leaving a shitty relationship can bring a huge sense of relief, it is often just the beginning of another period of turbulence and upheaval.

For the first year following my breakup I acted like Superwoman - I got a car, a job, a mortgage, I was Miss Independent with a capital "I" – Destiny's Child "Independent Woman" was my anthem... need I say more? I weathered the fury and fallout from my ex-partner, then just as the storm seemed to be abating and I could finally see the light at the end of the tunnel, I completely and utterly fell apart.

In all intent and purposes, I was now free to be my own person, but I discovered I didn't know how to be me. I didn't know who "me" was. Having spent such a formative period of my life being someone else's something and turning myself into god knows what to please, there was little sense of self left. This was so unsettling and destabilising that despite the initial joy and relief I had felt at being able to be with my children in a safe environment, I bottomed out with depression, stress, and anxiety.

Once more I reverted to type, I switched on the autopilot version of me, on went the mask, and every day I got up and went to work pretending I was okay. I would say hello with a smile to colleagues while inwardly feeling floored, depleted, and contemplating suicide.

During this time, I had a brief and disastrous first session with a counsellor who told me I should be feeling much better now things were "looking up" for me. It felt like a complete dismissal of my experience and the intensity of my feelings. As if I wasn't entitled to feel the way I did, that I had somehow failed at making a break because I wasn't doing cartwheels with happiness. After what I now call the "counselling fuckup," I didn't try to speak my truth or use my voice any more than I had in the past. I simply spoke out just enough to get prescribed the anti-depressants which kick-started my 10 years on/off relationship with chemical buddies.

By the time I arrived in the year 2000, my emotional stressors had been sky-high for half my life. I greeted the millennium as what you could describe as emotionally charged; like a highly-strung pony prancing through life - slightly skittish and a little mentally unpredictable! And then, amidst all the uncertainty, medication, and wobbling through life, a little karmic equalising swung my way and I met my future husband; the man who brought much-needed calm, joy, and love into my life.

This new relationship brought me stability, assurance, and above all, unconditional love. I, at last, began to feel as if my life was finally starting to come together. Depression and anxiety still reared its head from time to time, there was still a steady flow of stressful moments with much wrangling over the children with my ex-partner, but the stability and good times outweighed all the difficult moments. Because of this, it was very easy not to register the little warning signs that all was not well on a physical level - the onset of aches and pains and the general sense of feeling "off colour" most days.

In 2003, I was involved in a car accident in which I suffered a painful whiplash injury that left me feeling muscle pain much longer than it should have. The accident also triggered an increase in anxiety levels. But life was busy, I was planning our wedding, and with exciting times ahead I ignored the fact that I was feeling exceptionally tired much of the time. Now with the benefit of hindsight, there were so many early warning signals that I didn't pick up on that I was heading for a system failure.

In 2004, I was thrilled to become pregnant with my third child. Although without any major complications, I was drained by morning, noon, and night sickness that lasted a full six months of the pregnancy. Although I had no previous experience of alternative healing, out of desperation I tried acupuncture and was delighted to find that it finally stopped the sickness – I think it was this first introduction to the success of natural healing that stuck with me and encouraged me years later to explore the alternative path.

In October of that year, we happily welcomed our beautiful boy into the world. I loved being a mum, but by Christmas, the days were passing in a blur of constant fatigue. I found motherhood this time around to be far more exhausting than I recalled with my previous new-borns. But I put the fatigue down to the 7-year gap since my last pregnancy, the fact my gorgeous boy was of the non-sleeping variety, and the demands of breastfeeding a hungry 9lb 9oz-er. I didn't realise I was trying to do all the things a new mum did with a body that had already started to fail.

Caught up in the busyness of my life, I paid scant attention to the increased level of the niggling aches, random pains, and memory problems; happy to park the issues under the umbrella of being a sleep-deprived new mum and convincing myself that everything would magically get better once I got more sleep.

Two years further down the road, if sleeplessness was an Olympic sport, I would have been in contention for a gold medal. I was tired on top of tired, yet still chalking up my everyday feelings of total fatigue to our yet-to-sleep-through-the-night toddler and the general hustle and bustle of being a busy mum of three. I was blind to the fact that it was more than tiredness. Despite the lack of energy, I still felt the drive to begin a new chapter of my life and like many before me, I decided to channel my own difficult experiences in a direction that would be of help to others. With a determination to make a difference, to have something positive to show for my difficulties, and to give people a better counselling experience than the one I had received myself, I signed up to train to as Person-Centred Counsellor.

The counselling training was a lengthy and emotional process, one that involved digging deep into the dark places that I thought I had safely boxed up and hidden away from myself and the rest of the world. Unearthing and examining my personal history was a necessary process for my professional and personal development. Yet despite the cathartic experience that personal therapy gave me, it was at times emotionally stressful.

For periods of time throughout my training, as I examined my most inner thoughts and feelings, my life would often feel emotionally rocky. At certain times throughout the training process, my emotional equilibrium was completely unsettled. I often felt destabilised by everything from my past that was being brought to the surface for scrutiny. The re-living of some of the most traumatic episodes of my life caused an emotional upheaval that left me feeling wrung out and raw. When reflecting on how my health deteriorated over time, I have often wondered whether my personal therapy played a part in this process, if what I dealt with in my sessions was a contributory factor, the final emotional overwhelm that eventually tipped the scales. When I talk about the impact stress has on the body later in the book, it is easy to make a potential connection between this period of soul searching and the final cascade of symptoms.

Seeing as I believe that personal therapy had what others might see as a detrimental effect on my health, it may then seem a little strange that I am still such a huge advocate for it. After all, isn't the aim of therapy to make you feel better? I think the thing here to note once more is that I don't see this reflecting on my experience as looking for something to put the blame on. It is simply another connection I have made between my past emotional state and the development of illness - an exercise in recognising and acknowledging the circumstances around the onset of illness in my life and to demonstrate my understanding of how I got there - what the contributing/causative factors were.

There is no question that personal therapy changed my life for the better; because of the work I did in those sessions, as tough as it was, I believe I became a better person, a better parent, a better friend, a better wife; more tolerant, less judgemental, and far more well-rounded than I would ever have been had I not explored and cleared out all of my emotional baggage - it just so happens there was a lot of it!

The insights, wisdom, and strength I gained from exploring personal issues from my past during my personal therapy proved to be of great benefit to me in the future. It enabled me to cope better when I found myself living with illness. So much so that I remain convinced that the addressing of emotional issues in whichever way is best for an individual is an important part, in the first instance, of accepting a diagnosis, and then being able to move forward into recovery.

As difficult as it sometimes is, you just need to stir the pot! Dealing with the ripple effect from my therapy was undoubtedly stressful, and while I believe it may well have been a contributory factor in my final decline into ill health, I don’t feel it was the cause of illness per se. Although it’s feasible that the stress of reliving some of the darker and traumatic moments of my life may well have expedited the onset of symptoms, I feel that living with the internalised feelings brought about by trauma would eventually have led me to the same outcome regardless. On balance, it was worth the benefits I gained and unequivocally something I would do again.

CHAPTER 2

THE PATH TO DIAGNOSIS

By the time I qualified as a counsellor, there was no denying that I was struggling with my health. Daily life had become about battling my way through increasing fatigue. Although I no longer had children keeping me awake, I was falling into bed at the end of the day only to find that sleep either wouldn't come or wouldn't be deep enough to be refreshing. I awoke in the mornings just as tired as when I went to bed the previous night and remained that way throughout the day - every day. At that point, my personal record for being awake at night without so much as nodding off was four consecutive nights. The rest of the nights were broken snatches of half an hour here and there. As exhaustion became a constant companion, simple everyday tasks became more and more difficult: showering, dressing, food shopping, housework, and even thinking all left me feeling as if I've been trying to wade through mud. I remember once being reduced to a howling mess of frustration because I had put a t-shirt on back to front and didn't have the energy to pull my arms back out to reverse it - to this day I still wonder how I didn't just lie down and die from lack of sleep!

Trying to remain clear-headed and connect my thoughts was a constant battle with the brain fog. I had gone from being highly articulate, to, some days, struggling to find the right words or even complete a sentence without losing track. Out of all the symptoms, I found this one was the most distressing. Not being able to express myself fully, losing track of what I was saying halfway through conversations, and constantly trying to cover up these lapses really took its toll both physically and mentally.

I was such a communicator that struggling to hold conversations felt as if I was losing a big part of my personality. I started to feel anxious about even the simplest of interactions with others and would go out of my way to avoid conversations or meeting new people. For someone who considered themselves a real people person, being like this felt as if I was gradually being eroded away. This is exactly what I mean when I say fibro fucks with the very essence of you.

It was at this point that I was forced to give up counselling my clients as I no longer felt I was fully fit to practice. It had taken me five years to complete my training, and after only one year into practising this was a huge low point, and one that would add another layer of resentment and anger to my general "fucked off" with it all mindset.

During this period of time, I was still part of the furniture at the doctor's surgery, constantly presenting with what felt like an ever-expanding and endless list of symptoms. The frustration at knowing deep down that something was very wrong with me continued to build with every negative blood test and the doctor's failure to connect the dots that indicated that this was a systemic issue rather than a set of individual symptoms.

Although my instinct told me I was right to keep pushing, questioning, and searching for an answer, it was exhausting and demoralising trying to keep up with the task. When test after test proved negative my history of depression became the convenient out. I was often faced with the dismissive opinion that I was either tired because I was depressed or tired because I had been depressed! By that point, if I had presented with a broken ankle my doctors would have probably questioned self-harm, such was their determination to chalk it up to depression.

Despite repeatedly telling my doctors that just because my life had been plunged into a black hole it didn't mean my mind planned on joining it, they insisted that depression was the likely cause of all my ills. While I was willing to admit that it was true, I got depressed (not overly surprising with my back catalogue of life events), I was nonetheless absolutely convinced there was something else at play. Eventually, after much pushing, wrangling, and generally just making a nuisance of myself, I was referred to an endocrine specialist - I suspect the doctor only referred me because she wasn't sure what else to do with a person who kept on turning up at her surgery insisting something must be physically wrong.

In preparation for my consultation, I sat down and made a list of every single one of my symptoms; they filled an entire sheet of A4 paper. It was a sobering and hard-hitting moment. To see, in black and white, all the things that weren't functioning properly scared the shit out of me. I couldn't comprehend how I was still being told there was nothing wrong with me (apart from depression) when it felt like everything was wrong with me.

I hoped that this consultation would kick-start some sort of action and be a step toward obtaining some answers. Boy was I wrong! I waited 10 weeks to see the endocrinologist, but my expectations were crushed within the first five minutes of being in the consulting room. The consultant's bedside manner was non-existent. The symptom list that held so much importance to me wasn't given so much as even a cursory glance. There was a quick physical examination before it was briskly declared that no further tests were needed. I was surprised she didn't add, "And don't let the door hit your ass on the way out."

Although I felt immensely deflated, I tried to take the news as a positive sign that yet another set of potential life-changing conditions had been ruled out. However, the fact remained that once more I was at a loss, and day by day my life was changing beyond recognition. I had gone expecting further action, maybe a scan, more tests, or a screening, but not the nothingness. What I had thought might be a step forward felt like a step back to square one. The doctors seemed to think it was all in my mind and I had begun to think I was going out of my mind.

Now that I am looking back from a more educated position, I am astounded that given my symptoms and how prolonged levels of stress can negatively impact on the endocrine system, there wasn't even the suggestion that there should be a further investigation into my thyroid and adrenal function. If I had known then what I know now, I would have been a force to be reckoned with. There's no way I would have let that lame-ass consultation pass - this is an example of how gaining knowledge and having faith in yourself empowers you. Back then I didn't have either one, but now after years of taking responsibility for my own healing, I'm damn sure I would have given her one hell of a run for her money.

Post consultation with Mrs. "No Further Tests Required" felt like a huge anti-climax. Once again, I found myself in limbo with things continuing to go from bad to worse. I felt as if I was floundering and constantly trying to keep my head above the water. My life was a continuous struggle to find the energy to get through the day. I felt like I had exhausted all my avenues and I had all but given up hope on getting any answers from the doctors when I met someone who had fibromyalgia. As we talked about her experiences, I begin to see my symptoms mirrored in her own. These weren't just similarities. They were carbon copies of everything that was wrong with me!

This was another one of those pivotal moments, to hear someone else describing everything I was going through, to know that I might not be going crazy after all, was overwhelmingly reassuring. That one conversation produced an "ah-ha" moment that validated everything I was going through. It gave me the impetus and the kick up the bum I needed to get back on to pressurising the doctors for more of an explanation.

At the time I was so overcome with relief at having discovered this connection between our symptoms that I didn't stop to consider the fact that although this lady had received her diagnosis a few years previously, it was clear that she had made little progress recovery wise. I completely overlooked the fact that despite continued treatment and a regular increase in the medication, she was pretty much still in the same place as where she had started - experiencing much the same level of symptoms as the day she was diagnosed. None of those facts registered with me. I wasn't looking any further than trying to find answers as to why I was feeling the way I was. I was so caught up in this eureka moment that I hadn't realised this was an insight, a glimpse into the future and the ineffectiveness of the standard treatment for fibro.

Although all I had wanted to do was rush to the doctors to say,"What about this then, you knobhead? What do you think about it all being about depression now, huh?" I planned my next step carefully - I needed ammunition to shoot down the depression theory. I researched and educated myself on fibromyalgia. As I gathered the information, I recognised myself in every search, every list of symptoms, and in the stories people had shared about their fibro experiences. I couldn't believe that there were so many people struggling with the same bizarre symptoms as me, and equally, just how my doctors could have overlooked the possibility of this condition during my numerous visits. Sifting through information, I found the reading unsettling and sobering. The prospect of joining the ranks of fibro sufferers was unwelcome and scary, but there was also an element of comfort to be found in knowing I wasn't on my own with all this craziness.

Even though I had a growing sense of dread, I felt uplifted at the thought that I was finally getting somewhere. That as awful as it would be, this could spell the end of my search for why I had this long and ever-growing list of symptoms – little did I know!

From the hours spent trawling the Internet, I learned (or so I thought at the time) that a rheumatologist was my best bet for confirming whether I had fibromyalgia. I also discovered that I was incredibly fortunate to live within the referral catchment area for the Royal National Hospital for Rheumatic Diseases (also known as the Mineral Hospital). As part of its services, the hospital specialised in the treatment of Chronic Fatigue Syndrome and offered a Fibromyalgia Self-Management Programme. In a time of uncertainty, ever-increasing fears about my declining health, the frustration, and despondency, this small stroke of good fortune was a glimmer of hope. It felt almost serendipitous, an opportunity to finally get on the front foot in this seemingly never-ending quest to understand what had gone wrong with my body; a few weeks on from this point when I learned the full impact of fibro, I did not feel quite so fucking fortunate!

Locked and loaded with my newfound knowledge and information on fibromyalgia, I booked me and my take-no-shit attitude another doctor's appointment. I was a woman on a mission, and however things went down, I was determined not to leave without obtaining a referral to the Mineral Hospital - one way or the other I was going to get my answer.

Of course, life is never that straightforward. My forceful chat with the doctor didn't go quite as I planned. My request for referral was met with the question "Why?" Then, "Why exactly are you wanting this referral?" When I replied that I was looking to discover whether I had fibromyalgia, the doctor's response stunned me. "Well, I can tell you right now that you have fibromyalgia." Several seconds and several tumbleweeds moments passed as I sat there aghast and speechless at his flippancy. After all the wrangling (three fucking years) to get the various tests, the increasing level of frustration, and the dismissive nature towards my insistence that something was wrong, he dropped this bombshell! I was so incensed that despite not being a violent person I was tempted to beat him senseless with his prescription pad. However, not needing to add an assault charge to my woes, I settled for (in true British style) a tight-lipped expression (obviously meant to convey my disapproval) and a terse request that I at least receive official confirmation of the condition from a rheumatologist. And if necessary, access to their self-management course - how very proper of me!

I left the doctor's surgery like a rabbit caught in the headlights, stunned and reeling from his casual revelation and a head filled with so many questions! How could he have failed to mention this to me? When would I have got to hear about it? What if I hadn't gone to him with the suggestion? Would I have been left to just struggle on indefinitely? I was furious as a furious thing on a furious day at all the unanswered questions. As mad as fuck at how often I had been given the impression that all of the symptoms were just down to mental health issues and how I had been left to put the pieces together myself. Then, of course, fibro being fibro, after being on the receiving end of a big ole adrenaline surge from getting my knickers in a knot I had lie down for several hours to recover!

CHAPTER 3

D-DAY: DIAGNOSIS DAY

July 20th, 2011 was the big day. My consultation. What I saw as my chance to finally gain some ground, to become proactive instead of being just reactive to everything that was happening to me. As I sat waiting to be called in for my consult, I felt a mix of anxiety and hopeful anticipation. I was keenly aware that the next minutes, the space I was about to step into, had the potential to be a game changer. I had spent so long focused on just getting to this point that it wasn't until I was sat still in the waiting room that I realised just how much I had resting on the consult. The enormity of what I was potentially about to hear landed at that precise moment and I came very close to abandoning my search for answers and doing a runner out the back door.

After what felt like an age sitting with my own thoughts and feeling increasingly out of control, I was ushered into the consulting room. The rheumatologist, much nicer than Mrs. "No Further Tests Required," questioned me on my symptoms and carried out the trigger point test. I displayed a reaction to 17 of the 18 trigger points, ranging from "that hurts" to "if you touch me there again, I might have to kill you!" And then there was the diagnosis point. On hearing her words, "I can confirm you have fibromyalgia," I broke down. Obviously, as news goes it wasn't the greatest, but all I felt at that moment was a huge sense of relief. All the built-up tension and frustrations at having gone through so much just to get to this point, the frustration and hurt at not being believed, the fears for the future, just flooded out in rather incoherent ugly crying.

Part of me couldn't believe that three years of battling to be heard was reduced to 15 minutes. After years of confrontations with doctors and fearing for my own sanity, a 15-minute consult was all it took to receive confirmation that this place full of crazy symptoms I have been living in had a name; welcome to fibromyalgia-ville.

When I had ploughed through a considerable amount of the consultant's tissues while she sat awkwardly by, I eventually regained control of my emotions and I got the "what next" questions out of the way. I learnt that the next step was a referral to their management course and a letter sent to my doctor for them to take over treatment.

Not for the first time, I left an appointment slightly dazed and uncertain of the road ahead, but this time I was buoyed up by the confirmation that I wasn't a whiner or a hypochondriac. The feeling of relief at being believed and being able to give a name to what was happening to me was at the time immense. It was only later as I got further down the healing road that I would come to see that "fibromyalgia" was simply a label. Nothing more than an umbrella term to cover my yet-to-be-explained symptoms; a label handed to people like me because there is a fundamental lack of understanding of the root causes of illness and the building blocks needed for rebuilding and maintaining health.

By the time that consultation came around my world had been changed for a long time. I hadn't been living life as I had wanted to for years, but it wasn't until I stepped out the front door of the hospital that hit me just how changed it was and how I was totally unprepared for a future of ill health. I had spent so long searching for an answer, hitting brick walls, then trying to find a way over them that I hadn't actually prepared myself for when I finally got one.

As the hospital door shut behind me, for a few minutes, I stood perfectly still in the city centre of Bath, letting all the people bustle past me because I was struck motionless by the overwhelming thought – *"What the fuck was going to happen to me now?"*

CHAPTER 4

PAIN MANAGEMENT, PACING, AND PISSED OFF

October of that same year saw me back at the Mineral Hospital attending the first session of the 6-week management course. The interim period between my diagnosis and then had been a nightmare for symptoms. Following a big family argument my entire body felt like it had been ignited, and not in a sexy way. I had hives and rashes on top of hives and rashes and an almost constant feeling as if I wanted to scratch my own skin off. The pain was at a previously unknown level and sleep became something that I used to do. The medication my doctors had prescribed, was, as yet, doing little to alleviate anything and left me looking and feeling like a zombie. Never one to suit grey tones, I resorted to creating an illusion of health with the contents of my make-up bag, thus going on to receive many a "but you look so well" or "I can't believe you're ill" comments that for a long time would fuel a desire to make people understand my situation or to punch them in the face.

The first session of the course, I found myself sat in a semi-circle of about eight women. I remember casting my eye around my fellow course mates and seeing the same expression of exhaustion written on everyone's faces. Half of them look too tired to lift a pen or even form a coherent sentence. The thought that popped into my head was that they all looked like ghost women; a greyed, washed-out version of their former selves.

As I listened to their individual stories, I realised that a lot of the women had been at a debilitating level of symptoms for many more years than myself, and I was struck by the horrifying thought that this would be me. This was my future mapped out for me right there in that room. And I knew that despite the very best Maybelline had to offer, I was well on my way to becoming a ghost woman.

As the course went on, I didn't find the intended level of benefit. Instead of getting a handle on things, I found myself becoming more and more resentful towards my situation. Although helpful in some ways, the content of the course reinforced what I felt was the hopelessness of my situation.

The initial sense of hope I had felt after diagnosis had been worn away, to be replaced with the realisation of how little was understood about fibro and its treatment. It was slowly beginning to dawn on me that nobody was coming to rescue me, and nobody was going to fix this shit for me. At this stage of my journey I was feeling an ever-increasing mix of anger and resentment toward illness, my life, and just about everything in between - I was one seriously pissed-off lady, and believe me, seriously pissed off and seriously ill makes a rather arsey duo.

One of the main messages of the management course was that our lives now needed to be paced - daily monitoring of activities right down to energy spent on washing our hair, getting dressed, etc. In our self-help folders, we had a weekly chart to complete to monitor how we were expending that energy so that we could learn to pace ourselves appropriately. As my eyes scanned the list, I was stunned to see that reading was in the section for activities that required a high level of energy. Hang on, (record scratch) WTF?! What was going on here?

Reading had always been my life's blood, my escapism, I could easily whizz through a couple of books a week. Now this chart, this piece of fuckery, was telling me I needed to consider monitoring and possibly curbing my favourite pastime so I could attempt to preserve my energy levels. This innocuous suggestion was one of the moments when the cold hard reality of the condition hit home. It was a serious "up shit creek without a paddle" moment. It was also one of those straws that broke the camel's back moments that led to one of my more memorable meltdowns.

Although on some level, I knew pacing made sense, I grew incredibly resentful towards it. The charts came to represent everything that was now a struggle in my life, a constant reminder highlighting that the smallest of tasks took vital energy. The energy I no longer had to spare. Resting before I could go out for lunch with friends felt ridiculous and something my 95-year-old Gran would do. Life was no longer just doing stuff, it was about monitoring, measuring, and eking out my energy. This wasn't me. This wasn't supposed to be my life! I wasn't even 40 years old. I didn't want to spend my life pacing myself, compromising on everyday activities that most people didn't give a second thought to, just so I would be able to get through the day and hopefully ward off a flare-up (flare-up, god how I loathed that term). I didn't want to miss out on special occasions just because I'd washed my hair and given the house a clean in the same week and was now too exhausted to go. Every time I considered the pacing tool and thought about monitoring my activities in such minute detail, I could feel the spontaneity and joy draining out of my life.

As the course came to a close I was so pissed off at the thought of pacing that when I got home after the last session, in a fit of child-like pique, I completely threw my toys out the proverbial pram and ripped up my pacing chart into tiny shreds. I didn't want to know how much reading zapped my energy. I didn't want to use fucking coloured pens to map my life's coming and goings and see everything I loved, wanted to do, or be part of marked up like a traffic light system with more red lights than green. I didn't want to acknowledge just how big of a stop sign my life had come to.

By now, I practically oozed anger and resentment towards what I saw as the crap hand life's card game had dealt me. I'm not particularly proud, of this period, but I must say, I played my pissed off role exceptionally well - it was an Oscar-winning performance. I was completely 100% in victim mode and not even capable of entertaining the idea that I could get myself out of the hole I was wallowing in. Therefore, it was a substantial period of time and a lot of feeling sorry for myself before I reached the point where I realised that I was going to have to launch my own rescue mission.

CHAPTER 5

TAKING MATTERS INTO MY OWN HANDS

I spent nigh on a whole year holding a personal pity party and perfecting my role as victim. I was caught in a never-ending cycle of being angry at the world. I was angry at life, at myself, at people who could do what they wanted when they wanted, at people who could sleep, the list went on and on - I was even angry at the cat for having a better life than me. I was consumed with the unfairness of my situation, frequently lamenting to the skies with "Why me" and stuffed full of resentment. When I look back on this time, I think of all the energy I must have used up by being so angry at the world, at life, and what an absolute royal pain in the arse I must have been to live with!

My first step towards getting to grips with sorting out my situation was to return to personal therapy to help me learn how to deal with all the feelings I was experiencing since diagnosis. The counselling helped me to recognise that what I was experiencing was grief, and the realisation that I was working my way through the stages associated with the grieving process really helped me to cope with all the overwhelming feelings. During the sessions, I was able to talk freely about my anger and work on releasing it. It gave me the space to be able to listen to myself, to be honest with myself, and eventually to get over myself; get out of my own way. It freed up my mind space so I could consider other things, to start to contemplate my life in the here and now. I was able to see that there were changes I could make that would allow me to begin to regain a certain level of control over my life.

As helpful as the therapy was, it was the medication which finally propelled me to seek an alternative path back to health. I had been on medication for about a year at this stage and I was finding it to be of little benefit. A reduction in pain levels was barely discernible, nor did it seem to be doing much for sleep issues except to make me feel like a zombie. Although the tablets initially made me sleepy, I was still spending many hours awake at night and then finding I was practically having to prise my eyes open when it was time to get up. I would feel groggy, listless, and nauseous for at least the first couple of hours of the day.

At my next doctor's appointment, I raised the zombie-like feelings and was advised I should be taking the medication 12 hours before I wanted to be up and about. With my daily routine at that time, this meant that I would need to take the tablets at 7 p.m., resulting in my being asleep at approximately 7:30. My life already felt compromised in so many ways, and now this completely restrictive and impractical suggestion meant that I would need to be in bed earlier than my kids. Three young kids roaming the house while I slept, yeah, I could see that was going to work out well!

The final decision to ditch the conventional treatment methods came when I questioned the potential side effects of being on long-term medication. The fact that the doctor was unable to give me any clear indication of what might happen in the future set my mind whirring. If, like I was being told, the condition was chronic, I was looking at the possibility of a lifetime's worth of treatment. Universe willing that I lived to see a ripe old age, then how would my body react to possibly 40-50 years' worth of medication? What could I expect in 20, 10 or even 5 years' time? I already knew that it was more than likely that the medication would need to be stepped up over a period. My body would begin to adapt to its continued presence and eventually develop a tolerance. This knowledge, coupled with the unknown side effects of taking medication long-term alongside the fact that I wasn't even seeing much benefit, made continuing to take the tablets a poor trade-off in my eyes.

After making the decision to quit, I spent 12 weeks slowly tapering off the medication to avoid withdrawal symptoms. During that time, I also began to delve into natural ways to help myself, looking for what alternatives could relieve the symptoms. I didn't realise it at the time, but I was taking the first steps on the path to unearthing my root causes of illness.

The root cause wasn't a term I was even familiar with until I immersed myself in the world of alternative medicine. I think the fact that I wasn't even aware illnesses had root causes/causative factors is an indication of how little responsibility I was taking for looking out for myself. I was hooked into the mindset that conventional treatment was the only way to go. I knew nothing better than to turn to my GP and expect to be given the answers. I mistook symptoms for being the cause of what was wrong with me.

Until this point, I had been putting all my eggs in that one conventional basket without any awareness of just how many other treatments were out there waiting to be explored or how much impact I myself could have on my health. It wasn't until I began to see the progress in my health as a result of my own decisions that I began to feel more empowered and confident; coming to the realisation that nobody knows our own body better than we do.

During this time, I slowly began to realise that through educating ourselves on the different options and resources available to us, losing the fear and rebuilding our instinct to know what's right for us as individuals, we can become our own experts. And as we become more confident and trusting of ourselves, we then naturally begin to seek out the practitioners who are the right fit for us and can support us through our healing process; people whose ideas and treatments are truly aligned with our individual needs.

It was during my initial exploration of alternatives that I concluded that conventional treatment was never going to heal me. All it was ever going to do was act like a sticking plaster for symptoms. Whenever I considered continuing with the conventional path, I saw myself potentially taking an ever-increasing list of medication with unknown long-term side effects. I wasn't completely against taking conventional medicine; after all, it can be a lifesaver. I just felt that in my case it didn't fit the bill. I felt the best I could hope for would be a reduction in the severity of symptoms, but with the likelihood of a bunch of undesirable side effects which would probably require more medication as time went on. For me, it became a case of "Thanks, but no thanks!"

It was at this point I realised it was time to get serious, to take responsibility for my own healing, and start fixing the situation myself. The realisation that my recovery now fell to me was one of those big scary moments. The fact that I wasn't always going to be able to hand off decisions to a doctor and would be shouldering most of the responsibility for healing myself was daunting, to say the least. I wasn't sure where I was heading, or how I was going to get there, but despite feeling overwhelmed at the enormity of the task, I was for the first time in a long time hopeful of making progress.

I am not going to lie and say taking responsibility for fixing this shit has been easy. At times fixing my health has felt like too big of a thing to carry on with. There have been many times when I have wished I could have delegated it all to someone else and gotten them to take over the search for things to aide my recovery. There have been many times when I have been found weeping on the bedroom floor and saying that I can't keep on with it, or that I was just too tired of fighting for my health. I cannot tell you how many times I have had to regroup and gather myself up for one more push at it, hoping that whatever was around the next corner would be the next thing to move me on. But whenever I hit those patches, when it was all too much, when I was ready to throw in the towel and chuck it in the "fuck it" bucket, I tried to stay focused on two of the things that I believe help keep my foundation of healing steady: Self-responsibility and trust, alongside reminding myself that:

By being self-responsible for my health I could influence the outcome, change the odds that came with the diagnosis. There was always something I could do for myself to improve the situation. I always had the option to educate myself, explore, and increase my knowledge, and with knowledge came power and progress. That power, that education, and that knowledge are what enabled me to choose the right path and find the right kind of people to help me.

Trusting in the fact that we are born with an inherent self-healing capability and when we are given the right conditions, the right environment, the body will begin to heal. Trusting that the answers were out there, and I could find them. Trusting that my own instincts were still there beneath the fear and were sound enough to know when something was good for me.

CHAPTER 6

THE POWER OF THREE

When I began to work on fixing my health, I soon came to realise that I needed a plan of action. And almost without realising it, through formulating my action plan I created my foundational system for healing that I have since gone on to name The Power of Three.

The Power of Three is the combination of elements that have underpinned everything that I have explored and experienced over these past few years. The 3 S's - *Self-responsibility*, *Self-awareness*, and *Self-care:* This trio has formed the foundation of my healing, they are what have been the main pillars of my success.

Self-responsibility - the moment I decided to take responsibility for my own health was the first step of my healing journey. By no longer sitting back and entirely handing off my entire care to someone else, I started to do things my own way, and bit by bit I began to feel like I was back in charge of my life. Although, as I have already mentioned, taking over this task was a daunting prospect and at times overwhelming, I can also say it has been incredibly empowering too.

After years of feeling like I was being swept helplessly along by the tides of illness, once I started doing things for myself, I felt like I was navigating my own way. By becoming responsible for my healing, I began to claw back some of the ground I had lost to illness. Being more proactive propelled me forward. It enabled me to regain a sense of purpose and direction. This was something I had been lacking for a long time, and feeling it again after so long was a huge boost to my mental wellbeing.

Now, after years of taking matters into my own hands, I realise just how important it is to be responsible for yourself in all areas of your life. Our lives are not somebody else's responsibility, period; our happiness and health do not depend on others. It is up to us to make what we will of this precious life.

Of course, there will be people who can support, guide, and give us a helping hand, but ultimately the buck stops with us; the individual. This is not to say that I have gone it alone 100% of the time on this journey or that

I think we must shoulder all responsibility all the time - that would be an unnecessary burden. There is always going to be a time and place for asking for help, letting someone else prop us up when it's too much or while we are feeling vulnerable. There are going to be points when we will need to engage someone else's services, seek their expertise to get the best results. Self-responsibility is in part seeking out others to help us achieve our goals. However, what I feel is important is that we are still fully present in those moments with others, that we make sure that we are a participant, not just a passenger; a balanced relationship, a collaboration. Otherwise, it's easy to slip into allowing others to assume responsibility for us, which can be disempowering.

Something this journey has highlighted for me is that we and we alone deserve the opportunity to have the final decision over our lives and wellbeing, and we need to put ourselves in a position where this can happen. We need to have the faith that even when it doesn't feel like it, even when we are caught up in illness, we always have the power to make choices and decisions. That it is still possible for us to steer the direction of our lives and work towards where we want to go even if, at the time, we can only take the smallest of actions.

I think that when it comes to health issues, when we find ourselves weighed down by the enormity of diagnosis it is very easy to forget that we can still influence events. It's hard when we are caught in the vice-like grip of long-term illness to see that we still have lots of choices. Fear, pain, and exhaustion can cloud our judgement, disconnect us from our instinct, zap our drive, leave us wanting to stay hidden under the duvet and not have to face or think about our situation. When sickness becomes our every day, sorting things out for ourselves is often not high on the agenda, but to be honest, this is exactly the time when it is most important to do so.

I know that after I was first diagnosed, I just wanted someone to make it all go away. I wanted to be able to take something, have a silver bullet that would just fix the fucking problem. I spent a year dutifully taking the medication that the doctors believe is one of the best options for treating this condition, hoping that it would be that silver bullet. When I finally realised that there wasn't going to be a magic pill anytime soon and nobody was coming to save me, I stopped putting so much faith in conventional methods of treatment and started to look elsewhere for my answers.

In the past, I have often found myself slightly intimidated by doctors. I don't know if this was some hang-over from my childhood - not to question someone in authority. But for whatever reason, I would often find myself in mute agreement with them, holding the belief that they knew what was best for me or not empowered enough to question their opinion. Now, after several years of doing things for myself, I know that all along it's been me that knows what's best for me. Yes, I can seek their advice, expertise, and opinion, but it is not something I have to take as gospel nor agree with. I have the right to decide for myself, to challenge and then proceed with what I think is the best way forward for me. My go-to these days is to take on-board the advice I am given, do my own research, and then make an informed decision because I owe it to myself to take responsibility to do what is right for me.

For the record, I want to be clear that I do have respect for some doctors and the knowledge they possess, this is certainly not a doctor-bashing exercise. They save lives every day and are certainly worthy of praise, but the more I learn about health and how we get sick, the more I feel that conventional medicine is a much better fit for acute care. I'm really not sure how many of the conventional practitioners out there really understand what it is to truly heal or see healing as a process. Healing is not taking a pill and the symptoms being quashed. It's much deeper than that. It's not a sticking plaster to mask what's really going on. It's looking for causative factors such as our emotions, the connections in our past, the food we eat, the environment we live in, and much more. Above all, healing requires time, self-responsibility, and commitment. This is not something I have ever received on prescription.

In my experience, many conventional doctors do not seek to find the root causes/causative factors or unearth what is going on deep beneath the presenting symptoms. For many months after diagnosis I was like, "Oh, so fibro is what's wrong with me. This is why I'm breathless, I'm exhausted, I'm this and this and this..." but I was wrong, fibromyalgia wasn't the true reason I had so many things wrong with my body - it was just a label for the presenting symptoms (more on this later). What was wrong with me lay much deeper than that. It was in the layers underneath the diagnosis and list of symptoms; the root causes.

Initially, having a diagnosis was hugely important to me because it gave me a place to hang my hat. I felt like I finally had something of an explanation for myself, and just as important to me at the time, an explanation to give to others. There was a huge sense of relief that I now had something to pin how terrible I had been feeling on to and had a reason why I couldn't do the everyday things other people could. At that time, I really needed to have a diagnosis, to have a name for all the crazy shit that was happening to me. Once I began the healing process I realised that the diagnosis had also given my misfortunes a place to make a home and I had gotten a bit too comfortable there; resigning myself to my fate, believing this was the end of the road and labelling myself up as a "fibro sufferer."

I have often wondered if post-diagnosis relief may in some ways prevent people from seeking further answers, questioning deeper issues, or getting to the root causes of illness. How? Well, it often takes people such a long time to reach the diagnosis stage that by the time they come out the other side, I think that maybe they are so worn out by the process, the pain they're just so thankful to have what they feel is the answer. I wonder if this relief is so great that it leaves no space to question whether it's actually the full answer.

For me, a chronic illness diagnosis was like a double-edged sword. On one hand, it gave me a sense of comfort and validation, but on the other, I think it prevented me from exploring my health issues further. I also think that when we're handed a fibro diagnosis it can be quite easy to become enmeshed in a sense of despondency and develop a "there's little that can be done" or a "suck it up" mindset. I know that I spent quite some time thinking that the diagnosis was the end of my road, that I had my answer now and I just had to resign myself to living with a shit load of bizarre symptoms. It wasn't until I started questioning what my future would look like on my current treatment plan that I felt driven to dig deeper and take on the responsibility for my own healing.

I strongly believe that one of the first steps to achieving a good level of health is to take responsibility for yourself. From there you can reconnect with your instincts, listen to your body, and discover your individual needs.

Although I am waving the self-responsibility flag, I am fully aware that this is not the easiest of options. As you will have read, being responsible for my own health hasn't been a walk in the park. At times it's been confusing and lonely with more than one emotional meltdown (proper ugly crying), but it has got me where I am today. It has empowered me. It has enabled me to feel confident in trusting my instincts and encouraged me to at times going against the norm. It has given me the courage to challenge everything that I was once told fibro would be and not to settle for the life I was told I could expect to live. It has given me the drive and determination to explore the alternative avenues that have amazingly reversed symptoms that I was once led to believe I would be stuck with for a lifetime.

The results and progress I have achieved so far have exceeded my expectations. When I think back to how my life was post-diagnosis, I wouldn't have believed that my health could turn around in the way it has. Self-responsibility has been such an important element of my healing because it enabled me to delve deep enough to find the roots of illness. Without stepping up to responsibility, I think I would still have been treading water, firefighting symptoms, and living with a fibro diagnosis as my truth. This is why I wave that flag. This is why within these pages I am encouraging you to take a look at your current situation and consider taking steps towards being more responsible for your own health. After all, you just don't know just where it will take you!

Self-awareness - In my eyes, self-awareness is a really big deal. It's kind of one of those climb up on your "soap box" things for me. I can often be found on Instagram banging on about it and promoting the benefits of becoming more aware of ourselves. Why do I do this? Because I believe self-awareness provides us with so many answers and leads on to positive progress and drives personal development. It helps us discover the answers to how, what, and why we do the things we do, think the things we think, and feel the things we feel. It is key to understanding one's self better and unlocking some of the complexities of our lives. It is a gift that can help us in so many ways: communication, relationships, personal development, and of course health - it's a gift that keeps on giving!

Although, it is a process that never stops. I cannot tell you how fortunate I feel to have had the opportunity to develop a sound level of self-awareness through my counselling training because self-awareness has been such a big player in my recovery process. Understanding myself has been instrumental in my being able to put together some of the less obvious pieces of my life and health puzzle. It has helped me to track my downward spiral into ill health and make certain connections as to what has played a part in my getting sick in the first instance. Throughout the ongoing healing process, it has aided me in identifying what helps or hinders my recovery.

Through becoming more self-aware I have been able to...

- Recognise the patterns that were keeping me stuck in certain situations and relationships that were negatively impacting on my health. These included repeated patterns of unhelpful behaviour, feelings, thoughts, and events.

- Identify my emotions so I could more easily make the connections between a given situation and what I was feeling. This helped me to learn to abandon my fears so I could trust my instincts and opt for decisions that were better for my wellbeing, therefore creating a positive effect on my health.

- Gain a better understanding of my body's physical reaction to events, feelings, and thoughts so that I could work on responding in a more measured and healthier way, rather than just simply reacting.
- Identify the thoughts that were going through my mind and recognise what impact my inner dialogue was having on my wellbeing. I was able to learn to connect what I was thinking with how I was physically feeling. This helped me to maintain a more optimistic mindset, learn to be kinder to myself, and rid myself of some of the old and very deep-seated belief systems.
- Re-evaluate and re-assess my life to create one that is better suited to maintaining health.

Because the world we live in is so full on and busy I think it's so easy for us to bumble through life not really paying attention to just how much stuff impacts on our health. Relationships issues, personal crisis, thoughts, feelings, actions, other people's shit, and so much more can have a profound effect on our wellbeing, but often we're just too busy or caught up in whatever is going on to register how it may be affecting our health.

Becoming more aware of how I am existing in my world, delving into how I see myself, how I interact with and respond to the people and the environment around me has made a huge difference to my recovery. It has helped me to understand myself on a much deeper level, and through that I have been able to recognise and make the connections between how my life events, my responses, thoughts, feelings, behaviour, and emotions have contributed to the hot mess I found myself in. More importantly, though, it has helped me to pull myself back out of it, put my feet back on solid ground, and to gain a better command of my health.

Through gaining a greater level of self-awareness I have become much more clued into what is happening around me and within me. Don't get me wrong, I've not perfected the art. I still need other people to point things out to me, help me to see and understand things. In fact, only recently I have been working with an REBT (Rational, Emotive, Behaviour Therapy) therapist who has been helping me connect more with my emotions and tame some of the anxiety that I was still experiencing from time to time.

One of the big wins for becoming more self-aware is that I am now much better at steering myself away from unnecessary stress. Being able to understand myself and my needs more I can actively seek out the experiences and help that I know will benefit my health. These days I am much more discerning as to what or who I allow into my life, which allows me to control my stress levels more effectively, and I am able to make much healthier choices in all areas of my life.

Self-care - what can I say, this baby is huge! A real cornerstone for healing, and something that once again I have found needs to be a consistent thread running through all areas of my life. I don't know about you, but I used to think self-care was all about taking the time out to pamper yourself once in a while, trying to eat well, and making the effort to get more exercise, but over these last few years, I have come to realise that it is so much more than that. It's about safeguarding your mental health, having respect for yourself, and putting yourself first. It's striving for a greater sense of balance across all aspects of your life; nurturing yourself as a whole. It is having the courage in the face of what other people think to prioritise the stuff you know will enhance your levels of wellbeing, keep you healthy and sane.

Like the whole approach of this book, my self-care practice revolves around another powerful three elements - psychological, physical, and spiritual. These elements are interconnected; what is good for my physical body often has a positive effect on my mental and spiritual wellbeing too. If I was to try to define how I see my self-care practice, then I would say that the three main elements are made up of five further sub-elements that nurture all aspects of my life.

I go into more detail further in the book about some of the elements below, but in the meantime, here are the basics of what makes up my self-care practice.

My Five Elements of Self-care

#1 Psychological
- Maintaining a healthy mindset.
- Saying yes to new opportunities.
- Monitoring my thoughts and language.
- Learning new things and educating myself.
- Digital detox – disconnecting from electronic devices.
- Letting go of things I cannot change.
- Decluttering.
- Life-affirming affirmations/mantras.
- Meditation.
- Giving up watching the news.
- Limit my exposure to social media.

- One to one therapy.
- REBT therapy.
- EFT- Emotional Freedom Technique.
- Engaging in activities and interactions that are in alignment with my values, morals and principles.

#2 Physical

- Moving my body - daily stretching, regular exercise routine.
- Intimacy with loved ones.
- Eating nourishing foods.
- Staying hydrated.
- Breathing techniques.
- Sleep routine.
- Good hygiene practices.
- Diffusing essential oils.
- Dry brushing.
- Castor oil packs.
- Pampering - relaxing baths, skincare products, and routines.
- Osteopathic treatments.
- Natural supplementation.
- Energy work.

#3 Emotional

- Journalling - reflection time.
- Daily gratitude.
- Therapy.
- Human touch - hugging it out.
- Self-compassion, self-acceptance, self-responsibility, and being honest with myself.
- Saying no and creating strong personal boundaries.
- Letting go of perfection.
- Creative activities.
- Healthy support system - accepting help when overwhelmed.
- Allowing emotions without judgement.
- Understanding emotions through self-reflection and awareness-emotional intelligence.
- Coping strategies for tough times - things I know have worked in the past.
- Developing my self-awareness.

#4 Relationships & Social
- Prioritising close relationships.
- Spending regular quality time with like-minded uplifting people.
- Coffee (or in my case, herbal tea!) dates with friends.
- Belonging to uplifting and useful groups.
- Distancing myself from toxic or stressful relationships.
- Healing old wounds from previous experiences and relationships.
- A healthy balance between time for others and time for me.

#5 Spiritual
- Having a personal belief system.
- Meditation & mindfulness.
- Yoga.
- Getting out in nature.
- Reading inspirational material.
- Connecting with inspirational people.
- Doing what I love.
- Creativity.

One thing I have noticed on my journey is that my self-care is always changing and evolving. Over time, I have established a self-care routine to suit my individual needs, finely tuning it to fit where I am at any given time mentally, physically, or spiritually. Sometimes it involves focusing more of my time on my diet and other times it might be about putting boundaries in place to shield myself from external stress. It can be about the management of anxiety, the practising of a good sleep routine, or knowing when to just shutdown, kick back, and do nothing.

Although my list of the five elements looks long, I am not necessarily doing all the above all the time, but consistency is the key. Whatever I decide I need to focus my energies on, one thing I have learnt is that it's not something to dip in and out of. It is the consistent daily practice of taking care of myself that makes the difference. Self-care on all levels needs to be an integral part of my life. By consciously doing the very best for myself each day and every day I know I can participate more fully in life and give more to those around me – one of my biggest learning points around becoming okay with prioritising myself has been that self-care is not selfish in a bad way or self-absorbed it is simply looking out for one's self and it is a non-negotiable element of maintaining health.

When planning out how I was going to write this book, I decided in part 2 to break the different aspects of my healing process into three holistic elements – Mind, Body, & Soul. "Simples," I thought, but as I began the writing process, I realised that this was not quite as straightforward as it first appeared.

Through my own healing experience, I knew that everything about us is connected, but in trying to break things down into the three parts (Mind, Body, and Soul), I became even more aware of just how interconnected these elements of self are and how they cannot ever really be completely separated from one another. The same goes for the 5 elements above. One element is an integral part of the other; they are, if you like, cogs of the same machine, working in sync with one another to make a whole.

In the following pages I have included certain topics under just one heading, but as you come with me on this journey, I would like you to bear in mind that so much of the stuff I write about is interchangeable and one element often impacts on another. Topics are situated in this book where they are to save me from repeating the same content under the different headings (although sometimes you may find me doing this). Often something that I have written as being good for the Mind will also be also good for the Soul or the Body or both. I feel that this really highlights how our body's functions and our wellbeing are connected on so many different levels. And I feel it is a perfect reflection of why a holistic approach is needed for healing from long-term illness.

In my experience of conventional medicine, there seems to be far too little attention given to how all the different aspects of a person's life can impact on their health. There is not enough recognition of how there needs to be a good level of balance in all areas for us to be able to function well in life. From the conventional perspective, symptoms are often seen as individual issues, not part of a whole, or dismissed as being part of a condition without the understanding of just how they are part of it.

When there is an overwhelming list of presenting issues which standard tests can't seem to fully explain, then I believe that is often when a diagnosis such as fibromyalgia can come into play. And once that diagnosis is given, it's then a quick hop onto a standardised medication route for the "condition," with little or no consideration given to an individual's biochemistry, lifestyle, environment, history, emotional traumas, etc.; all the things that could be a person's causative factors/root cause of illness. When we become aware that ill health can come from imbalances and dysfunction in all aspects of our life, we can see that treating it holistically makes the most sense. We realise it isn't logical that medication alone can overcome dysfunction that is coming from multiple areas such as lifestyle, gut health, chronic stress, trauma, mindset, etc. Yet it is often the dysfunction that is having a tremendous impact on a person's health.

My biggest reasoning for championing a holistic approach is that we need an all-encompassing healing process for an all-encompassing illness. If we take the all-invasive nature of fibro, if we consider the sheer range of different symptoms, the come-and-go nature of them, and the way in which fibro can simultaneously affect various parts of our body from our mind to our gut, then how can popping a pill or multiple pills bring all this back into balance? To suppress (not cure) all those symptoms we'd probably need a bucketful of different pills. These days, I wonder how on earth increasing amounts of Amitriptyline, Tramadol, or Lyrica can fix impaired adrenal function, correct gut issues (see Body section) or deal with the emotional trauma that has manifested in a physical illness?

I'm sure, like me, that when you received your diagnosis you thought you had a definitive answer for everything that had gone wrong with your health. Especially all that weird shit. You know what I'm talking about. Those voodoo doll type stabbing pains, forgetting how to empty the Hoover you've had for the last 5 years, or the inability to make simple decisions, such as what to eat. And yeah, those 200 other things you have going on. I'm going to wager that you have probably had numerous tests come back waving the all-clear flag or have been told your tests results are within range and marked "no further action needed," leaving you feeling as if you've ruled them out or have no grounds to pursue things further. Along your route to diagnosis, there have more than likely been a few other conditions identified as contributing to the overall diagnosis and you've just had to accept it for what it is. But what if there are some missing pieces? What if this is not the whole picture?

Okay, so this is the moment where I stick my neck out and say that there may be a possibility that what truly ails you, what's underlying that fibro diagnosis of yours, could still be a bit of mystery even if you don't think it is! You might want to read those few lines again just to make sure you heard me correctly, because of course you know what's wrong with you and I'm just being plain ridiculous, right? Or am I?

The further I have got in the healing process the more I believe that many of us have been given a fibro diagnosis as a label, and it's a label that prevents us from getting to the root causes; or the diagnosis is correct on some level but there could still be improvements to health or a reversal of symptoms if doctors took more of a holistic approach to treatment. I am convinced that many conventional doctors simply do not know enough about this condition to be able to be 100% fully confident in their diagnosis. I think many people are given the diagnosis because:

1) doctors do not know what to do with someone who keeps presenting with health issues that can't seem to be explained through standard testing.

2) because not enough time is spent investigating other possibilities that sit outside of the normal diagnostic ranges that they have at their disposal.

3) there is not as yet a definitive marker for fibromyalgia.

I have come to the conclusion that fibromyalgia is often a diagnosis that is given as a coverall explanation for a multitude of symptoms that are impacting on a person's ability to lead a normal life. I see it as an umbrella term meant to provide an answer for what's happening to someone without truly identifying their root causes or without taking into account many other contributory factors such as a person's individuality, biochemistry, and history.

Now, before you get all pissed with me, get your knickers in a knot, or perhaps get tempted to lead with the, "Well, my doctor with his medical degree knows best," or, "Been consulting Dr. Google again, love?" Just take a moment to consider this. If what you have going on with your health is being driven totally or in part by other things, then this IS good news! Yes, it is! While it may mean you have to let go of that hard-won fibro diagnosis, it also means you have something to work with and improve on.

I know the whole "doctor knows best" is probably still hanging there for some, so I want to just take a moment to explain why I feel that the standard treatment (medication) doled out by them may not always be the best way to go for treating fibro. If we take a moment to recap on things; how there can be many factors in a person's route to illness, how emotional stress, environment, personal history, and more can lead to ill health, and then look at how current medication works, we can see some potential pitfalls.

If all the above can contribute to illness, then what are the chances that standardised medications that purely focus on the central nervous system in the brain and are designed as a one-size-fits-all can fix absolutely everything that's gone to shit? Where does our individuality and unique route to illness fit in here? Therefore, what could an approach that takes into account all areas of our life (Mind, Body, and Soul) do? Could it be that a treatment plan that addresses all those areas, the mechanics of our whole life, not just what the brain is doing, would stand a greater chance of success? My answer to that is yes. Having been down both paths and seen how the natural approach has brought my life and body back into balance, I know for sure which one gets my vote for success.

On many occasions, I have read on health (or should I say ill health) forums, people's comments that they are on ever-increasing amounts of medication, that they are combining 3, 4, 5, or more different types of drugs at high doses yet are feeling no better or getting minimal benefits. I see Amitriptyline being combined with Gabapentin being combined with Tramadol and more, and I feel saddened that there are many people out there who have been led to believe that this is the only option. It seems to me there are so many people who have been diagnosed with fibro who are in a cycle of taking multiple medications and increasing doses with minimal benefit. Maybe there are people out there who'd disagree, but I have yet to come across anyone who has said, "These drugs are fucking amazing, I'm symptom-free." Instead, all too often I hear that the drugs, at best, offer a little relief in exchange for a whole heap of side effects.

Now, before I plough on. I want to be clear that I'm not making any judgement on how people are managing their illness. I totally understand why they are doing what they are doing and how they may have gotten to that point of taking multiple medications. I understand that they may have other health issues that require medication, or they may see benefits from taking certain medication and need to stick with it. The reason I am drawing attention to this is because I hear time and time again that people are not getting good results from medication and I am convinced that no matter what someone has going on, whatever symptoms they are experiencing, how or if they are getting relief, there will still be some health issues that can be alleviated or even reversed by a more natural approach.

Of course, I am not advocating that everyone launches their prescriptions out the window. Folks have to do what is right for them, but I am never going to be convinced that the standard conventional treatment route of using a drug that just targets the central nervous system is going to give the majority of people with a fibro diagnosis the resolution they are looking for or deserve. All I want to say to anyone who is in the situation where they are taking drugs or multiple drugs in return for little benefit is this - isn't an alternative approach worth at least some consideration? Would it be worth trying it if it helped you to overcome just one or two symptoms or helped you to reduce or come off just one of your medications? I simply want to encourage people to be curious about their diagnosis and their current treatment plan. I want people with this diagnosis to question if they are really on the best path for regaining health or could they try something new, explore a different avenue. Would it not serve them to take another look at how they might deal with their health issues?

I realise that people who are on medication cannot just switch overnight, it would need to be a slow process with monitoring, but there are still many things that can be done in conjunction with medication - people don't need to come off their medication in order to eat better or up their self-care.

I am not going to deny that considering a completely different way of doing something is more than a bit scary and challenging. I totally get that when you have been on a set course for a period of time it can be hard to consider something new, especially if someone can't tell you exactly what it is you need to do! A big part of the apprehension, the shit that's going to prevent you from kickstarting this process, is going to be good old-fashioned fear of the unknown. There's going to be a "better the devil you know" situation going down here because, well hey, that sounds a whole lot safer. But what if, by staying in the same old same routine or mindset you were missing out on an opportunity to bring a greater level of health into your life? What if you could have something more just by taking the time to explore the alternative path and taking a few steps into the unknown?

As one of my favourite quotes goes, "*You cannot swim for new horizons without losing sight of the shore*." Unless you are willing to be open to alternative methods then you may never know what benefits may lie in wait for you.

Also, worth a mention

During my research into fibromyalgia, I came across Dr. David Brady, and I feel that his work and perspective are worthy of noting when it comes to gaining an understanding of a fibro diagnosis or possible misdiagnosis – yes, I did just say misdiagnosis because my own investigations and Dr Brady's work are some of the reasons I believe this may be true for some.

To date, I have watched several of his interviews, read his articles and what I find particularly interesting is the point he makes as to whether everybody who is diagnosed with fibro truly has what is known as "classic fibromyalgia" (a pain processing disorder in the brain), or whether they have other issues that are causing the same symptoms.

When I first listened to Dr Brady, I was completely shocked. I was all, "Pah! Of course I have fibro!" But once I got over my initial indignation that somebody was trying to wrestle my diagnosis off of me, I was able to entertain the idea that it was possible I might not have what he describes as "classic fibromyalgia." For one, it would certainly explain why I and many other people I have come across with this condition do not respond to the standard fibro medication. It stands to reason that if we don't have a true pain processing disorder in the brain (classic fibro), then drugs that target the central nervous system via the brain will not work. I know, I know, you've had all the tests under the sun, right? Surely this can't be true because you've run the gauntlet of blood tests and all manner of diagnostics and they've revealed nothing - you've ruled out things like thyroid, coeliac disease, and more - or have you?

Something I have learned over these past few years is that often standard tests are just not in-depth enough or their ranges too broad. Take, for example, a thyroid test. For one, different countries have different ranges, so in the UK you may be deemed as not in need of treatment, yet somewhere else in the world you would. I don't know about you, but that doesn't seem to make any sense at all!

There is also the argument that individuality needs to be taken into account when considering potential thyroid issues. Yes, a test may show you as being within range, but as an individual, you may need to be at the optimal end of the range to feel well and function properly; mid-way or bottom of the range could see you experiencing symptoms that have a huge impact on your life. I know of people whose thyroid tests have been within range but have later found a doctor to treat them based on symptoms, not test ranges, and have seen a vast improvement in their health.

Another example would be magnesium and potassium testing. Many GP surgeries just test the levels of magnesium using a standard serum test as opposed to the red blood cell test (RBC) that gives a more accurate picture. The same goes for potassium testing: an RBC test is a better indicator of what your levels are. The standard serum test may show levels within range, but the RBC test can indicate a deficiency sooner. You will not believe how many symptoms of imbalances in magnesium and potassium levels are a perfect match for fibro symptoms.

Let's look at cortisol. This usually is tested through a blood test, but that can only give you an indication of whether you are high or low at that point the blood is drawn. It will not give you a full picture of what your levels are doing throughout the day. High night-time cortisol can prevent you from sleeping and can create many health issues which yes, you've guessed it, can be a match with fibro. A 4-point saliva test can provide more of an overall picture, yet it is one that is rarely offered here in the UK. In some countries like the US, they also offer a test which draws blood at several times throughout the day, which much like the saliva test gives a wider picture as to what is going on with cortisol levels and how they may be fluctuating over time.

Now let's take anaemia, a patient may be being treated for anaemia based solely on a ferritin blood test, yet they could have an issue with making iron bioavailable and actually have excess iron building up elsewhere, causing pain in joints and tissues (sound familiar?), In which case taking iron supplements will only offer temporary relief before going on to compound the issue further - my ferritin blood test put me in the low iron category, yet further, more in-depth testing revealed I had high iron levels elsewhere, my iron just wasn't getting to where it needed to be and I was experiencing symptoms because of it.

Believe me, I know how when you think you have the answer in the form of a fibro diagnosis it is hard to wrap your head and emotions around the possibility that it might be time to question the validity of it. After all, you've probably been given the news by your GP, consultant, or rheumatologist, by someone who knows what they're talking about, right? Well, according to Dr. Brady, when patients who had previously received a fibro diagnosis were put in front of a panel of fibro experts, 66% of them had been misdiagnosed!

So, what if that's you? What if you're a 66%er? And if there is something else going on, wouldn't it be a sound idea to check things out, to question and dig a little deeper? The way I see it is you have absolutely nothing to lose and everything to gain by questioning and taking a fresh look at things. This is the exact reason why I advocate taking responsibility for your own health, because sometimes you need to go elsewhere for your tests and answers.

To this day I can't say I am 100% sure if I had the correct diagnosis. Many of the things I've had going on in the past match the in-depth diagnostic criteria that Dr Brady uses, but equally, there are some things that are not a fit. I can't help but think that even "classic fibro" is a label for something going on at a deeper level - that other things have resulted in the pain processing issues. Short of flying over to Pittsburgh to meet with the man himself and telling him what symptoms I used to have, this will have to remain a mystery for now. The one thing I do know is that by working on "other things" I have overcome symptoms and I'm functioning at a high level on a day-to-day basis.

What I do know is that conventional treatment didn't help me and investigating other potential root causes has led to a greater level of health. I, for one, am extremely grateful for the likes of Dr. Brady because although I fought hard to get a diagnosis, after reading his research I found I was prepared to consider letting go of it. His reasoning allowed me to become more open-minded as to what could be wrong with me. Most importantly of all, his work creates hope either way; while he opens us up to the possibility of other diagnoses and invites us to explore other avenues, he also doesn't see "classic fibro" as unfixable either. His alternative approach makes a refreshing change to the "this is irreversible" message that goes hand in hand with a fibro diagnosis.

Mind

PART 2: CHAPTER 7

MIND

The mind is an incredible thing. It holds so much power over us. Our memories and thoughts alone are enough to evoke complex emotions and intense feelings. And it is the driver of many of our actions and behaviours and influences our health greatly. When at its best it can be our strongest ally, an invaluable tool for personal growth and a huge boost to our wellbeing. When troubled our mind can be our own worst enemy: sabotaging progress, keeping us stuck in unhelpful cycles, creating pain and discomfort both on a mental and physical level.

In the following paragraphs, I am going to demonstrate some of the ways the mind can influence the physical body - the mind-body connection. The reason I do this is to encourage you, the reader, to start to consider possible connections between your own state of mind, thoughts, beliefs, and the physical symptoms you experience.

The mind-body connection is something that can be often overlooked or downplayed when dealing with illness. Yet it plays such an important part in our health because our thought patterns, feelings, behaviours, and beliefs can all influence both our mental and physical health; what goes on in our heads can contribute to imbalances within the physical body. Thoughts, beliefs, attitudes, feelings, and emotions are all mental states and research shows that these states can positively or negatively affect our biological function. If you're not quite sure what I mean by this, then a very simple example of the mind-body connection is that butterflies in the stomach feeling we can get when we're excited or nervous.

Through a messaging system of hormones and neurotransmitters our immune, endocrine, and nervous system are in constant communication with our brain, and our state of mind can have a considerable impact on this messaging system. For example, being in a state of anxiety produces stress hormones, which creates a physical stress response from the body. Staying in this stress response for a prolonged period of time can, therefore, have a detrimental effect on health.

Many studies show that the cells in our bodies are capable of responding to vibrations. This is an important aspect of the mind-body connection since we express our thoughts through language and the words we use carry vibrational energy. Not in the words themselves, but in the intention and emotion behind them. What this means is that the things we say, the thoughts we express verbally, can physically affect the cells in our body. This may then account for how things such as positive affirmations, hypnotherapy, and adjustments to mindset can influence our physical health.

There is no question that our bodies can feel emotions, you only have to look at tension headaches and upset digestive systems in times of stress or fear to know there is a link between what we experience on an emotional level and subsequently our physical state. Therefore, it is not such a great leap to think that our state of mind, particularly when we have prolonged periods of negative thoughts and feelings, can create imbalances within the body, contributing to ill health or preventing us from healing.

It is well known that our thoughts, emotions, and feelings can create stress and anxiety. What we don't always think about is the effect this can have on the body. Stress and anxiety can cause an imbalance in cortisol levels, affect inflammatory responses, and more. Dysregulation of cortisol levels and being in a state of continuous inflammatory response can over time lead to illness. Science has proved that emotional trauma and stress can physically change our genes - the study of epigenetics has shown that the environment (psychological, microbial, social, nutritional) we are exposed to throughout our lives can impact on our DNA in how our genes read information.

It is widely acknowledged that stress and anxiety can cause physical illness; however, what is often overlooked is the root causes of the stress itself. Stress and anxiety can be the result of many things: our thought and belief patterns, the way we interpret and manage events in our lives, the blueprints which we have "downloaded" from our past that are subconsciously influencing us in the here and now and more. As individuals we all experience life differently, and there will often be a spectrum of factors as unique as we are that are influencing our state of mind and therefore our physical health. It is also important to note that one person's stress or anxiety may be another person's walk in the park. Which is also why we all respond differently from one another to our inner and external world.

If a person is not fully aware of how they are functioning in life, how they see the world, their thoughts, and behaviour patterns, etc., it is possible for their system to be placed under stress without them being entirely conscious of it - another example of why investigating potential root causes can achieve more balance, harmony, and health in life and why self-awareness is so important.

Over the years, I have witnessed a number of people who have a fibro diagnosis become outraged when it had been suggested to them that cognitive behaviour therapy (CBT) can be an effective treatment for their symptoms. They are often offended by the suggestion that emotional issues may be a causative factor of the condition. But what cannot be denied is that science has proven that prolonged emotional trauma and stress can be linked to autoimmune diseases. Since fibromyalgia does in some professionals' opinion comes under that autoimmune umbrella, then yes, whether you are happy about it or not, cognitive therapy can be useful.

To regain health, we need to look at the mind as something that needs to be nurtured, supported, and sometimes re-trained to improve our physical health - therapies such as CBT and REBT among others can do this.

So, before I boggle your mind with more talk of how the mind influences the body, let's move on to the things that I have worked on to help my mind and in turn improve my physical health.

CHAPTER 8

MINDSET

I would say that mindset, is if not the most important element of the healing process, it was the very first thing that I needed to address before I could even begin to make any progress. I soon worked out that if I was trying to improve on something, not just health, if I wasn't in the right mindset then it undermined everything I was trying to achieve.

Our mindset is heavily influenced by our knowledge, beliefs, and thoughts. It's often determined by how we see ourselves in life and the world around us. It can act as a kind of filter or lens through which we interpret and react to situations. This is why it is so important for us to be self-aware and get into the right kind of mindset that will be able to move us forward.

After I was diagnosed, I held a year-long pity party. It was very much a case of "poor old me, life is so unfair." I veered between feeling extremely sorry for myself and lamenting the skies in rage with cries of "why me." Life was shit, my body was shit, and a lot of the time I felt the whole damn world was shit. I immersed myself in what I thought was the hopelessness of my situation and I well and truly wallowed in self-pity - think hippo and mud. I resented the fact that other people could lead normal lives and developed quite the "it's all right for them" attitude. I was a fully signed up member of the "fuck my life" club. I couldn't see beyond what was wrong with my body or all the things I had been forced to cast aside. I thought just because my health was totally shit then my whole life was shit

I can't really pinpoint the exact moment when the turning point came. There wasn't one of those ground-breaking eureka moments where I realised that I needed to make a shift in mindset. I wasn't struck by enlightenment; more of a slow burn that came with the awareness that if I was going to get well, I needed to make changes. One day I just realised that I had been asking the wrong question. Instead of asking, "Why me?" I needed to be asking, "What is this trying to tell me? What do I need to be doing? Who do I need to be now?" When I started to ask those questions, then the "why is this happening to me?" became less about pity and more about discovering what had gone wrong with my health.

It was this shift in perspective and mindset which suddenly put an entirely different slant on my situation. It enabled me to see that my body was trying to communicate to me through the symptoms I was experiencing that changes needed to be made. Instead of seeing illness as the end of the road, I now saw that illness was re-routing me onto a new path. The realisation that I needed to take this new and different path from the one I was currently on switched me from wallowing and inaction into action. I began to stop thinking, “Why am I here?” in a “poor me” mindset and started to think about trying to work out how exactly I had got there. Later, I went on to gain a more spiritual perspective to the “why am I here?” question. I began to feel that I had a lot to learn from the struggles and challenges I was facing from a life-lesson perspective. Yes, it’s out, I am one of life’s woo-woo people.

The second biggest shift in my mindset came from the decision to stop talking about illness and immersing myself in it. Once I had been diagnosed, I spent a lot of time checking off symptoms against lists I found on the Internet or with other people who had fibro. Every morning when I woke up, I would lie in bed and mentally perform a body scan to identify what was hurting or not functioning properly. Before I even stepped out of bed, my mind was full of everything that was wrong with me. Now, when I look back on this habit, I think what a bloody depressing way it was to start the day!

When I first set about changing my mindset, I remembered that I had once read that the frame of mind you start your day with is what sets the tone for how the rest of your day will be. If that was true, then my morning mental checklist of doom was a pretty crap way to start things off. So, I made the decision to switch my focus to the things that were still good in my life. Of course, I still felt totally horrendous in the mornings, and many times it was a challenge to switch my focus away from the physical pain, but to start my day with a list of the good things in my life put me in a much better place. On my worst days, I would fall back on being grateful for simple things like my super comfortable bed, a hot cup of tea, or the fact I was still breathing! - anything to switch my mindset from drifting to the checklist of doom

ACCEPTANCE

I am going to talk more about acceptance in the next chapter on dealing with emotional issues, but it does need a little shout out here because it played an important part in getting myself into the right mindset. Once I was able to accept my situation for what it was, I was able to step aside from a lot of the inner conflict that being ill was creating in my life and switch my focus towards healing. Acceptance allowed me to progress forward and to realise that I had options and choices ahead of me. I began to be able to look forward instead of continually looking backwards and yearning for what was in the past.

SHUTTING THE FUCK UP

As I mentioned above, making the decision to stop talking about my symptoms and the shitty situation I was in made a big difference to my mindset and overall mood. I stopped talking about and dwelling so much on the big 'F' and began to make a conscious effort to watch the words I was using in my everyday conversations and interactions.

For a good period after I was diagnosed I had developed a habit of telling people I had fibro. Most of the time it was in response to the dreaded, "So what do you do?" question. I'd tell people about the illness to explain why I wasn't working or why I had opted to start a business that was an on-and-off type of set up. On other occasions, I would tell people to cover brain fog moments because I feared they'd think I was stupid. There were times where I'd tell a person about the condition only minutes into meeting them, such was the compulsion to explain myself, excuse, or gloss over the everyday things I was struggling with or wasn't achieving.

I remember a situation once where I was battling with my brain cells to recall the correct PIN to put into the debit card machine at the supermarket. Embarrassed by this brain fog moment I found myself telling the checkout operator I had fibro. I mean, come on, did she really need to know? Of course not. Did she care? No. Were there other people who'd forgotten their PIN that day? Probably. But this was an example of how much fibro was popping into my daily interactions, it was so forefront in my mind, part of my everything, that it became my automatic "go to" for covering awkward moments that other people would have perhaps taken in their stride or found a way around. Moments that other people didn't even notice, or to be honest, probably couldn't give two fucks about.

In the beginning, fibro was like the sulky alter-ego that would shove me out the way and take over my conversations with talk of illness, difficulties, and struggles. It was like dragging around an unwanted and boring sidekick that made my life very, very dull. That was, until I realised that I mentally had control over it, I had the power to put it in a box and tell it to shut the fuck up. Once I began to do just this, the better I began to feel about myself. I was able to see that there was still so much more to me as a person than illness.

Again, I'm not sure what precipitated the decision to stop talking so much about fibro, there wasn't one stand out moment. I just remember becoming so damn tired of hearing myself talk about the ill effects of being ill. I was sick of being that sick person. I was fed up with most of my conversations revolving around the same subject and acting as a constant reminder as to how much I couldn't do, how tired I was, or how much this or that was a struggle. And I was sick of the looks of pity I was getting from other people because of what I was bringing to the conversation. One day I just became aware that if I was boring myself rigid with all the fibro talk, then god knows what it was doing to other people - I wanted to eye roll myself, so thank you to all those people around me who refrained from doing so during that time.

It was at this point that I also became aware that by constantly affirming fibro's presence in my life through my interactions and conversations, I was allowing it to overwhelm, control, and define me. I was making it my identity. And while yes, I did need to acknowledge and accept that it was coming along for the ride, I didn't need to make it the biggest part of me. Somehow along the way, I had given it too much room in my life. I had allowed it to overstep the mark and overshadow everything else about me. All of the skills I still possessed and the roles I played in life had been pushed further and further back into the shadows. I had lost contact with so many of the other things that made me, me. I had forgotten that I was more than an illness. I was more than fibro.

So, I stopped. I stopped giving my husband, family, and friends a rundown of every symptom I was experiencing or how bad I was feeling every time I talked to them. When asked how I was I started to respond with things like, "I'm working on it," "taking it easy," or "being gentle with myself." Obviously, there were times when I did need to talk about it, burying or denying something completely doesn't help at all, but I stopped inviting in into my day, every day. I found other things to talk about or focussed on using more positive language when I did find myself on the subject. I stopped telling everyone and his mother that I had fibro. And (this is a big one) I stopped trying to make other people understand what it was like to be me.

For a considerable amount of time after I was diagnosed I spent a lot of time, energy, and talk trying to get people to understand how life was for me. How difficult it was being me. I was very much in the mindset that I needed them to know what it was like for me, to understand how or why I couldn't do things. I would get angry when people would say things like, "Why don't you come out for a night out? It will do you good." I'd end up getting myself in knots emotionally trying to make them understand just why it wouldn't do me good at all or how it would actually make me feel worse. This was one of those frustrating repeating patterns I got stuck in for some time until I had one of those "newsflash" type moments.

What was my moment of clarity? This... I was never, ever going to be able to make other people understand what it was like to live with long-term illness. I was never going to make them see what was invisible. They were never going to understand what it was like to be me simply because they weren't me. Some people would want to try and understand, some people just weren't interested. There would be people who understood my limitations, had compassion for me, and would do their best to support me, but equally, others would not. In my newsflash moment, I realised all of this was fine. I didn't need people to understand. I was wasting my time and precious energy trying to push for it. In fact, I was being unfair getting all resentful and angry towards those who couldn't. Hell, to be honest, half the time I didn't understand what was going on, so how could I expect others to grasp it? And most importantly, it wasn't serving any purpose. Getting my knickers in a twist over other people's lack of understanding wasn't benefiting me in the slightest.

This little revelation allowed me to create even more space in my mind to focus on more useful things and also to re-evaluate the people around me. I was able to create a network of genuine support with those who did understand or at least were empathic and let go of my resentment towards those who didn't. If people didn't get it, they didn't get it, and that was okay. By becoming okay with people not understanding my situation I found that some of my relationships improved because I was lowering my unfair expectations. I was able to accept that they were just human and had their limitations. I stopped blaming people for not getting what it was like to be me, and this relieved an undercurrent of tension in some relationships that had been present for some time in my conversations and interactions with them.

When I wrote earlier that counselling sessions helped me to "get over myself," this was in part referring to me being able to let go of my need to have people understand. During my therapy sessions, I had the space to get what you could call a bird's eye view of my situation and see that I was, in fact, being unreasonable. Interestingly, it has been my most recent therapy (REBT) that has given me another level of insight - that by trying to force people into understanding I was actually making the demand "you must understand me" and that was irrational.

Now, without going down too much of a therapy rabbit hole, let us just say that where there is a demand being placed on someone, it can be the product of an irrational perspective with many other thoughts and feelings going on beneath it. In my case, it was a playing out of my feeling of lack of value and a need to be heard, which you will have read earlier, links into my past history. The reason I have slipped this little paragraph in here is that I think it highlights perfectly the importance of self-awareness and learning just what is driving our actions, thoughts, and behaviours. In a time of crisis (illness), I developed a need for people to understand what I was going through because that need was being driven by a whole heap of stuff from my past. It wasn't really about the illness per se, it was about my sense of value. Continuing to push for understanding wasn't helpful to me at all; in fact, it exacerbated the situation and caused me extra stress that I didn't need. Addressing this created one of those small shifts towards feeling better.

Of course, this may not apply to you at all, but if you find yourself really needing people to understand what you are going through, if you can often be found saying stuff like, "You just don't understand what it's like," a LOT with feelings of anger, hurt, or frustration, you might want to consider just why it is you need that understanding. What is driving that need? And can you do yourself a favour by letting go of that shit so you can move on to something more proactive and healthier?

STOPPING SWIMMING IN THE SAME POND

This is the part where I talk about some online fibro groups and forums. Now, don't get me wrong. I'm all for the support, people helping other people, the benefits of shared experiences and such. In fact, in the past, I've run my own FB group and may do so again. These are some observations about myself and about some other people's (please remember I said "some") behaviour in some groups and forums, and as to why I don't feel they are always such a good place to be long-term.

This is also the part where, depending on how what I'm about to say sits with you, you may or may not want to bash me on the head, burn my book, or write me a "how fucking dare you" comment.

Warning potential contentious moment ahead

Okay, deep breath, here goes. Sometimes some online fibro forums and groups can feel like just one big ole moan-fest and pity party. Eeek! Do ya hate me? Did that feel harsh? Are you pissed off? Enraged? Well, to coin an earlier phrase, I'm sorry, not sorry! There is a reason I say this, and to probably compound things further, I'm going to pop in the quote "misery loves company." AND just in case the pitchforks aren't quite raised yet, I'm going to throw in the observation that surrounding oneself in the kind of negative vibe that can be in a some of these groups day in and day out is not good for anyone's health.

Now, I just want to say, Woah Nellie! Before anyone gets all up in my face over this, please just hang fire while I add something else. Let me add that I've met some fantastic people in fibro forums and groups that have become friends. I have also found little gems of advice that have helped further my recovery. Group/forums and such do have their rightful place in this world (the more proactive ones that actually offer useful advice and feel the love are best). They can help people feel less alone, they can be a safe place to vent, they may be a person's only place of support and understanding. But unfortunately, there is a flip side to some of them too that I feel is important to note, and that is the sense of doom and gloom they can bring into our lives.

Initially, I was a very active member of in certain fibro groups. For a while, I was in one or another on a daily basis before I realised that although there were occasional benefits to be had, these were outweighed by the fact that I was regularly opening myself up to a high level of negativity. Of course, the very basis that places are built on (illness) doesn't exactly promote a party vibe or an abundance of cheeriness - how can it? I'm certainly not judging anyone for being negative. After all, everyone is sick and thoroughly fucked off. However, I found that exposing myself to a huge amount of daily negativity when I was already low wasn't healthy on a long-term basis - listening to bad news over and over has to do something to your brain, right? Well, yes it does. Scientific studies have proven that negative thoughts, words, and phrases can have an impact on the brain and in turn our wellbeing.

Negative talk and thoughts can interfere with the production of the neurochemicals that are produced to protect us from stress. Just hearing negative words increases the number of stress-producing hormones in the brain, which can impact on the way we communicate, process language, and how we reason. Negative or fear-producing words can increase activity in the part of our brain (the amygdala) that decodes emotions and detects danger. Although not directly responsible for causing us to feel fearful, the increased activity can kick start a type of fear response (secretion of chemicals) in the brain, which in turn floods the entire body with fear-producing hormones; a chain reaction response that triggers our adrenals, cortisol release, and our flight-or-fight response. Believe me, this is not something we want happening to our body when it is already under considerable stress. When we look at how words, thoughts, etc., can have a lasting impact on us, then we can see how it's possible that regular prolonged exposure to a lot of negativity can contribute to poor physical health – the mind-body connection.

Despite the negative aspect, I do think that some forums and groups can be a good resource because they give us a place to ask questions and seek advice, feel less isolated, especially in the early days after diagnosis. They can provide comfort and understanding, but I think perhaps it would serve people better if they were to dip in and out of them or use them only as a "as or when" type of resource. I feel that sometimes when we get totally absorbed with a group of people who are all in the same boat as us it can unwittingly become an invitation to get caught up in our misfortunes longer than is good for us. I guess what I am saying here is that I feel it's important for mindset to not make online fibro groups and forums a permanent or only place of support. That it is healthier for us to look for support in other places - join some health groups, seek out the support groups that are more upbeat and focus on things that can make life better or connect with stuff elsewhere on a daily basis that will help boost our wellbeing and raise our vibe, not lower it. The main point I'm making here is that when considering which groups to join, choose wisely - go for the ones that are trying to help move us forward.

I eventually made the decision to leave fibro groups and forums altogether; stop swimming in the same pond - I just saw one too many of those "if you could only see fibro, it would look like this" images with the aim of making fibro pain visible and endless infographics listing all the symptoms, limitations, and struggles. You know, on the one hand I get it, this fibro shit is a soul sucking bastard. In fact, in the past I used to post things like that myself, but in reality, what is it all for? Does it really change anything? Does it actually make us feel better? Or is it a constant visual reminder in our social media feeds that keeps us caught up in the awfulness of it all? I don't know about you, but I have never sat back after posting or reading something like that and thought, "Wow I feel much better now." For me all did was reaffirm how awful things were and invited me to dwell on health issues. These days I no longer see any benefit to this sort of stuff, giving my attention to these types of posts or allowing them space in my thoughts- if our heads are filled with negativity there's no space for optimism. Again, this brings me back around to the point of wasting valuable time and energy on stuff that isn't going to move us forward or be of any direct benefit to our health and wellbeing.

THE ILLNESS PAYOFF

So, this is another one of those moments where I feel that I might need to get light on my feet so I can dodge the missiles some readers might want to throw at me when they read the following paragraphs. Now, if this hits a nerve I'm going to ask you to just stick with it, not go with any knee-jerk reactions, throw my book out the window, or dismiss this whole thing just because you may be feeling outraged, pissed, indignant, or whatever first leaps into your mind when you read on.

Ready? Here goes...

When I started to be able to view my situation from a more objective perspective I was able to see that although I desperately didn't want to be sick there were some hidden payoffs to the situation I was in (subconscious secondary gain)

Yes, (holds up hands) I did just say that. Now, I'm not saying this definitely applies to you, my reader, but it is something I have observed. I feel is worth consideration because what I've learned from being in this healing game is that progress can come from the smallest of shifts in mindset, and to make those shifts it can mean digging deep, looking into stuff that is really uncomfortable, and unearthing hidden thoughts , mechanisms and behaviours.

When I talk about there being a payoff to illness, what I am drawing attention to is that sometimes, out of our awareness, we can find ourselves "stuck" in certain situations or struggling to find our way out because there can be a subconscious emotional need being met by the situation we are in. And when that happens, our brain will do its best to convince us that we do not need to change our situation.

On a conscious level, in our everyday thoughts, we find our situation far from comfortable (illness is not comfortable, period). Consciously, we know we want to be anywhere else but in pain, brain fogged, fatigued, etc. However, there can, at times, through the subconscious fulfilment of an emotional need, be a hidden payoff to our current situation. It is this sense of fulfilment (that is running subconsciously in the background of our lives) that can make it more difficult to sustain the will to make the changes we need to become healthier.

How's that sitting with you so far? I think before we go on, I might need to give a voice to some of the thoughts you might just be having right now. Are you currently doing any of the following...?

"WHAAAAT?! You dumb ass crazy woman!" "Did I really just read that?" "WTF. Did she really suggest that there was something to be gained from being sick?" "Don't you think I'd be well if I could?" "Of course, I don't want to be fucking sick you moron!" "How dare she suggest I'm benefitting from this shit!" "I'm not reading any more of this stupid book!" "Fuck you"

Okay, if any of that is you, this may be a bit of a big ask after what you've just read, but I'm going to ask you to suspend your outrage, hurt etc., and read just a little bit further and allow me to explain the reasoning behind this "light the touch paper" moment of mine.

To explain things, I'm going to need to introduce you to some of the clever but seemingly cray-cray things our mind can do. The brain being the clever thing it is can perceive when an emotional need is being met, even if, like in the case of illness, the need is being met from a really shitty source. It simply doesn't register that this source is a place our conscious self is less than thrilled to be in.

You see, this brain of ours is not fussy, in fact, it's a bit of a floozy - it doesn't care where the satisfaction comes from, just that it's satisfied; that the need is met. Think of a child who is perpetually acting out to get attention. They don't want to be naughty and get into trouble all the time, but subconsciously any kind of attention fulfils their emotional need to be noticed. The brain of the child doesn't care that it got attention from being told off, it's just happy to complete its "attention met" tick box. Meanwhile, the child falls into the cycle of getting attention through bad behaviour and unfortunately becomes known as a giant pain in the arse in the process.

To help explain things further, I'm going to use my own experience of what I call the "illness payoff" as an example. I can say that 100% in my conscious mind I did not want to be sick, I had plans for my life, and that certainly did not involve being too fatigued or too pained to achieve it. Back then I would have been absolutely outraged at the mere suggestion that I was getting a payoff from being sick, but as I have discovered, that is exactly what was happening, and what's more, it was interfering with my healing.

What was my payoff? Security. In an irrational way (operative words) illness provided me with a sense of security. Now, that may sound absolutely crazy, but being able to stay at home, not to have to put myself in what I viewed as positions of vulnerability - out in a regular workplace or in the big wide world as much as I would have done if I had been fully well, met my emotional need for security very nicely. It wasn't in my awareness, but my brain was perceiving that on some level my current situation (stay at home ill person) was keeping me safe and comfortable, which meant that my emotional need for security was being met. A need that was formed from all the years I had previously spent feeling threatened.

Now because one of my brain's priorities was to keep me safe and protected, what happened next was that it created little mental blocks in the form of unhelpful thoughts which sabotaged my motivation and helped to perpetuate the belief that I couldn't get well. Thoughts like, "what's the point," "this thing is incurable," "pushing myself will just make me feel worse," "I'll try tomorrow," and all the other little thoughts that would zap my desire to search for things that might help me feel better. Why did my brain do this? Because it was doing its job. It was protecting me and keeping me safe from having to experience situations that might make me feel insecure, anxious, or uncomfortable. Something that is also important to note here is that the brain cannot distinguish between a real threat and what is imagined, it just goes into protection mode whatever the circumstances.

Of course, I knew I wasn't happy to be living a life of illness, who would be? But my brain (my subconciousness) was so clever at running the show behind the scenes that I didn't realise it was sabotaging my own desire to get well. It also needs to be said that at this point I was busy dancing on the table at my own pity party, so these thoughts also matched up nicely with my victim mindset of the time.

What I wasn't aware of at the time was that when illness enabled me to avoid things I didn't like doing, when I had a valid reason to cry off from situations I was uncomfortable with or avoid people and places that stressed me, my brain was busy congratulating itself on a job well done. Having people look out for me, being able to read a book anytime I wanted, take a bath anytime I wanted, and watch back-to-back episodes of "Criminal Minds" three afternoons a week also made my subconscious mind think I was safe, secure, and that everything was tickety boo. As crazy as it sounds, in my subconscious mind, regaining my health was a threat because it opened me up to the possibilities of an unfamiliar life, and for someone like me who craved who security, that was scary. If I was to create a formula for my situation at the time it would look something like this: Illness = not having to do uncomfortable/scary shit = security.

As harsh and as uncomfortable as it sounds, I had to deeply question my desire to get well. I had to ask myself the difficult questions, "What was illness giving me?" And, "Was every part of me ready to get well?"

There is no doubt this kind of self-reflection is one of those "squirm in your pants" situations. Asking yourself to consider that on sub sunconcious level illness might be keeping you stuck in some way because it's meeting some kind of deep-seated emotional need is not pleasant in the slightest. In fact, on face value, it's pretty fucking offensive. After all, who wants to think or know that their mind might be in some way holding them back from addressing their health issues? And having someone else suggest it well thats just beyond the pale. But something I have learnt over the years of healing is sometimes the biggest shifts come out of the most uncomfortable and unexpected places.

I am not saying this is something that everyone is going through. You may not connect with this at all, you may be thinking, "I don't have any of this going on, thank you, lady," "I don't need to ask myself those questions." Maybe you don't but let me just pop in another example. I had an acquaintance with a chronic illness. Prior to her becoming sick her relationship with her husband was fairly rocky - she felt invisible, that her husband paid little attention to her, was too wrapped up in his work, and often didn't seem to care how she was or what she was doing. When through illness her life became challenging, her husband surprisingly stepped up. He became more caring, attentive and paid more attention to her needs.

Can you see where I am going with this? This person's situation was far from ideal, she absolutely hated being ill. In her conscious mind, she wanted nothing more than to be well, but the hidden payoff (her secondary gain) was her husband's care and attention – something she craved and the thing that had been lacking in her relationship when she was well. Subconsciously, her brain was thinking "Bingo!" Because her emotional need for her husband to be more attentive was being met. Therefore, her mind started to throw a spanner in the works when it came to sustaining the desire to get well. There was an unspoken and possibly unconscious fear of "what if I get well and my husband goes back to ignoring me," so it became easy for her subconscious mind to influence her thoughts and behaviour and divert her away from taking any action that might threaten her new reality: a reality in which her husband was attentive - the "illness payoff."

Just to clarify things here, I don't want you to go away from reading this section thinking that I am suggesting that you are not trying to get well or that you are enjoying being ill. I 100% know that is not the case. There is no blame apportioned to what is essentially a behavioural mechanism that creates a trap. The key bit of information here to hang our hats on is that our subconscious mind controls approximately 95%-98% of our actions, thoughts, behaviours, etc. - for all of us who were thinking that we are consciously in control of our lives, think again. Stuff that is hidden in our subconscious mind includes our reactions, desires, beliefs, habits, and repressed feelings. All of this hidden stuff can either work for us or against us, which is why getting to know ourselves can help us to discover if something may be sabotaging or hindering our attempts to get started on healing.

To be honest, my own subconscious shenanigans were not the biggest roadblock to my healing, but they did have a walk-on part in this drama, so they get a mention because recognising and dealing with them was a small yet meaningful factor in my being able to get into the right mindset to start making changes.

Whatever you feel about what you have just read, I would still say to ask yourself those difficult questions and really dig deep. If you come up empty-handed then cast it aside. If you have a tremendous amount of resistance to the notion, or emotive response then ask yourself why? Sometimes this can be an indication of something hitting too close to home for comfort because it holds an element of truth we do not want to look at.

If you do think it resonates, then firstly, high five for an impressive display of self-awareness. Secondly, maybe you can create a shift by addressing it. Wherever you land with this information, I don't think there's a need to get too hung up on this matter. One way or the other it's good, it either gives you something to disregard or to work on. Just by looking at the possibility around this subject you are getting to know yourself more, and as I am always saying, self-awareness is key to progress!

NOT LETTING THIS SHIT OWN ME

During the early days of illness, it was as if fibro and I were existing in some kind of inseparable partnership. An intense relationship where an unwanted other half was controlling and overshadowing everything in my life. Where I went, fibro came, it dominated conversations and made its presence known at every opportunity. I was permanently struggling to get out from under it and it was beginning to define who I was. That was, until I started to sever some of the ties I had with it: the groups, stopping bringing it into my daily conversations, and consciously giving it less attention. I stopped letting it own me. How? By distancing myself from it, by creating a psychological boundary.

You will see in this book that I never refer to fibro as "my" anything, I don't say things like "my illness," "my fibro." (go on, have a quick scan, I know you want to), I don't form any personal connection with it in that way. This may seem like an insignificant action, but on a psychological level, it played an important part in my being able to push fibro a little more into the periphery of my life. This is not the same as denial (I did that too - it doesn't work), it's more about having an acceptance of fibro as a place/space I was in but not something that was my identity. As far as I was concerned, although it was a part of me, it was just a state of being, not what actually made me, me. I felt it didn't warrant an equal place alongside my values, beliefs, and how I saw myself in this world because there was so much more to me that came before it.

In the self-help field, there is a lot of talk about owning experiences. While I think it's important to acknowledge and accept situations, take responsibility for our thoughts, actions, and behaviour, there is a difference between owning an illness and an illness owning you. And in the beginning, I found it very easy to slip into the latter. You may disagree with me on this, you may feel that illness does define you and you are okay with that. Personally, that doesn't work for me. If I let it define me, I let it own me, and that just isn't going to happen on my watch. I am determined that although illness has been life-changing, it doesn't need to be something that defines me. The way I like to phrase it is with this little mantra of mine: "It may be life changing but it doesn't need to be life-defining – it's how I choose to respond that defines me."

There is no question that illness has shaped my life and my decisions and to some, that may be the same as defining, but for me, I would describe it more as having an influence over my life. This influence changed me as a person, at times it has dictated outcomes, but it hasn't completely defined who I am as a person. I am a mother, a wife, a friend, a sister, a daughter, an aunt, an author, a communicator, a coach. I am creative, resilient, funny, determined, tenacious, strong-willed, stubborn, and many more things depending on how you find me. Fibro deserves a place at the bottom of this list. It's something that has sat alongside all the things I am. Something that I have acknowledged and accepted, but I have found from a mindset perspective that it is healthier for me to not make it one of the primary things that describe me as a person - not to make it foremost on my "I am" list

When we have a chronic illness, of course, it is part of us, there's no getting away from it or negating the enormity of illness when there are so many limitations forced upon us. It can't be ignored when it's having such a huge impact on our daily life, but I do feel that it is important not to allow it to become the most important part of us. Not to make it the sole focus of our lives or continually orbit around it as if it was the centre of our universe.

SHOWING UP

This is one of those things that was very much my own personal experience and I want to be clear that I am not making any judgements on other anyone else's situation.

I feel that I was fortunate to have small children when I became ill. To some that might seem an odd thing to say because, on the one hand, it complicated things by having to find the energy to care for someone other than myself. Undoubtedly it made things harder, but having to do this also kept me in a sense of routine. I had a purpose and that was good for my mindset, otherwise I think I would have sunk without a trace. The majority of days I was forced to get up and do the school run, without which I think I would have remained in bed all day.

The small actions of washing and dressing, no matter how hard, had to be done because most of the time I simply didn't have a choice. On the whole, it was a non-negotiable task, but it was one that forced me to show up for the day ahead. Granted, there were many days where I spent a great deal of time laying down after the school run, but this enforced morning routine of mine kept me from surrendering to my bed for days on end. I still rested, but I would either lie fully clothed atop the covers or rest on the sofa with a blanket. On a day-to-day basis I rarely got back into bed, because it was important to me from a mindset perspective that I could claim getting up and dressed as a small victory against illness. There were of course some times where I was forced back into bed after completely tanking myself after doing more than my ordinary (reduced list) of things but on the whole, I was regularly showing up in the way I described above.

In my mind, sticking to this routine created a sense of normality. I felt as if I was sending the message to myself that on some level I was still functioning and facing the day. In the early years, there were days (mainly school holidays) where I didn't get up or didn't bother getting dressed, but catching sight of my pyjama clad self with sticky unwashed hair in the mirror at 2 p.m. just made me feel worse about myself. Staying in bed, not washing or getting dressed, always made me feel groggy and sluggish, it created a slump that had a knock-on effect on my whole outlook for the hours ahead. It set an uninspiring tone for the day and created a melancholy that I would then struggle to shake off.

Showing up for the day in this way kept a bit of a boundary between me and illness and gave me something to build on. It drew a line between my day and night, and I believe that this helped me to establish a better sleep routine later on. Getting out of bed signalled to my brain that my bed was the place I was supposed to get into for sleep, not somewhere I spent all of my days - although I might have been spending a lot of time on the sofa there was still this dividing line between the two spaces.

As you will well know, with chronic illness it's those simple everyday tasks that can feel like climbing mountains. It wasn't, by any stretch, easy to get up and dressed. Sometimes my husband would have to help me to step into my knickers, and to this day dry shampoo is still my best friend. But despite the difficulties, it did give me a sense of achievement and satisfaction. I kept my morning routine low key and simple. Some days it would just be refreshing my face, tackling my underarms, and liberally applying the dry shampoo, other times I made it into the bath or shower. A lot of the time I also stuck to a simple make-up routine, applying a little BB cream, doing my brows, and waving some mascara around because it helped me to feel like myself. I dressed in comfortable clothes that still made me feel good about myself. (I could probably make the Guinness Book of World Records for the number of long-sleeved tees owned). I developed the mindset that if I was going to be sick, I was going to look half decent and have a "fuck you" attitude while I was doing it - sick but sassy was the order of the day. While it might seem a bit crazy to some that I got dressed and put some slap on just to lie on the sofa, it was important to me on a psychological level that illness wasn't reflected in my clothes or my face. I didn't want to dress like a sick person and my make-up reminded me I was still winning on some level despite feeling so ill.

The stuff we wear and the way we present ourselves does have an impact on mindset and mood. It's a known fact that certain colours can influence mood, feelings, and emotions. Of course, I can appreciate that not everyone is able to get out of bed because their symtoms, fatigue, pain may be too great. Thinking about washing hair, let alone adding a dash of lippy, etc., is the very least of concerns for some. However, I've found achieving those little daily things that were easy to let slide were what helped me to retain a sense of self, keep a connection with what made me feel more together and capable.

I am not saying everyone should or can get out of bed but I do honestly believe no matter what the situation is, even if we're a million miles from where we want to be, even when we're sick and every day is an uphill climb, there are still ways to make small shifts that will bring a little bit of light back into our days and help us to feel like we are showing up. Even if it's having a selection of the most fabulous print pj's, or leggings to wear while we're holed up in bed or asking someone else to help us with the little things like a face or hair wash to makes us feel more like ourselves.

COMMITMENT TO MYSELF

This subject kind of sits with self-responsibility, but also helped to keep me in the right mindset. Once I realised that I was going to have to be my own knight in shining armour, I made a commitment to myself to do the best for myself. When times got tough and I couldn't see the wood for the trees, when I found myself being sucked into that unhelpful spiral of "my life is shit," "it's so unfair," "it's too hard," etc., I would remind myself that I had chosen to commit to this path and that I alone had made the decision to take it. Nobody was forcing me to do it. I told myself I could stop right there if I wanted, I could step away from everything I was doing and stick with how things were, and weirdly, like some kind of reverse psychology mind game, this worked. When I gave myself the option to quit I never fully took it. Sometimes I took a day or so out to surrender to it, to lie on the floor, cry, and hold a mini pity party. But then I would resurface and regroup by asking myself, "What next?" What little step could I take next to keep my commitment to myself to heal and to get me back up into that saddle?

There is no denying that healing is a commitment, to fully heal you need to fully commit. It's the time to go all in, to push your chips into the centre of the table and bet on yourself. There will be many tests and challenges, but I feel this is no different than other situations in life. People who commit to things like marriage, a burning cause, or children face challenges all the time, and the same goes for recovery from long-term illness. The choice as to whether you stick with the commitment to heal is entirely up to you, no one is making you do it, but equally, nobody will do it for you. One thing I will say is that if you have stuck with or by any other long-term commitment in your life before this, then you are more than capable of sticking with this too.

PUTTING MYSELF FIRST

Getting into the mindset of making myself a priority, becoming numero uno, and placing my stuff above others was difficult. I used to be the sort of person who would drag myself to events feeling like death for a fear of disappointing or letting other people down. I was the type who, when feeling myself coming down with one of the bouts of tonsillitis I was prone to, would whizz around the house like a whirling dervish tidying, organising, and putting washing on, etc., because I knew I would soon be out of action for at least a week (I know! How bat shit crazy is that?). I was also, without a doubt, one of life's people pleasers. I used to put so many other things and other people's needs before my own. I would take on stuff, commit myself to do stuff, that often turned out to be to my own detriment, especially when it came to maintaining energy levels.

It took a considerable while for me to see that putting myself and my own needs first wasn't an unecessary selfish act. That it was okay to cancel an appointment, reschedule a meetup, or break a commitment because I needed to take care of me first. Nor was it too selfish to distance myself from the situations or relationships that compromised in any way.

When I first started putting myself first it was mighty uncomfortable. I felt guilty for bailing out on a pre-planned event and then spending the time quietly reading a book and recharging my batteries. I experienced a lot of "I should be" when I chose to stay home and rest instead of driving half an hour to catch up with someone. For a while, I worried that changing my mind and rescheduling came across as being flaky. I felt like I was going against everything I had built myself up in my own mind to be - If I was asked to list my attributes, dependable, reliable, and committed would be on that list. These were important personal values and aspects of my personality to me. Initially, when I first started making me my number one priority, I felt like I was somehow reneging on these qualities. Now, I realise that changing plans, etc., didn't negate those attributes. Cancelling a lunch date didn't make me any less committed or worth less. In fact, it meant that I was committed to taking care of myself - It is not lost on me that when I was doing all that self-sacrificing stuff, being there for others more than myself and putting my needs at the bottom of the pile, that meant I was continually negating my worth anyway.

I used to have a friend who was brilliant at putting herself first. She thought nothing of cancelling plans last minute if she wasn't feeling up to it. At the time of our friendship, I would have conflicting thoughts over her actions. On one hand, I admired her ability to focus on herself and on the other a small part of me used to think, "Really? Could you not have tried harder to make it?" (pure projection of my at the time skewed standards). It wasn't until sometime later when we were no longer in each other's lives that I realised that she had it right all along. I finally got the memo that you shouldn't have to try harder to push yourself when self-care needs to be your priority. You have every right to cancel stuff if you're not up to it for any reason. It doesn't have to be another person's version of a good reason; it just has to be what's right for you in the here and now. I also learnt that there are no medals given for dragging yourself about the place, acting the martyr or doing shit in the misguided hope you'll retain the title of Most Reliable Person of *insert year*

I feel the key here is about learning to help ourselves before helping others, all that cheesy stuff we see in motivational quotes about filling our own cup before giving to others and the in-flight advice about putting the oxygen mask on ourselves first. It's all true! Putting ourselves first is a form of self-care; caring for ourselves and caring for others are not mutually exclusive. One enriches the other and prioritising our own needs will often be reflected in a deeper sense of inner contentment, which can lead to less resentment towards the tasks we need to do for others.

This wasn't to say that putting myself first meant that I bailed on everything I didn't want to do in life. As we know, there are many times in life when we still have to do shit even when we don't want to. Sometimes it's because it's a commitment or obligation we can't dodge, like making sure our kids are kept alive and sometimes like exercise, simply because it's for our own damn good. For sure there were certain roles I had in life that came with non-negotiable tasks. As a mother, I was responsible for three other little people. There were certain things that I had to do. There were many times where their needs had to come above my own, but as I started to put myself first more in other areas, I came to realise that in the past I had been putting too much stuff above my own needs and there were things I could let go of. I learnt that delegating and asking for help and not being such a bloody martyr meant I had more time for addressing my own needs, so I broke off my long-standing friendship with Miss Martyr and struck up a healthier relationship with Miss Delegation instead.

I also found that as I started to put myself first more, I was more able to say no to the things that weren't non-negotiable that I didn't enjoy or that didn't sit comfortably with me. The things I had always gone along with for the sake of peace, through fear of upsetting others or concerning myself with what others might think of me if I didn't. Saying no wasn't an easy task for me, I was naturally a yes person, and as I have said, a people pleaser. When I first started to say yes to myself and no to others, I felt the need to excuse why I couldn't do something or be somewhere. After a while, it dawned on me that by providing a detailed reason for my no show I was trying to justify to my decision to others and to myself. I was excusing myself and in a roundabout way apologising for being me. I finally realised I didn't need to provide an excuse or reason, and I certainly didn't need to apologise for making myself a priority. I stopped apologising and giving long-winded or self-justifying reasons and switched to using simple statements such as, "I can't make it that day," or "That doesn't work for me," without tagging on those extra sentences as an explanation.

The bonus to this new approach and natural progression of this way of being meant that I started to gravitate more towards people and experiences that were more aligned with my values and principles. I felt more confident in the stuff I was doing on a day-to-day basis, which brought about a level of contentment that had eluded me until then. I created boundaries and stuck with them. I found myself happier and more settled, which of course helped me both on a mental and physical level.

By making this adjustment and prioritising myself I was no longer wasting precious energy on things and people that weren't a good fit for me. I was able to use that energy to be more productive and work on things that would benefit me from a health perspective. Because I was no longer engaging with situations that caused internal conflict and left me feeling out of sorts, I was able to let go of the resentments that had built up over time from all the stuff I felt I should be doing. One of life's little lessons that came out of this situation was that when your actions are coming from a place of resentment or a misplaced sense of duty it can be stressful and a big drain on your energy.

It was taking responsibility for tackling illness that led me to become better at respecting myself and putting my own needs first. As I healed it became more and more important that I spent the time that I was clawing back from illness in a way that continued to move me forward. Therefore, it seemed much more appropriate and healthier to spend my increased energy levels on living my own best life rather than allowing other people and their priorities to dictate the flow.

As I discovered, if we're not used to doing it, learning to say no can be really uncomfortable. It can be met with surprise from the people around us who are used to us toeing the line or always being available. We can face pressure from some folks who'd like us to get back into our "yes" box or the mould they help create for us because the new person we have become makes them uncomfortable. However, I can assure you once you get the hang of it, it's liberating, empowering, and slightly addictive!

Saying no has the power to release us from underlying stressors, unhelpful patterns of behaviour, it allows us to set strong boundaries and free up the time and energy for focusing on the stuff that really matters, and is beneficial to our overall wellbeing.

QUITTING THE COMPARISON GAME

Some time ago I started to reduce the amount of time I spent on social media. I stopped spending so many of my precious hours scrolling through endless showreels of other people's lives because no matter how hard I tried, I would still get sucked into the comparison game. Despite knowing that it was likely that minutes before that picture-perfect family shot was taken the kids in it were probably trying to bicker their way into the Guinness Book of Records. Even though I knew that most people only post the edited golden highlights of their lives, I would still find myself comparing my life to others.

When I was really sick, I used to constantly compare the life I wasn't able to lead to the lives of healthy people. Then, as I began to heal, I switched to comparing my level of healing to others I thought were on the same path. That was, until the day I discovered that our unique biochemistry means we all heal in different ways and at different paces. With that realisation, it dawned on me that I was wasting valuable energy and time focusing on how someone else was going about their life. It really didn't matter what they were doing or when they were doing it because my life and healing path would always be different from theirs.

This past couple of years I have discovered that comparing my life with others and spending time wishing myself into somebody else's life is a distraction, a mood zapper, and quite frankly, a fucking monumental waste of time and energy. It fuels procrastination and it's not in the slightest bit helpful when trying to keep in the mindset that is needed for getting stuff done in my own life, like healing. I now try to look at comparing from the perspective that if it inspires me, then it's useful. If it drags me down or brings out the worst in me (critical inner bitch), then I need to let it go. When I do find myself slipping into comparing my progress with other people or wishing I was more like other people, I ask myself these two questions: "Is this helpful?" "Does it put me in a good mindset?" This usually sorts out the wheat from the chaff and helps me to filter out all the unhelpful stuff that can have a negative impact on my mindset and health.

WATCHING MY LANGUAGE

I think it's obvious by the swear words that are liberally scattered throughout this book that I'm not talking about cursing here. (Although I did once give up swearing for nearly 3 years as a New Year resolution) No, what I am referring to is how I learnt to check in with my self-talk, tune into and overhaul the language I used to describe myself, my situation, and most importantly, the things I was saying to myself. As I mentioned earlier, when talking about support groups and the like, negative words and phrases can have an impact on our wellbeing because of the way the brain perceives them, and the subsequent physical responses to what we say, think, and hear can have a lasting impact on our health.

Something that I find really cool (nerd moment) is that just like a cute puppy, our brains can be taught new ways and become quite well behaved. Yep, that old brain of ours can be steered away from old pathways of negative thinking into positive pastures anew. I'm not going to venture into the complex subject of neuroplasticity here, so basically, here's the low down.

By watching and being more mindful of how we are speaking to others and to ourselves, by learning to use more positive words and phrases in our day-to-day talk, we can use our brain to improve our general wellbeing. By learning to hold more positive words in our minds and use more positive language we can transform our outlook on life and even alter our reality... Woah! Seriously cool, huh? - Or is that just me?

Is this sounding a little too woo-woo or sci-fi for you? Or do you find the prospect that we can create a shift in our reality with our language as mind-blowing (excuse the pun) as I do? Regardless of which side of the fence you're sitting on with this subject, let me just drop a bit of a science bomb and share with you this excerpt from Andrew Newberg, MD and Mark Robert Waldman's book, Words can Change Your Brain:

"By holding a positive and optimistic [word] in your mind, you stimulate frontal lobe activity. This area includes specific language centers that connect directly to the motor cortex responsible for moving you into action. And as our research has shown, the longer you concentrate on positive words, the more you begin to affect other areas of the brain. Functions in the parietal lobe start to change, which changes your perception of yourself and the people you interact with. A positive view of yourself will bias you toward seeing the good in others, whereas a negative self-image will include you toward suspicion and doubt. Over time the structure of your thalamus will also change in response to your conscious words, thoughts, and feelings, and we believe that the thalamic changes affect the way in which you perceive reality."

You see, our language, our thoughts, how we phrase things, really can affect our perception of ourselves, others, and the world in general. Therefore, on some level impacting on our day-to-day reality. To keep all of this nice and simple and in line with the topic of fibro and regaining health, what this boils down to is the more positive language we use in our talk and thoughts, the greater positive effect it has on the brain. This can make us feel better physically and mentally, and helps us to gain a much healthier outlook and perspective on life and other people. Which in turn makes us more receptive to opportunities.

We have already looked at the how the mind-body connection impacts on health - this is another example of how that connection works, how through a relatively small action such as monitoring our talk, using positive affirmations, choosing gratitude, etc., we can take a step towards a healthier future.

What this subject is leading to is how much things changed for me when I learned not to be so hard on myself, not to beat myself up with my thoughts and language, and became more aware of what was in my head and what was coming out of my mouth. When we are struggling with a long-term illness it's very easy to become frustrated and fixated on our lack of ability to do stuff. I used to be really hard and critical of myself, I really bore the brunt of my own frustrations. I would regularly say things like, "My body's useless," "If it wasn't for this stupid body," "I hate…" I would always be thinking about how pathetic I was because I couldn't do what other people could do. I held a huge amount of negative thoughts and beliefs about myself, and because I do like to share, at times I extended my frustrations to others - criticising and bringing them down too.

When I realised all of this being down on myself and being a critical knob-head towards others wasn't helping my healing a jot, I found kinder ways to talk to myself and others. I switched my talk to the more positive end of the language spectrum using phrases like, "My body is doing the best it can." I stopped belittling myself, quit the not so funny self-deprecating shit, and learnt to appreciate how well my body was trying its best to function under difficult circumstances. I stopped ruminating on everything that was wrong with me and focused on small victories - yep, there's that gratitude thing again!

I write more about this in the chapters ahead, but all in all, taking note and being more mindful of my language helped me to develop a greater sense of self-compassion, something that is most definitely needed when we are trying to heal ourselves.

PUTTING ONE FOOT IN FRONT OF THE OTHER

Keeping motivated in life at the best of times is hard enough. Chuck in long-term illness, especially one that causes pain and fatigue, and you can watch motivation drain faster than a bucket full of holes. If we then add to the mix the feelings of guilt, inadequacy, and frustration that bubble to the surface when we know there's stuff we could be doing to help ourselves but we just can't seem to get on with them - what we get are days when it can feel easier to climb back under the duvet, wait it out, and hope that we might feel more motivated tomorrow. The only problem with that is that A) Nothing gets moved forward, and B) All those crappy feelings it evokes add up to extra emotional pressure nobody needs.

Throughout my healing journey I have frequently struggled with motivation. You'd think being ill would be motivating enough, but it seems at least in my case, it doesn't work that way. (P.S. Thyroid issues can induce apathy like a motherfucker.) Because motivation has always difficult for me to summon up and often deserts me, until fairly recently my healing progress came down to two things: willpower and perseverance. Over the years I have relied heavily on this duo to help push me through the challenges and obstacles I have faced.

When it comes to motivation, I have never really known what it would take to really spur me on except maybe a rocket up the backside. Which brings me to the point about how I got around the lack of motivation without having to continually call upon my willpower and perseverance.

Some time ago, I happened upon an interview with Mel Robbins: a motivational speaker, coach, and creator of the 5-Second Rule - an idea that was originally inspired by the countdown of a NASA rocket launch. Now, I can't tell you how many times I've wanted to throw in the towel on this journey, where I told myself I couldn't be bothered to do this any longer, that it was too hard, yada, yada, but the day I stumbled across this lady's interview was the day I began to feel much better about my lapses in motivation. It gave me one more tool to add to my self-help toolbox that has enabled me to bypass the mental battles I have often experienced when trying to keep on track with healing.

Discovering this fresh take on motivation turned everything I had previously thought on its head. The first point in this interview that really hit home was the statement that motivation is "total BS;" a complete load of baloney. That statement instantly made me feel a whole heap better about the times I lacked the motivation to continue with my healing.

According to Mel Robbins, we'd all be better off if we stopped trying to get motivated…

Really?! Yeah, I know, right? This completely goes against everything we're told! But just how can that attitude be helpful when trying to heal? Well, this is how it all works. First, we can stop with all that searching and trying to gear ourselves up to get cracking with making changes because here's the thing… we're wasting our time with that. As humans, we're naturally programmed to kick back at making changes because change can be scary, uncomfortable, and overwhelming - yes, it's that subconscious brain protection thing again.

Okay, so I kind of knew as much, I knew that many of us shy away from doing what's uncomfortable, but what did that have to do with lack of motivation? Isn't that the moment where motivation is needed it the most? No. Apparently not. Now, this is the part that really surprised me in this interview. Mel

Robbins discusses why we're NEVER going to feel ready or motivated to do the things that are scary, uncomfortable, and such. This was a real "aha" moment for me. Things suddenly made more sense. It explained the many times I promised myself I'd start tomorrow and the hours of procrastinating I did before finally getting down to it. The times I felt inadequate for not being able to get on with or restart the simplest of things which I knew would help me; it turns out I had been waiting for a motivational train that was never going to arrive at the platform.

Why do I feel this important to anyone thinking of starting a healing journey? Because I think we can waste a lot of time waiting for our motivational train to arrive and we can get caught in the habit of mentally beating ourselves up for failing to catch it. Although the 5-Second Rule is something that I have only more recently incorporated into my healing process, it's one of those things that I wished I had come across sooner. I think it would have helped me to feel better about not feeling motivated to heal and enabled me to avoid some negative self-talk and unhelpful mental conversations with myself.

Right then, so now we're all feeling better about not having to hang about waiting for motivation to strike - What's this rule all about? Basically, it comes down to the fact that by nature as human beings, we are not necessarily designed to do what's uncomfortable or scary (getting yourself out of illness is both of those things). But obviously, the rub here is that to make changes and progress in our lives we are often called upon to step outside of our comfort zone - to do the very things that challenge us and push us to face our fears.

The 5-Second Rule explains that when we are faced with challenges, uncertainty, and fears, our natural instinct is to hesitate before taking action. When this happens, the brain goes into protection mode because to our brain hesitating equals discomfort, which equals potential harm. Now as we have already witnessed, our brains are totally amazing. One of its many functions is to protect and keep us safe from any perceived danger - it will always look for a way to protect us. Therefore, with its clever arsenal of mental tricks, the brain will pull us away from any sort of action that it thinks will cause us harm. It will convince us to think that we shouldn't do something and will get up to all sorts of mental tricks to dissuade us from heading in that direction. The end result of all this mental trickery is the mother of all de-motivators, and shit like apathy, procrastination, hiding under the duvet, and more. When we are faced with doing stuff, we're uncomfortable with, we tend to hesitate. A microsecond of hesitation is all it takes to send a stress like signal to our brain, a signal it then interprets as a sign to go into protection mode… hello, lack of motivation and duvet dwelling. These few seconds of hesitation are also more than enough for our mind to automatically switch to those unhelpful, negative, and sabotaging thoughts that prevent us from acting in our own best interest.

What this all really boils down to is that as human beings we are only truly going to feel motivated to do the things we enjoy or are comfortable with. This means we're never, ever going to be fully ready to make that leap out of our comfort zone which, let's face it, isn't exactly good news for this fixing our health business.

I promise you I'm going to get around to telling you how the 5-Second Rule works in a minute, but before I do, I just want to add in something else around motivation and getting started on a healing journey.

Like a lot of things in life, there is never going to be the right time to embark on a life-changing path. There will always be something in our way or we will always find things to put in our way (welcome, procrastination). We all make excuses for not getting on with stuff and getting started on the healing process is no exception, only now with this handy little rule, having a lack of motivation is no longer one of those get outs.

The 5-Second Rule is something that really changed my perspective on motivation and helped me over some of my "I can't go on" moments. This strategy has not only been good for helping me to keep on putting one foot in front of another when I don't feel like I can keep on with healing, but also in life in general. It has completely changed my mindset around motivation. It has stopped me waiting for that motivation train to arrive, stopped me overthinking and procrastinating, and has done away with my old belief that I needed to be fully ready for my next move. It has also helped me to trust in those first instinctive thoughts that I know are directing me to healthier decisions such as getting out for a walk, choosing something healthy to eat, etc.

The biggest realisation I have had since learning this rule has been that at any given time I am only ever one split-second decision away from changing my life; improving my lifestyle, my health or relationships, and that I don't necessarily need motivation to be able to act. All I need to do is to rely on my instinct to work out what is my next best move and use the rule to get me started. Working with this technique has made me more aware of the fact that a lot of the time when looking to make changes I have to get out of my own way. That it's not simply about lack of motivation, but more how my brain is capable of creating obstacles and excuses when I'm faced with doing something that is uncomfortable or scary. This shift in perspective has allowed me to see that during moments of hesitation my brain likes to jump in to steer me away from doing the challenging and scary stuff and this is why I find it hard to summon up the motivation, not just because I'm crap at staying motivated!

Nowadays if I find myself struggling to get off the ground with something, instead of beating myself up over my lack of drive, I use the 5-Second Rule alongside intentions and goals. The process is simple: I use goals and intentions to set the next step that I know will help to move me forward. I then throw in the rule to bypass the hesitation stage that puts my brain into protection mode and prevents me from getting shit done.

If you fancy learning how to do this too, then here's what you need to know.

The 5- Second Rule

Mel Robbins devised the 5-Second Rule to launch herself into action when she was going through a really tough period in life where she had lost all motivation. The rule is a simple yet effective way to flip our brain out of self-sabotage and into making decisions that will lead to action and results.

The counting process interrupts the automatic thoughts, habits, and behaviours that we are often unaware of, but which keep us stuck in patterns of procrastination, excuses and avoidance. The counting fills the few seconds where we hesitate and allows us to access a small window of opportunity that can move us from having an intention about doing something into actual action.

The rule uses the action of counting backwards from 5 to 1 (the NASA rocket countdown) to awaken the action part of our brain. This is the part of the brain we need to change our behaviour and thoughts and learn new ways. When we reach number 1 it acts as a prompt and a trigger for getting us going. With practice, it teaches us to become a person who thinks and steps straight into action. When I first started using it, I couldn't believe how simple it was or really believe that it could work, but I was proved wrong. It really is as easy as it seems - You simply count backwards from 5 to 1 for any situation that you want to turn around.

There are many more ways that the 5-Second Rule can help to change situations. I have found it to be particularly effective for kicking me out of procrastination and jump-starting me into action. I focus on the thing I'm wanting to achieve, set the intention, then I do the countdown to activate it, i.e., get out the door for a walk, getting out of bed on time, picking up the phone to make a call I've been putting off, getting started on a healthy meal instead of grabbing something easier but less healthy. All the little things that

I know are good for keeping me on track with my health but are so easy not to do because I don't feel like it or have lost the motivation.

I have noticed that the rule has also helped me to change my thought patterns. I can countdown myself away from negative self-talk and replace it with thoughts or mental visualisations that make me feel more uplifted or confident. The same also goes for flipping feelings or emotions from a negative state to a more positive and helpful one. Incorporating this rule into my life has made me re-evaluate the need to be ready or to have the motivation to get things done.

It has taken away the pressure off trying to find ways to get or stay motivated. I have found that it has made it easier to switch myself out of a negative mindset when I am struggling to make new changes or keep on top of the things that require sustained action. Mel Robbins' perspective on motivation and her 5-Second Rule has been one of those little gems a person stumbles across from time to time - a simple yet effective tool. (You can find a link for her book in the "Useful Websites & Stuff" section at the back of this book.)

DECLUTTERING MY ENVIRONMENT

You may have heard of that expression "tidy desk, tidy mind." This is something I used to strive for back in my admin days. Having clutter-free desk helped me to focus on the task at hand, and when, thanks to illness, I found myself occupying far more hours at home than I had intended, I started to apply the same principle to my home environment. I got rid of all the unnecessary crap, created designated places for stuff I didn't want to lie around but needed to keep - bills, paperwork, etc. - and I cleared out all of the stuff that I no longer needed. It has become a standing joke with one of my friends that I have a cupboard for everything!

Decluttering is good for the mind. Spaces that are cluttered tend to be a distraction we don't need and can actually impair the brain's ability to process information – if you have brain fog then you'll know anything that helps your brain to process stuff has got to be a good thing!

When we're surrounded by mess and clutter, especially if it has accumulated through our lack of energy to deal with it, then it can become a stressful element in our lives. Piles of stuff laying around the place, encroaching on the surfaces around our home, can be a constant reminder that things are getting away from us. The more it accumulates, the more overwhelmed we can get. Having a tidy living space can help us feel more settled, and for me, that has always been an important factor. I found that having a long-term illness was really destabilising, so being able to exercise control over how my home environment looked and felt made me feel more grounded. It was good to know that there was one area of my life where I could still maintain a sense of order.

Now, I'm going to break with my own rule of not being too directive here, get my Boss Lady on, and be straight with you, because I can hear some of you saying stuff like, "I can barely get dressed, woman, I haven't got the energy to tidy." Well, if that's the case then I have one word for you: "delegate." Yes. Grab the nearest family member or get someone over, get yourself a pointing stick (or you could just place a sticker on everything you want to get rid of), start pointing out stuff you want to get shut of, and get them to bag that shit and ship it out. If you have the resources then pay for a one-off whole house decluttering/cleaning service, that's going to take the weight off your shoulders. If you don't have the funds, then ask friends for a favour and hold a decluttering party - whatever it takes to make your home environment a cleaner, simplified, and calmer space. Remember it's okay to ask for help, you'll be surprised how most people are willing to help out when asked.

It's surprising how the state of our physical environment can reflect and influence our state of mind. Our stuff symbolises a lot: periods of our lives, memories, etc., and there can be a considerable amount of emotions and feelings attached to them. Getting rid of any items that transport us back to the more challenging or unhappy periods in our life can help us to stick with the here and now and keep our focus on what we can do in the moment. If our eyes are constantly alighting on piles of clutter and we feel overwhelmed by the mess around, then our thoughts can become cluttered too. When the spaces that we live in are clear and calm it is reflected in our state of our mind: calm environment, calmer mind. Studies show that a tidy and clean home can have a physical effect on our bodies too, by helping to lower cortisol levels, which as we've already seen, can impact on our health.

The wardrobe is often one of the areas in the home where many people are prone to letting the clutter creep in. Statistics show we only wear something like 20% of our wardrobe 80% of the time. That's a whole heap of superfluous clothing! Plus, if you are anything like the old me, there's possibly more than a few "one-day" items lurking in the back of your closet - you know, that stuff we hope we'll fit back into again one day. Trust me, you do not need reminders like that, especially when you're not feeling tip-top because of illness. It's like trying to walk forward with your head twisted back over your shoulder - try it, it's uncomfortable and unnecessary! Our wardrobe should consist of things that we feel good in now, items that will give us a mental boost, not remind us of days when we thought we looked better.

It's likely that there are items in the other rooms in your home that you could easily do without too; items which could be reduced by applying the "if you haven't used it in 2 years then lose it" rule.

Not sure if any of this applies to you? Take a look around you, how do you feel about your home environment? If it makes you feel disheartened or want to sigh with exasperation, then it may be a sign it is causing you unnecessary stress or anxiety. If you find yourself overwhelmed, stressed, or just feeling bleurgh about stuff in your home, then maybe it's time to be ruthless. If you have things that you no longer have a need for, stuff that's broken or expired, items that hold unhappy memories or make you feel less than your best, then it's time to ditch them and create a home that makes you feel relaxed and peaceful. This sense of peacefulness will not only have a positive impact on your mindset, but on your general wellbeing too.

Decluttering, tidying, and cleaning can completely change the energy of a room and give an instant boost to wellbeing. It may not seem like the biggest of shifts, but it's surprising how good it can make you feel when your surroundings are less cluttered. This whole holistic approach is about taking action in both big and small ways and remembering that it's often the small actions that come together to make greater things.

GETTING MY GRATITUDE ON

As I have already mentioned, when I was initially diagnosed, I spent a great deal of time focusing on how bad my life was, dwelling on everything I had lost, and yearning for a future that was no longer on the cards. It wasn't until I reached the point of acceptance that I began to climb out of the hole that the grieving for my losses had put me in. By accepting my current situation, I was able to make a start on flipping my everyday mindset by consciously and actively making the choice to shift my attention towards the things that were still good in my life.

Whenever I found myself re-issuing an invitation to that pity party of mine I would mentally give myself a window of time to allow a little wallowing, and then I would park it and choose to think about what I was grateful for. Sometimes I would talk to myself out loud, telling myself that although this or that wasn't working so great or I was feeling this pain, I still had x, y, z in my life. This was a way for me to shut down and override the voice of illness.

Today, I do my best to make gratitude part of my every day. At night before

I go to sleep, I think of a few things that I am grateful for. When I write in my journal, no matter how much of a moan or vent I've been having, I end each entry with three expressions of gratitude. I have a mantra that I do my best to live by, and that is "no matter how challenging my life is there is always a pocket of beauty to be found within it." In the past, on difficult days my "pocket of beauty" may only have been the smallest of moments – a helping hand, kindness or gesture of support from someone, reading something inspiring, the sunshine through the window, someone making me laugh, a beautifully cooked meal, or simply just fact I was still alive!

When I began to make mindset shifts I was able to see that there had always been a ton of lovely things on the side-lines of my life, but I had been so wrapped up in illness, caught up in the mess of emotions and thoughts following diagnosis, that I had stopped noticing them. Making a conscious effort to re-focus my attention on what I was grateful for enabled me to reconnect with all of the stuff that could still brighten up my life if I let it. Giving my attention and taking the time to log all of those little things that could still put a smile on my face helped to shrink the beast, to reduce the amount of time I spent thinking about big "F." Through expressions of gratitude I came to realise I had a choice about what I focused on. I could choose to give all of my attention to everything that was wrong, or I could actively look for the mood-boosting things. It wasn't always easy, sometimes I had to really force myself to be grateful, but eventually, it became a habitual part of my life.

The place in which I stand today, believe it or not, I can even give thanks to illness for what it has brought into my life. Trust me, nobody was more surprised than me with this shift in mindset. Never in my wildest dreams would I have thought I would be thanking the very thing that shattered my life. But as we all know, this thing called life is a weird and wonderful place, so, despite illness being the worst thing to happen to me, in some ways it's also been the best thing to happen to me. Much to my astonishment, I have a great appreciation for what illness has taught me.

There have been many things that have changed during my experience of illness. Along the way, I've have had to accept that I've lost a lot of the old me, but as it turns out, that hasn't been such a bad thing after all. This may not be what I had planned for myself, but as they say, "The best-laid plans of mice and men often go awry." Like a bizarre twist in the game of life, I can now see that the thing that once brought my world crashing down is something I am grateful for. In a strange and challenging way, it has gifted me many opportunities to rebuild my life on many levels and in a better, stronger way.

I am grateful that on my journey, I have met so many fabulous, inspirational, amazingly, compassionate people. I have encountered generosity and the very best of human nature. I discovered how positive and liberating it can be to build something back up from the ruins and to re-invent yourself in the process. Today, in many ways, I think I stand here a better version of myself. I know for sure that because of what I have been through, I have a much healthier and more tolerant perspective on life in general.

Now, you may be thinking this is all very rose-tinted spectacles, so just in case you're doubting this picture I am painting and thinking that I'm constantly skipping through meadows revelling in the rediscovered beauty of my life, let me tell you that I still have days when I think the world can go and fuck itself. Days when I'm overwhelmed by doing my best to stay well and just want to hide under the duvet. I've not some morphed into some kind of eternal positive princess always raising a half-full glass salute whenever life slaps me in the face. While it's true I've gained many positive things from such crappy life events, I haven't become a "make lemonade out of lemons" type. When life hands me lemons, my first thought will always be - shall I pop 'em in a gin and tonic and work out how to deal with shit. I am pragmatic enough to acknowledge that you can't negate all your woes and turn a disastrous situation around with an attitude of gratitude, but I do believe you can choose which perspective you want to take and how you respond to the stuff that happens to you. And I do believe that practising gratitude can help to raise your energy vibration level, which is something that can also influence your state of health.

My experience of this life-changing event has taught me a great deal. The lessons, without a doubt, have been brutal, but it has led to a belief that no matter what life throws at you or how many times it brings you down, you can still move forward through the smallest of actions. That's not to say that I wouldn't have liked to have received my important life lessons in a gentler fashion, but to be honest, if they hadn't have happened in such a seismic manner, I'm not sure I would have paid enough attention to learn what I needed to learn.

Of course, there are still plenty of days when I wish I'd draw a better set of numbers in life's lottery, but the way I see it is I have two choices: I can either choose to focus my attention on everything I have lost and been forced to surrender to illness, or I can lean into it and choose to look towards the good that has come out of the situation and the insight I have gained from it. So, while I may not have a lemonade factory for those life lemons, I do on my optimistic days have this little bundle of positivity to share with you - the more insightful stuff I have gained from my experience. I'm going to be recapping on a few things here, but sometimes I think it helps to hear things twice!

Take responsibility - Our life is nobody's responsibility except our own. Nobody is coming to save us; we can't look to other people to fix this thing for us or make us happy or healthy. They can support us, but ultimately, it's down to us to get ourselves back on solid ground. It's also a waste of time blaming other people. Shit things happen to good people, people do shit things to others, but what's done is done. Blaming someone or something for a situation we find ourselves in is a complete waste of time, energy, and focus. We may or may not have been responsible or played a part in how we ended up in a certain situation, but it's going to take US to get ourselves out of it and that means taking responsibility.

Trusting instincts - Often in life, we lose touch with our instincts. They get dulled by fear, experiences, buried by other people's judgments and opinions. The truth is, we know what's best for ourselves, we are our own expert. Spending time reconnecting with ourselves, becoming more self-aware, sorting our emotional issues, addressing our fears can help us to get back in touch with that instinct. Sometimes it takes difficult life events to force us to do just that.

How resilient us humans are - it can take adversity to realise just how amazingly resilient and strong we are - to reveal our superpowers. It's not until life tests us that we discover our strengths and skills. When we come through hardship, we realise we have the ability within us to dig deep. We have the skills to pull ourselves through, and this can give us the confidence to face future challenges.

Sometimes, we need to take a blind leap of faith - we can't always be in control of the outcome, we can't predict what will work. Sometimes we just need to take the leap, trust that our parachute will open, and work shit out on the way down. We won't always know where we are going to land, either, but that's okay because life can have a funny habit of placing us just where we need to be - even if we don't like it there! We don't need to let the fear of the unknown or unfamiliar stop us from trying to work towards a healthier future. When we surrender to an unknown outcome it makes it easier to go with the flow of the here and now.

Mindset is key to surviving challenges - this is not about positive thinking, that can be nigh on impossible when the chips are down, but we don't need to be positive to get into the right mindset for pushing through. We can be a realist about our situation and still choose to remain actively optimistic that we will see brighter days. We can learn to live alongside the negative aspects of our current situation without constantly orbiting them - wallowing is to be expected and allowed, but it's a good idea to put a time limit on it.

Self-awareness is a foundation of self-development - when we get to know ourselves inside out, we become more in tune to our own needs and what we want from life. We can then begin to align ourselves with people and experiences that can provide us with the opportunities that will help move us forward. Difficult life events have a knack of exposing self-truths alongside providing the opportunity for us to have honest and enlightening conversations with ourselves and others.

We always have a choice as to how we will respond - when we experience a life crisis, we can tend to be more reactive to what's happening to and around us. There can be a lot of knee-jerk reactions to events, especially as things spiral out of control and our emotions run high. In the bigger picture, these reactions may not always be our best course of action. While we may not be able to control a situation, we can still choose how to respond in a healthier way.

There are pockets of beauty in every situation, even if they're tiny things - when life is super shitty, it can seem like there's nothing good going on, but I'm a firm believer that even in the darkest of moments there are silver linings to be found. It might be something as simple as your faith in human nature being restored by people's kindness or finding out who your real friends are. I promise there will always be something somewhere to grasp onto if you make the time to look.

To ask for help - when we're going through a difficult time it can be hard to ask for help. Sometimes it's our own fears about how others will respond that can prevent us from asking, but as they say, "If you don't ask, you don't receive." At times it may feel like people can't help because nobody truly understands what we're going through, especially when it's a long-term situation. Remember my newsflash moment? - we don't need people to understand our situation to be able to help.

Who to turn to for support - There's nothing like a big life event or crisis for discovering who our real friends are. Difficult times have a habit of revealing some interesting traits in others. Learning who we can and can't count on in these moments can be a harsh and painful lesson, but it does clear the space for the people who truly want to be there for us. Through adversity comes truth, and we often learn who we can let go of and who's a keeper.

There is always an option - It may feel like our back is against the wall, but much of the time there are still options open to us. We just may not have considered them yet or need to create the space to be able to see them, but they are there. Our life may not be what we had planned, but that doesn't mean there aren't different options open to us. Often, as tough as it is, it comes down to accepting and realigning ourselves with a new reality and allowing ourselves some space to regroup and rethink before taking our next step.

Gratitude - It can be pretty hard to conjure up feelings of gratitude when our life has gone to shit, but there are still many things to be grateful for. Even on my roughest of days, I did my best to come up with something that I was grateful for... sometimes it was just the fact that I had survived the previous 10 minutes!

DAILY AFFIRMATIONS AND PERSONAL MANTRAS

How many times have you wanted to slap the next person who tells you to "just think positively?" Let's be honest, trying to maintain a positive outlook when you're feeling like crap day in and day out sucks. The trouble with trying to think on the positive side all the time is that

1. It's plain old tiring trying to remain upbeat all the time.

2. It can become a constant mental battle with the reality of your situation.

Positivity can be great but pushing too hard for it can get in the way and act as a distraction. Forcing positivity can prevent us from fully looking at the things we don't want to look at it or acknowledging the full impact of an event - two things that I believe are needed for us to be able to reach acceptance of a new reality. Pushing ourselves to remain positive when our life has been turned upside down can become an extra pressure we can do without when trying to heal. If we fall back on good old science and revisit our physics lessons, we know that when something is forced it creates resistance. Sometimes forcing oneself to keep in a positive mindset can just make the negative stuff push back harder and make the whole thing feel like a huge mental battle - not good for our health!

Don't get me wrong, I'm all for a spot of positivity. I like a good, optimistic, inspiring quote as much as the next person, but I feel there has to be a good balance with a healthy dose of realism. Early on in my recovery I tried to take the "must keep positive" stance, but like many things in my life, being a perfectionist I tried to perfect the art, which just led to a whole load of unwanted thoughts and feelings as I struggled to maintain it. By trying to constantly put a positive spin on my situation I didn't allow myself the chance to fully reconcile with the reality of what was happening to me. My positivity was a form of denial and delayed my transition into acceptance.

Eventually, I got tired of trying to keep myself sat on the positive side of the fence and discovered a way that was better suited. I found what worked for me when dealing with challenges that ill health created was to stop trying to gloss over what I was experiencing with happy thoughts. Instead, I gave myself time to acknowledge the situation I was in, warts and all, to sit with the ugly truth of it, and give myself the chance to feel everything connected to it before looking for how I could create a shift in my mindset. This helped me to keep things real, stay connected with the reality of my situation, while still being open to the things that could help move me into a more positive space. I found that creating positive affirmations and personal mantras enabled me to combine a sense of optimism for the future while still being able to "be present" and accept my situation for what it was. By using this self-help tool, I was able to create little positive shifts in my mindset.

For example, when I was going through my toughest days, I would repeat to myself, "I am always in the place I am in, at the time I am meant to be there." This wasn't negating the impact of what was happening to me at the time or false positivity. It was faith and optimism that gave me something to hang hope on to. To help keep me open me to the possibility that what I was going through was a part of a bigger picture, one that I would eventually find some value in.

I also created daily affirmations and visualisations that fit with where I saw myself in the future, the reality I wanted to create for myself, along with what felt were my attributes. My favourite affirmations that I have used for the last few years are, "I am healed," "I am strong," "I am confident."

I am healed
The mental image I hold for the state I wish my body to be in.

I am strong
Confirmation of the strength I have to overcome challenges.

I am confident
Confidence in my body and mind's ability to heal.

To some of you, this may seem a waste of time. You may hold little faith in the power of words and affirmations, or perhaps you have never heard of this practice. Maybe this really resonates with some people reading this.

Perhaps you already incorporate affirmations and mantras into your life? Whatever your viewpoint, it's written here because I know that it helped my mindset. Many times, it stopped me from spiralling too far down the rabbit hole of hopelessness.

By using affirmations and mantras I was able to channel my thought process into a different direction. If you're not sure if this is your thing, as with many things in this book, it's a question of what have you got to lose by giving it a go?

CHAPTER 9

GETTING MY EMOTIONAL SHIT TOGETHER

In Part One of the book, I wrote how emotional stressors and trauma from my past contributed to my ill health, and how the mind-body connection is something that is often neglected when looking at the causative factors for the onset of illness. Following my years of research and learning, I am surprised that this is something that is not more fully investigated by doctors, particularly when a patient presents with widespread and not easily explained symptoms. It is a proven fact that emotional trauma can be a factor in increased inflammation in the body. Prolonged heightened emotional states, trauma, and chronic stress can lead to imbalances throughout the body such as cortisol levels, mineral levels, nervous system issues, and increased inflammation, all of which can be linked to many symptoms and illnesses. Studies show stress and emotional issues can cause or worsen chronic pain.

Traumatic events (remembering that what quantifies as trauma is different for everyone) can trigger the nervous system into survival mode. If the nervous system stays stuck in this heightened state for a prolonged period of time, then stress hormones such as cortisol are pushed out of kilter putting the body into a state of constant stress. Since cortisol controls blood sugar levels, blood pressure, the body's ability to regulate inflammation, and metabolism it's easy to see how cortisol imbalances can be connected to many physical symptoms and conditions such as adrenal dysfunction/ fatigue. Stress, anxiety, and emotionally demanding situations can deplete the body of essential vitamins and minerals too. Magnesium, potassium and other essential minerals, do not respond well to stress - the body dumps vital mineral at a fast rate when under stress. I write in more detail about this in the Body section of the book, but let's just say in this modern world it's very easy to become deficient in minerals such as magnesium and potassium and these deficiencies once again produce many of the symptoms associated with fibromyalgia.

Can you see where I am going with this? Emotional stress/ trauma/unresolved emotional issues = physical illness. Oh, and by the way, it's no coincidence that many people with a fibro diagnosis often have a history of emotional stress, trauma, or the like in their lives. This is the reason why I feel it's so important for us to review our past and consider all of the events, situations, experiences that may have been causative factors in our personal route to illness.

You have previously read just how incredible the brain is at interpreting signals and protecting us from uncomfortable situations, thoughts, etc., and this comes into play more than ever when we are experiencing emotional stress. The brain is capable of creating physical pain (psychogenic pain) to protect us from the fallout of emotionally painful experiences. Some specialists say that physical aches and pains can be the brain's way of distracting a person from becoming conscious of repressed emotions. Others say that when we can no longer keep a lid on emotional issues they can manifest into physical symptoms.

This is not to say that the physical pain or physical symptoms we feel are not real, or they do not have a physical cause, this is not saying that all pain is being imagined. I know many of you will have had this suggested to you in the past and that this particular subject can be an emotive one.

So, let's set the record straight: the pain is very real, your pain is very real, nobody is denying that. However, I do believe there is something to be said for investigating at a deeper level as to where the pain or some of the pain may be originating from. I feel it is foolish to dismiss a potential connection between emotional stress or trauma and what is happening to the body on a physical level. I do not think it is wise to ignore the possibility that emotional stressors, past or present, could be driving pain levels and physical symptoms just because it feels too uncomfortable to consider that there may be a mental health component to illness.

Despite great strides being made over the years to make mental health issues and emotional difficulties less of a taboo subject, I have found that many people still find it difficult to accept that dysfunction within the body or difficulties in certain areas of their lives can have a connection to emotional issues from their past or issues they are currently experiencing. I have seen many a comment on social media from people with fibro getting enraged at the suggestion that there may be a connection between their emotional and physical state.

Maybe it's because of my previous life as a counsellor, but I personally firmly believe that the majority of people need some form of therapy at some point in their lives simply because life is life. Life throws so many things at us that I find it odd that we often do not take the time to consider the impact of our life experiences on our wellbeing. Why would grief not trigger a physical illness? Why wouldn't a child's experience of their parent's bitter divorce not result in anxiety later in life that affects their physical health? What about abuse and the many other traumatic events a person can experience? Why would all this pain and emotion not be expressed in a physical form further down the line from the traumatic event?

I feel it has to be noted here that I have heard people say that they have never experienced a traumatic life event, had a happy childhood, etc., yet they are ill. While I am open to the fact that not all illness may have an emotional cause, I am also willing to bet that there is an emotional connection in many chronic conditions, and often it is not always immediately obvious as to what that may be. A person doesn't necessarily have to have experienced some kind of hugely traumatic event or had something completely derail their life for there to be a noticeable impact within the body. Low-level emotional stress that has been present over a long period of time can have as much of an impact on health as a single traumatic event. I feel that we also need to be aware that while an event may not initially seem that significant, the consequences and fallout from it can over time can create issues which have an affect our wellbeing. Something that is very rarely mentioned in connection to illness is what is called "Intergenerational Trauma." This is a subject that is a way too complex of an issue for me to cover in this book. A quick overview of this subject is that we can "inherit" issues caused by unresolved trauma from previous generations. If you are wanting to delve deeper into this subject for your own healing journey, you can find a book listed in the "Useful Websites and Stuff" section at the back of the book.

I know that there are some who shy away from the idea that emotional stress can cause ill health, but when we take into consideration the mind-body connection and how stress of any kind can impact on the body, I don't think it's a case of if emotional issues contribute to ill health, but how do they. One thing is for sure, this will vary greatly from person to person. For some, it may be the root cause of their illness. For others, it may be something that is exacerbating symptoms. Whichever it may be, resolving emotional issues is something that can greatly aid our healing.

So, if there is an emotional connection with physical illness, how is it the case that some people weather difficult life events and others don't fare as well? Why doesn't everyone who's been through challenging times become ill? Well, this all comes down to that individuality thing again, everyone is different. Everyone has different biochemistry, some people have better immune responses, good mineral levels, a better support network, the list goes on. To put it simply, some people just come from a stronger foundation and are more robust physically and mentally to deal with life's ups and downs. This is not a judgement on how people cope, but a statement as to how it is to be human. When we're trying to figure this stuff out, we always need to bear in mind that what is stressful or emotive for one person may not be for another.

There is no doubt that the benefits of working on my own emotional issues have been reflected in my physical progress. Coming to terms with, unpacking my past trauma and difficulties and reducing the emotional impact they were having on my life helped me to release an emotional tension that had been present for many years. An emotional tension that, until I started work on all of this stuff, I wasn't even aware was having such a detrimental effect on my health.

ONE TO ONE

As I have written in the first part of this book, when I trained as a counsellor it was compulsory for me to enter into personal therapy. After diagnosis I voluntary returned to one-to-one therapy to sort through all the feelings I had around what I felt at the time was a very gloomy prognosis for my future.

The therapy sessions gave me the time and space to really connect with how I was feeling about being ill. Away from the sessions, I was able to bury my feelings, distract myself with other things, pretend to be Miss Positivity. But during that one hour a week, because of the commitment I made to myself to be open and honest, there was nowhere to hide. I was encouraged to confront the full extent of the effect the diagnosis was having on me, and early on it became quite clear that I was overwhelmed by the prospect of having to lead a life different from what I had planned. I felt a huge sense of loss, I felt cheated and betrayed (by my body, by life, by the Universe), and I was experiencing a deep sense of grief at what I felt was my lost life.

During the counselling sessions I was able to rage, rant, cry, sulk, and give a name to all of the stuff I was feeling without judgement, without anyone trying to make me feel better, tell me what I should do, or give me that sort of well-meaning but useless advice. I came to realise just how much stuff I was holding, how many emotions and feelings I had in relation to my situation. Until I got to this point of dealing with my emotional shit, there was no space for any thoughts of healing because I was so full up with resentment, anger, bitterness, injustice, sadness, and about a million other thoughts, feelings, and emotions – all of which were then being channelled out from my inner negative Nancy.

During the sessions, it was clear that I was pretty much at full capacity with the enormous amount of emotions and feelings I was holding onto. While sifting through all of these I became aware of how much of an impact my emotions were having on my thoughts and actions; how much it was draining me. The emotional stress was adding an extra burden that I didn't need and the sessions gave me a place to put that burden down, a place to unpack my emotional baggage, come to terms with the changes in my life, and discard all the stuff that was preventing me from moving forward. I offloaded a huge amount of superfluous baggage during those sessions, and when my therapy came to an end, I felt ten times lighter.

Through therapy, I was able to pinpoint that a lot of what I was feeling was grief, and from there I was able to then work through the five stages of grief, denial, anger, bargaining, depression and acceptance. I was able to see more clearly where I was with my feelings and thoughts, which helped me monitor and track my emotions throughout the different stages.

There's no denying my therapy was a messy business. I left many sessions feeling raw and wrung out, but like healing, grieving is not a linear process; I bounced back and forth through the stages. One week I would be in denial, another I would be depressed or mad as hell, and some weeks I was a combination of a few, but the great thing about my sessions and my therapist was that they met me just where I was on any given week. They gave me the time to work through each of the spaces I found myself in. I could tease things apart, identify what was pushing which buttons, examine why I felt the way I did, and eventually release stuff's hold on me. Having the time every week to just be, to sit with how I was feeling without anyone trying to fix it, allowed me to deal with the sense of being overwhelmed, the feeling that it was all too big to cope with.

The sessions enabled me to roll with the waves of my emotions so that I was no longer being pulled under and drowned by them. To continue this ocean analogy, and at the risk of sounding super cheesy, after my therapy, it felt like I had weathered the initial storm of diagnosis and I had finally washed up on the shores of acceptance. Reflecting back on this process, I feel that it was around this time where my mindset began to shift away from thinking everything was hopeless to questioning what I could do about it.

This is not to say that I never went back to any of the other stages of the grieving process. Over the years, in response to my situation, I have still experienced times of anger and depression, sometimes at the same time. Occasionally I've popped back for a visit with denial, but when that has happened I have been able to move past it and return to my normal service much quicker.

Therapy not only gave me the time and space to come to terms with the diagnosis, but it also gave me the tools to cope much better with the fluctuations in feeling and emotions that have arisen in the times since. The self-awareness I gained during those sessions has since enabled me to recognise how my emotions, feelings, and thoughts have impacted on various areas of my life, not just in the past but in the here and now.

Through this awareness, I have been able to work on breaking the thought and behaviour patterns that were unconsciously feeding physical symptoms - these days if I'm feeling out of balance in any way my first port of call is to check in with myself on an emotional level. I take time out to look at the thoughts, emotions, and feelings I am having and what part they may be playing in how I am feeling on a physical and mental level. This often helps me to work through and resolve issues that have arisen far quicker.

ACCEPTANCE

Acceptance probably has a different meaning for different people, so, let me talk about what it has meant for me. By saying I gained acceptance, I mean that was able to reach the point of being okay with the reality of my situation. I didn't like it, I still wished it wasn't what it was, but I was able to acknowledge that although a fibro diagnosis was on the list of the worst things to ever happen to me, it had happened. And what I was experiencing at that point in time was what it was.

Looking at my situation from this new perspective, I was able to view illness more objectively, which allowed me to sidestep some of the emotions that were clouding my view. This meant I could see more clearly that I still had options and choices, that the situation wasn't completely hopeless. I was able to acknowledge that although this wasn't the life I planned for myself, it could still be a good life and eventually, I was even able to admit that there were some aspects of my life and myself that were better because of the changes illness has brought into my life.

Acceptance didn't mean hanging my hat up in defeat, but more of a letting go of resisting and raging against the situation. Letting go of the resistance and the rage meant I could start to lean into the experience instead of constantly pushing against it. Through this action, I gave myself permission to move past it, which presented me with the opportunity to re-orient myself with my new reality. It wasn't a case of being resigned or surrendering to being in this situation for the rest of my life, it was an acceptance of where I was at that precise moment in time. It was a refocusing of my attention on the reality of my current situation and a letting go of what had gone before so I could start to pave a new way forward.

Part of my acceptance process was letting go of the old me, and the realisation that I needed to stop trying to get back to the old me was a painful one. For a long time, this was my only wish, the only thing I wanted the most, and accepting that wasn't going to happen was extremely difficult. One of my turning points came when I read a simple passage in a book that spoke of how we are forever evolving and being shaped by our experiences, and because of that, the person we are today is different from who we were yesterday, last week, last month, or last year. That simple statement made me realise that regardless of illness, even if my life had been going swimmingly, I was always going to be moving away from the "old me." This realisation somehow made it easier to accept there wasn't really an old me to get back to.

Acceptance of my new reality pulled me out of a melancholic yearning for the past, stopped my obsession with trying to predict my future, it placed me in the present moment so that I could open my eyes to the options available in the here and now. Being more accepting of who this new me was meant I was also able to acknowledge what I could and couldn't change, and then move on to really re-evaluating my life. It created the space for me to acknowledge the role I was playing in my current situation, ask questions of myself so I could identify the things I was or wasn't doing that were holding me back from making progress.

By accepting where I was in the moment I changed my whole perspective on a living life with illness. From my new viewpoint, I was able to open up the space to reconnect with the things that were still good in my life and to count my blessings more than my losses. This helped me to maintain a more productive mindset, identifying the life skills and tools that could help me to climb back out the hole illness had put me in and re-establish a sense of hope.

The most important shift that came from acceptance was that it enabled me to regain some control over the direction my life was heading in. By finally acknowledging the current reality that my life was a struggle, I gave myself the option of confronting those struggles. By facing everything head-on, through seeing the true scope of my situation without having the distraction of worrying about the past or the future, I could make the choice to work on the things that I could change. In taking that option I made the shift from hopelessness to a more empowered position.

How did I get to the point of acceptance?

- Being responsible for getting my arse into therapy.
- Sticking with it and being okay with the uncomfortable.
- Allowing myself to go with the flow of the process.
- Being totally honest with myself and open to challenges from my therapist.
- Identifying what I was denying and trying to push away.
- Acknowledging that this shit didn't just happen out of the blue, there was a history and connections.
- Realising that whether I was happy about it or not, I was in part responsible for the outcome of my life, the place I found myself in.
- Letting go of the old me.

RE-ASSESSING AND RE-EVALUATING

My therapy sessions also highlighted how important it was for me to establish boundaries, let go of the things that were causing me unnecessary stress, and distance myself from the stuff that was having a negative impact on my life and therefore adding to my health issues. Although at times it was uncomfortable for me to implement them, I came to realise that these actions were a form of self-care and by doing them I was doing the very best for myself.

I started the ball rolling by taking a long hard look at myself, my situation, and those around me. I worked out what I was prepared to give my time and energy to, what actions, situations, and people were draining me. Sometimes the decision was easy as pie. Other times I had to make a pros and cons list before showing stuff the door. Occasionally, as difficult as it was, I had to admit that some of the emotional crap that was zapping my energy was of my own creation. By taking an audit of my life I was able to simplify it, and in doing so it removed certain stresses that were adding to physical symptoms.

SETTING THE BOUNDARIES

In the mindset section, you will have read that I used to be a people pleaser, the type who'd often put everyone and their mother's needs before my own, and you will have seen that I eventually turned my back on that part of my personality and started to put myself first. I began to set personal boundaries and I started to say no. I became more familiar with my feelings, tuned into how certain situations and relationships truly made me feel - I was totally honest with myself as to why I was doing certain things, i.e., being a martyr.

How I created my boundaries:

- Core values - I made sure I was 100% clear on what my values were, what was important to me, all the stuff I wanted to safeguard. Health, energy, wellbeing, honesty, and family topped my list. Some of these values were influenced and still are through my experience of long-term illness; e.g., it is highly important to me that I maintain my health, energy, and wellbeing. I greatly value honesty. I believe it to be the foundation for a lot of things in life. I value it in others, and I believe in being honest with people and with myself, which has helped me while I have been healing. My family is precious. Illness meant that I lost time and missed out on certain experiences with them, which is why having more energy and time to be with them now is of such great value to me. My family was one of the drivers behind my desire to heal.

- Taking note - I began paying greater attention to what affected me and how. I learned to gauge my responses to places, situations, and people, developing, if you like, my own personal barometer. If something made me feel drained and depleted, I made a note. I paid attention to what made me feel more energised or inspired. By becoming more aware of my responses and the impact that everything in my life was having on me, I was able to identify the areas in my life where I needed to create boundaries to help support my health and recovery.

- Recognised my limits - Once I had my list I took the time to consider what exactly I was willing to tolerate and accept within the areas I had identified. I paid particular attention to how it would impact on my values. If things were compromising my values, then I looked at what boundaries I needed to set to ensure this wasn't happening or was at least reduced. I adjusted my limits according to where I found myself and what I needed more or less of in my life at any given point. Boundary setting enabled me to send the message out to others about how I wanted to be treated and helped me to develop a much healthier level of self-respect and worth, all of which boosted my mental wellbeing.

I have written about boundaries in the emotional section of this book. However, like so much of what is written within these pages, it could have equally found itself at home in the Body or Soul section. Having healthy personal boundaries has a positive effect on our mental, physical, and emotional states. It is residing here in this section because for me, setting boundaries had such a positive influence on my emotional state. By creating them I gained a greater sense of empowerment, and that enabled me to figure out how much I was willing to emotionally invest in other people and situations. Through boundary-setting I created a stronger connection between myself, my feelings, thoughts and emotions. And because of that, I was able to separate my own feelings from other people's and realise how other people's emotions could potentially dictate my own. It was like creating a roadblock, a buffer between myself and the situations or people that emotionally drained me. This prevented me from getting caught up in the shit that I would have previously let drag me down an emotional rabbit hole.

Of course, the ripple effect of a process such as this meant that the benefits have not just been on an emotional level. I found that I became more confident in my own abilities and making my own voice heard, which put me in a much more positive mindset for going on to achieve things. The boundaries helped me to reduced stress and conserve valuable energy, which meant I was more physically capable in other areas of my life. On a soul level, it allowed me to feel more connected to myself and my values, more grounded and open to listening to my own intuition.

LETTING GO OF PERFECT

Up until the age of 40 I lived by the statement "if a job is worth doing it's worth doing well." I applied this to every area of my life: work, relationships, housework, garden, DIY, you name it. I'm not what you could fully call a type A personality, but I definitely share some of the traits - perfectionist for sure, highly conscientious - tick, sensitive to stress - yep, and driven - well, let's just say at times I can have laser-like focus.

Although on face value that statement doesn't seem like such a bad thing. However, combined with those personality traits of mine, it became clear to me that they were a contributory factor in stoking the fires of ill health (see bullet point no 7 on my reaching acceptance list). My need for things to be perfect coupled with a strong tendency toward self-criticism (which I have since learned is called maladaptive perfectionism) at times drove me to exhaustion and resulted in my taking on tasks that were detrimental to my wellbeing. Even something as mundane as gardening would see me pushing myself beyond my limits to get everything looking "just so."

On reflection, I think this is why I had such an extreme reaction to the idea of pacing my life - it just didn't fit with my personality. I was so used to pushing for myself to achieve perfection that the whole concept made me feel totally uncomfortable and out of sorts.

It seems that my being a maladaptive perfectionist and finding myself on the receiving end of a chronic illness diagnosis is not something I am alone in. A study reported in the Journal of Psychotherapy and Psychosomatics concluded that maladaptive perfectionism promotes self-critical thought. This not so delightful combo can affect a person's ability to cope with stress in a healthy manner, and because there is an element of self-blame in this mix, it can contribute to prolonged chronic stress. As we have already looked at earlier, this chronic stress can have a negative impact on health, the immune system, and more, so no surprise here that my perfectionism was making things worse.

If we fast forward to my 45th year of life, you will now find me trying my very best to live life by the new rule "done is good enough." There is no question that this has been a challenge. When you're naturally driven to perfectionism it is something that you have to consciously work on. I have had to learn to let go of perfect and settle for good enough. It's not something that comes naturally or easily to me, but I have found that it has been another of those little shifts that have helped me to heal.

I have also learned to lower my expectations of myself and others, something which I feel went hand in hand with my need for everything to be perfect but which all too often led to feelings of frustration, disappointment, and disillusionment. When I was living my life out of a place of perfectionism, although I couldn't see it at the time, I often had unrealistically high expectations of myself, other people, relationships, events, and such. Much of the time I would pin my happiness on these expectations, which I now realise was a precarious bet simply because life rarely lives up to expectations, especially unrealistic ones!

There is no doubt that I set the bar really high when it came to myself and my achievements in life, but what I hadn't realised at the time was how these high standards were spilling over into other areas of my life and colouring my perspective. I would often struggle to understand why other people couldn't live by the same morals and principles that I held. To me it was simple, but now I can see that unless I somehow developed the ability to clone myself this could never have happened - it was a completely unrealistic expectation and demand. It was these unrealistic expectations that would often cause me hurt and upset when I found my gestures, consideration, or kindness weren't reciprocated by others. When I found myself in those moments my feelings frequently snowballed into thoughts of not being good enough or worthy of being treated well. I don't think I need to go any further for you to see how this once more highlights how our past history, the baggage we carry from the past into the future, can be intrinsically linked to emotional stress and ill health.

As is often the case, it can be the small things that create a big impact. All it took for me to re-evaluate my perspective and break my pattern of unrealistic expectations was a simple comment from a friend. During a conversation I was explaining to her (or should I say moaning to her?) about how hurt I had felt by a mutual friend's actions, and she replied with, "But you've have always had quite high expectations of friendships." That was it, not exactly earth-shattering in itself, but that simple statement opened my eyes wide to how I had been going through life putting my high expectations onto others. It was enough to create a shift in my perspective. It made me step back and take note that the times I was putting these unrealistic demands on myself, others, and life I was creating unnecessary emotional situations and stress. Stress that was adding to an already complicated life.

BUILDING EMOTIONAL RESILIENCE

In the past, I would have described myself as too sensitive for my own good. From an early age, I just didn't seem to be as emotionally robust as other people. I frequently experienced a high level of emotion that most of the time was out of proportion to the situation or event at hand. I would often feel wounded by off-the-cuff remarks of other people; I would take far too much of the little things to heart and I would struggle to let go of what I saw as criticism from others. When I found myself in these situations, I would only be able to see as far as the immediate feelings I was experiencing, I had no awareness as to why I was feeling the way I was - I just felt. I wasn't able to see that it was my reactions to events, people, etc., not the event or person itself, that was often the cause of these emotional rollercoasters.

During my training to be a counsellor, between my coursework and personal therapy I developed a greater level of self-awareness, which helped me to become more emotionally resilient - able to cope more effectively with the shit that life threw at me. I was able to identify then build on the skills I did have and use them as tools; create an emotional "toolbox" to help me with challenges. When illness rolled around, once the dust had settled and I was in the acceptance phase I was able to access this toolbox to help me to roll with the bad times better than I would have previously done.

It goes without saying that when I was in full pity party mode, I was not displaying much emotional resilience. In fact, for a time I forgot I possessed the skills to help myself; my toolbox was gathering dust somewhere at the back of my mind. More often than not, my emotions about the situation I was in overwhelmed me and all I capable of was bouncing from one emotional reaction to another as more health issues arose. However, once I began to resurface from my wallowing, my resilience eventually kicked and began to lend a helping hand to get me through the rough days. Once I was no longer in the "my life is fucked" mindset I was able to see my difficulties, not as a disaster, but as a challenge I could overcome. I began to switch from "why me" to "what can I do?" and I was able to move past the emotional disturbance that had created the post-diagnosis paralysis that was preventing me from moving forward.

My emotional resilience has played an important part in my being able to move through the process of healing. It has been a tool I have relied on from the point I began to emerge from my paralysis right up to the present day. Below are some of the most important things that it has helped to work out on me this journey.

- To acknowledge the enormity of my situation but not to remain stuck in emotions such as fear and grief.
- To maintain a belief and confidence that I can cope with and overcome what illness throws at me.
- Allowed me to step away from victim mode and meet challenges head-on.
- Enabled me to adjust my sails and sail in a new direction when faced with obstacles.
- To take an alternative perspective and actively look for what this new reality has brought into my life rather than focus on what it has taken away.
- Acceptance that life is going to change one way or the other - that's life. Sometimes those changes are as unwelcome as shit through the letterbox but embracing and leaning into these changes is the only way to move past them.

The way in which we navigate the challenges that life throws at us and our level of resilience is often as unique as we are. It can depend on factors such as our past experiences, age, role models, and the level of trauma we have been exposed to. Just how well we adapt to stressful situations and life-changing events can have a huge impact on our general wellbeing.

While it's true that some people are more naturally resilient than others, and although it can be said that we can't necessarily change the factors that have shaped our emotional responses and psyche, something to hang onto and remember is that we can learn to become more emotionally resilient. This can be extremely helpful when trying to heal.

In this life, there are some people who have been fortunate to have been born with an inherent emotional resilience that allows them to roll more effectively with life punches. Unfortunately, I wasn't one. If, like me, you need to develop and build resilience, you may now be thinking, "How do I get me some?" For me, therapy was the first steppingstone, it helped me to access and develop the personal skills and tools that I needed to cope better with life's ups and downs. Having said this, that is not the only way. I am confident that there are some things outside of therapy that can help us to build emotional resilience.

For readers who are interested in increasing their emotional resilience, below is a list of the things that I have found that have helped me to build on and maintain mine. They are the things that I can fall back on for when life, which invariably it does, throws me another curveball.

On this list, you will see that some of the stuff I have already written, and you will recognise some of the things in the coming pages. Although I may be in danger of sounding like a broken record with this message, this list once again highlights how elements of the holistic approach are linked, i.e., getting in a better mindset can help us to build our emotional resilience, which in turn reduces stress when we face a challenging situation. A reduction in stress is beneficial for the mind and the body.

A higher level of emotional resilience can not only help us to manage emotionally challenging events more effectively, but it can also benefit us in other areas of life, such as helping us to build a stronger, healthier relationship with others and ourselves, both of which can have a positive effect on our physical and mental wellbeing.

12 Ways I Built My Emotional Resilience:

1. Mindset - Balancing a more optimistic outlook while remaining realistic about the world and my current circumstances. Acknowledging the negative side of my situation but not getting permanently stuck in negativity by actively seeking positive aspects of my situation. This helped me to open up choices, steer me away from a victim mentality, and minimise the setbacks.

2. Empathy - Practicing empathy for others helped me to notice and regulate my own emotions which enabled me to manage stressful situations better.

3. Journalling - Writing down my worries and making a note of my emotional responses helped me to reduce stress and gave me an insight into how I was dealing with events. This helped me to identify solutions or ways in which I could adapt in order to cope better.

4. Sense of humour - This one can't be readily applied to every situation but being able to laugh at myself and at life's difficulties helped to alter my body's response to stress and diffuse tension. Laughter also releases endorphins and boosts the immune system too.

5. Social Support - Surrounding myself with a trustworthy supportive network of people helped me get through difficult and stressful times by building up my own emotional strength. Sharing thoughts and feelings, asking for feedback, and connecting with good friends who were my cheerleaders all helped me to strengthen my resilience.

6. Self-care - Looking after myself on all levels, healthy eating, healthy relationships, exercise, rest and relaxation. Establishing a good self-care routine nurtured my self-worth and confidence and boosted my physical, mental, and emotional strength.

7. Reflection - Learning to reflect on how I dealt with past situations and experiences helped me to recognise my strengths and weaknesses. I was then able to identify what worked well for me and what didn't and use that knowledge to help me during future challenging times.

8. Identity - Developing a strong sense of identity helped me to become more self-assured with who I was and develop more confidence in my ability to cope with what life throws at me.

9. Acceptance - Being able to accept my changed circumstances for what they were, a new reality caused by illness, helped me to reconcile my

feelings and start working through my pain, stress, grief, etc., sooner. Accepting my emotions allowed me to move into them, rather than side-stepping them. Being able to fully feel taught me that my emotions were nothing to be feared. Sometimes the fear of feeling can prolong the impact of an event.

10. Self- awareness - Increasing my levels of self-awareness allowed me to develop a higher level of trust in my instinct and become more in touch with my emotional needs. It helped me to more readily recognise the subtle changes in my mood and body, making it much easier to identify what I was feeling. Once I knew which emotion I was truly feeling and why, it became easier to manage them. Understanding what I was feeling and why helped me to move through my emotions and come out the other side instead of becoming paralysed and stuck by my emotional responses. Becoming more self-aware and emotionally intelligent also helped to stop me from being "hijacked" by my emotions and slipping into overwhelm when confronted with unexpected changes or challenging situations.

11. Mindfulness helped to reduce the time I spent dwelling on challenging and emotional situations- stopping me from repeatedly going over events and creating a negative viewpoint.

12. Personal Mantra - Creating a personal mantra acted as a reminder of my own power and abilities, i.e., "I am strong, I am courageous, I am resilient."

MINDFULNESS

To be honest, I have never been much good at mindful meditation in the traditional sit in silence sense. While I know the point of this practice is to let your mind wander and allow your thoughts and feelings to come and go, my thoughts often refuse to "pass like clouds" through my mind or float away "like a balloon." I end getting drawn more and more into my thoughts and end up with enough "thought balloons" for a balloon release. But because I know that mindfulness is hugely beneficial, instead of having a specific sit-down silent mindfulness time I prefer to practice mindfulness moments when I am going about my everyday tasks.

On the whole we often tend to go about life on autopilot, especially when carrying out familiar and routine tasks, i.e., brushing our teeth, eating meals, and sometimes, although probably not the safest, driving to familiar places. Because so much of our everyday involves a set routine it can be really easy to switch off from what we are doing. When this happens, we become disengaged from ourselves and what is going on around us in the here and now. Our minds tend to drift to other things and if we are going through struggles it can be easy for our thoughts to get caught up in how difficult life is, our pain, worries, and fears. Mindfulness acts as anchor in the sense that it keeps us firmly in the present moment by turning our attention to our body, our breath, and our senses.

Mindfulness may seem like a modern modality, but it has been around for many thousands of years and can be beneficial for:

- Reducing stress and fear.
- Managing depression, anxiety, chronic pain.
- Gaining a new perspective on events - prevents catastrophising, overanalysing, and downward spiral of thoughts.
- Increasing emotional resilience.
- Boosting creativity.
- Improving concentration and memory.
- Giving you a moment to breathe better- (see "And Breathe" section for benefits).
- Supporting the immune system.

As you can see, the practice of mindfulness not only has a positive effect on the mind it also can help with physical issues. This practice is also considered to be a gateway for connecting with Universal energy on a Soul level.

I'm going to give you a little how-to here because this is one of those areas where I feel I can be more directive and that it can benefit the majority of people. It does need to be noted some people have been known to experiencefeelings of disassociation or intense anxiety when practicing mindful meditation (for most people it reduces anxiety). Also, if you have symptoms of psychosis this practice may not be for you, or you should at least seek advice before trying - note that these are rare occurrences but something I feel I am obliged to draw your attention to.

Bringing mindfulness into everyday life is really very simple, all it takes is a conscious effort to focus the mind. The easiest way to bring this practice into your life to help your healing is to first gain awareness of the times that your thoughts tend to wander to your problems, painful memories, concerns, worries etc., this could be any part of your day - getting dressed, driving to places, your lunch break. Just take the time to work out when you get caught up in your negative thoughts and feelings.

Once you have established the above you can then move onto practicing mindfulness during these times. Next time you find your mind straying into negative territory or dwelling on difficulties try the following:

Draw your focus to what is happening with your senses. What can you see? What can you hear, taste, touch? Don't get too bogged down in it all, just recognise what is going on and acknowledge it.

Let any thoughts and feelings come but keep bringing your focus back to what is going on in the here and now with your senses.

Next switch your focus to your breath, inhale through your nose and notice what the breath is doing. Focus on feeling the air coming in as you inhale and going out as you exhale. Don't force the breath but let it be smooth, calm and steady. (see "And Breathe" section)

You will find that you get distracted but the more you practice the easier it becomes. It's a bit like exercising a muscle. Remember you only need a few minutes each day to make a difference - 5 minutes of quality practice is far more beneficial than sitting still for 20 minutes trying too hard.

This is a fairly standard way to practice mindfulness. Another way I like to practice is to fully direct my attention to what I am doing. For example, if I am folding laundry, I focus on what my hands are doing, what the different textures feel like, the clean fresh smell. In the past I used this technique a lot, especially in the earlier days when it seemed all I could focus on was how shit I felt. When I made a cup of tea, I would focus all of my attention on the different steps in the process: filling the kettle, listening to the sound as it boiled, noticing my hands stirring the tea bag, and then how it tasted. Doing this gave me little windows of time where I was not thinking about or allowing my thoughts to drift to everything that was wrong. It gave my brain and nervous system a little break from all the intense feelings and stress that were connected to my situation.

Mindfulness be done anytime, anywhere. You can practice mindful walking, eating, cooking, and just about anything else in between. It can also be undertaken with a therapist as part of cognitive therapy such as MBCT (mindfulness-based cognitive therapy) and CBT (cognitive behavioural therapy).

Remember to allow time for this practice to be of benefit - it can take 8 weeks for practices such as meditation to physically change the neural pathways of our brain so it's going to take a tad longer than giving it a go for 5 minutes one Tuesday afternoon.

EFT: EMOTIONAL FREEDOM TECHNIQUE

Emotional Freedom Technique, or what is also known as tapping, is something that I came across about 2 years ago and is a holistic tool I have used for anxiety, emotional distress, and releasing emotional obstacles. EFT has been proven to be effective for a wide range of issues including PTSD, chronic pain, emotional issues, phobias, stress, depression, and those really unhelpful beliefs. You know the sort, that negative self-talk, etc., that has a habit of sabotaging our good intentions or attempts to move forward. The type of thoughts that start with things like "I can't do this," or "I'm useless."m

Tapping has its roots in Chinese medicine, working on the acupressure points of the body to stimulate them. It helps to release stored emotions that may be affecting us mentally and physically. This form of therapy has been used with soldiers suffering from PTSD, so you get an idea of how powerful it can be. It works by systematically tapping on some of the body's 12 major meridian points.The meridians are channels that direct the flow of energy throughout the body just like the circulatory system does with our blood. Below is a diagram of the points that are used in this therapy.

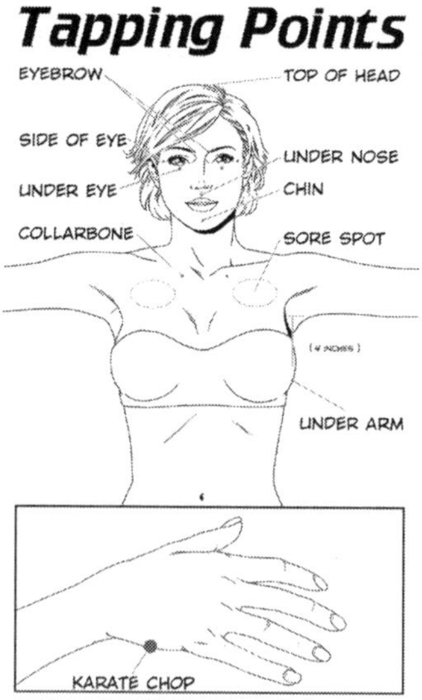

Courtesy of www.ThrivingNow.com & www.Joy-Connection.com
Visit us for free reprint information and energy tapping tips
© 2009 - Reprint information and links must remain with the image

Each meridian point in our body corresponds with and regulates a particular organ and is part of a meridian system that's interconnected - think of it as an energy superhighway. In Chinese medicine, our energy flow is called Qi; our circulating life-force (I feel all Star Wars-y when I imagine this). If our system is imbalanced then our life force is interrupted, which can result in ill health. Tapping can help to release blockages and bring our system back into balance, enabling Qi to flow more freely and promote good health.

The thing I love about tapping is that like many of the alternative practices, it's about treating the body as a whole and bringing it back into balance. It helps to break cycles that lurk behind the emotional issues that hold us back and can help to release some of the emotional baggage that weighs us down. I think it's amazing that by practising this technique you can tap (literally) into your own energy healing and trigger the body's innate ability to heal.

In case you're finding this a bit on the "woo-woo" side, then let's just remind ourselves of that mind-body connection and how emotional trauma and pain can manifest into physical illness, and negative thoughts and emotions have a disruptive effect on the body. If we apply that knowledge to this context, then what we are saying is that all that negative shit disrupts our energy flow (Qi) throughout the body. We can also look at this from a law of physics perspective. We know from the study of physics that the Universe is made up of energy. We can't see that energy, but we trust the physicists, so we acknowledge this to be true. Well, the same goes for the human body. We are made up of energy that we cannot see and just because we can't see it doesn't mean we should ignore the impact a disruption to it can have on our health or how beneficial bringing it back to balance would be - kind of makes sense when you put it like that, huh?

There is so much more I could go into about EFT it. In fact, I could probably write a whole book on this subject alone, but that is something I will leave to the many people who have already done so. I have included EFT info in the "Useful Websites and Stuff" section in the back of this book, a section designed to stop me banging on too much or boring you to death with certain subjects like this!

I will round up talk of this technique by saying it is something that you can easily do at home. There are of course many benefits from learning one to one with a professional instructor, but it is, something that you can learn and apply yourself through books, YouTube, and instructional videos via the Internet. This is how I did it, I read up on the technique and tapped along with videos until I was confident to do it alone. Doing it this way, without an instructor, might not have given me the full benefit out of this therapy, but I have been happy with the results it produced for me. I found tapping particularly helpful for dealing with the aftermath of emotionally charged situations, the sort that can capsize your life if you don't address the fallout. I also found it resolved a long-standing fear of the dark.

For many years I had an irrational fear of sleeping alone in the dark. I'm not entirely sure where it came from (I'm sure my penchant for crime novels probably didn't help), but in the wee early hours I would often lie awake or bolt out of sleep with my grownup version of the monster under the bed, which obviously was not ideal for someone with cortisol issues! Tapping banished the monsters for good and I was amazed by the speed with which it did so. I kid you not, three nights of tapping on the emotions I was feeling connected to this situation, and I was able to kiss goodbye to that fear.

For me, tapping is one of those things for which I can say I don't know how it works, but it works and that's all I need. Something that can resolve an issue like my fear of the dark in such a short timeframe comes under 'A' for Awesome - If you knew me you would know that "awesome" is not a word I often bestow on anything, so please take this as a sign that I was super impressed.

Although I experienced a super-fast resolution of my fear of the dark, I think it's important to note that in general EFT is like many things in alternative healing: something that requires patience and commitment. It is said to take a minimum of 21 days to break a habit and longer to form a new one, so I think that would be a sound guideline for anyone wishing to give this technique a go. In terms of helping with fibro symptoms, I think anything that can alleviate emotional stress can only be good and will have a knock-on effect on things such as pain levels, sleep patterns, stomach issues, and concentration. Along my research travels I have read that tapping can directly impact on pain levels, so if you want to read more on this, then check out some of the links and research articles at the back of the book.

GRIEVING

It wasn't until I dipped my toe back into the therapy pond that I became aware that a lot of what I was feeling around being ill was connected to grief. The emotions, thoughts, and feelings I was experiencing were creating a cycle: increase in the level of symptoms because of my emotions surrounding illness, and a prolonged highly emotional state because of the impact of the symptoms. This cycle was keeping me stuck in illness, each driving the other and leaving me very little head space to consider my options or take on board anything that might help me.

Although I had anticipated receiving a fibro diagnosis, I soon learnt that emotionally anticipation and confirmation are two very different things. I thought I was prepared for it, but on an emotional level, I was nowhere near ready. For a time until I came to terms with it, I saw it very much like an ending. Not only was it the end of a 3-year battle to discover what was wrong with me, but also at that stage, the end of hope. These endings left me floundering around with nothing but grief to keep me company. I was grieving for so much: the years that I had already lost to illness, the loss of the future life I had planned and everything that went hand in hand with that. I can remember sobbing to my therapist how now I would never be able to climb Machu Picchu. When she asked me if that was something I had wanted to do, I wailed that I didn't know but the diagnosis had robbed me of any chance I'd ever have! Today, recalling this conversation makes me laugh. Just for the record, I have never had the slightest desire for mountain climbing (it was a pure drama queen moment), but at the time it was representative of how keenly I felt the loss of my freedom of choice.

I think it is fair to say that back then I was consumed with everything I thought I had lost to illness, even potential mountain climbing. I was clouded by grief and without a doubt, the illness situation was compounded by the feelings I also had around lost opportunities in my previous abusive relationship. The feelings of grief surrounding the chronic illness diagnosis reignited the sense of loss I felt from my past relationship, culminating in an emotional maelstrom. Throw into the mix a hefty family argument, and the result was my physical symptoms were being driven Thelma and Louise style over a cliff by all my emotional shit.

Recognising that it was grief I was experiencing was one of the first small steps I made towards getting better. Once I had identified the cause of a lot of the emotions that were making the physical symptoms worse, I was able to begin working through them. As I have already mentioned, the therapy sessions helped me to work through the grieving process and reach the point of acceptance from where the healing processes really started to take root. Without these sessions, I don't think that I would have realised as soon as I did that I was mourning the loss of the life I thought I was going to have.

I think in our society our overriding impression of grief and loss is usually connected to death. We do not automatically connect that a life-changing diagnosis can impact us on a similar level as the loss of life and that the feelings can be as intense; therefore, we do not always recognise the enormity of these other life events. One of the things I had to work through during my therapy was not minimising or dismissing the grief I felt. Although there may not have been a physical loss of someone or something in my life, my feelings of grief were still valid.

Grief had such a direct effect on my physical and mental health that after experiencing the release and relief by dealing with it, I feel that on every recovery journey it is important for us to identify our losses, sit with them, and work through how we feel.

HEALING THE PAST

Our history, whether we are aware of it or not, has a marked impact on our lives in the here and now. As a child our most formative years are from birth to the age of 8 years. This is kind of where the architecture of our brains is shaped. Our early childhood provides the foundation for our social, physical, emotional, and mental development. The things we learn during these years help us to create our "blueprints" for how we see ourselves, others, and the world, in general, influencing everything from our decision making to our interactions with others and our relationships.

How we experience these early years may determine how rough or smooth our path through life will be. The life events and experiences we have outside of childhood can also impact greatly on how our lives unfold. This is why it is so valuable to our future wellbeing to identify and resolve any past emotional issues that keep revisiting us in the present.

I think it's fair to say that most people have shit from their past that they would benefit from offloading, but I feel this is particularly important when we are trying to heal our physical body. To heal fully is to heal all areas of our lives. I feel confident in having the opinion that often there is an emotional element to many illnesses. Whether it may be a direct driver of symptoms or a contributory factor, either way, I believe that it is vital that they are resolved in order to heal. Healing past hurts and wrongdoings is not easy. Unearthing and sifting through our personal shit pile can at times feel as emotional as when events first occurred, but as difficult as it is, it is a process that can move us forward in the healing process.

When it comes to forgiveness. It is not for me to say that people must forgive anyone who has caused them pain or hurt. I realise that for many people the hurt may be too great, but I do feel that for us to be able to fully move forward we need to find ways to release ourselves from the hold our difficult past experiences can have on us. Addressing past hurts is a very personal journey, it's one that needs to be done at a pace that is comfortable and safe, but nevertheless I feel it is something that needs to be done if we are to give ourselves the best chance at forgiveness, or at least find a way to live more comfortably alongside our history.

From my own personal experience, I can honestly say I don't know if I have reached a level of forgiveness towards the person that caused me so much hurt. After all, what exactly does forgiveness feel or look like? How do you know when you are in full forgiveness mode? What I do know is that when I think of my past with this person, I feel very ambivalent towards it. There is a feeling of sadness for the other person, I don't hold any animosity towards them, and I truly wish that they could overcome their demons so that they can lead a peaceful life. Is that forgiveness? Maybe.

While reaching forgiveness may be considered the ideal outcome to healing past hurts I feel that it is still possible to move forward by accepting that you are not ready to forgive someone. Sometimes it can be as powerful and freeing to lay aside the need to reach a certain state of being and revisit it in another time and space. It can be stressful and delay progress trying to force ourselves to feel something we are not ready to feel just because everyone tells us it's the only way forward. Laying down the need to find forgiveness for someone that badly hurt us, to just cut it free and place it to one side can also help us to move forward. I believe it's possible to be okay with not being able to forgive someone if the emotional issues connected to this person and their actions can be worked through and resolved.

For me, it's not really that important to confirm whether I have been able to forgive or not. It is good enough that I feel like I am at peace with that part of my life, that I am okay with knowing my past is what it is. Of course, if I could have the time again, I would do things differently, I would rewrite that part of my life script but there probably isn't a person alive in this world who wouldn't do some things differently if given a second shot at life.

I am not denying that occasionally there are certain situations that arise in my current life that still have the power to ping me back to my past and resurrect certain feelings, but the emotions that are attached to this connection no longer hold any real weight. Any emotions that are present are manageable and do not interfere with my day to day, nor do they have the power to totally overwhelm me.

I think that healing the past isn't just about reconciling ourselves with other people's actions or behaviour towards us, it is also learning to forgive ourselves. It means letting go of our own past actions and finding a sense of peace with the less than desirable parts of our past. The past is the past, and no amount of beating ourselves up, feeling guilty, or wishing it away will change what has gone before. As they say, "what is done is done." Keeping ourselves tied to the past mentally or emotionally through our feelings, thoughts, and actions is a drain on our energy. It also prevents us from fully being present in the here and now and open to what that holds for us. When we are too emotionally connected to our past in a negative way, we cannot always see the doors that are open to us in the present. We miss the signals, signs, and opportunities that can be of benefit to our wellbeing.

I appreciate that for some this is a big ask. It is not easy to release the past, especially when there have been experiences that have been emotionally catastrophic. It is not something we just wake up one day and decide we will move on from, but I do think with work, some of the connections and ties can be cut to give us more emotional freedom and I do think we owe it to ourselves to try. We deserve to be released from our past trauma and bad experinces.

Because certain life events can be so emotionally overwhelming I'm not entirely sure whether I believe we can ever completely resolve all the complex emotions attached to our past experiences, but I do believe we can reduce the impact that they have on us in the present. I believe that we can reach a place where they don't cast such a dark shadow over our everyday lives. A place where we can learn to live alongside our experiences without them sabotaging our wellbeing or contributing to illness.

I must confess that I am one of those slightly irritating people who has signed up to the belief that it's not what happens to us but the way we choose to respond to it that counts. You might be with me on this, or you might want to roll your eyes at me, or even tell me to fuck off but I'm leaving it out there as a reminder that there is always one thing in life that we always have control over, and that is how we choose to respond.

REACTING VS. RESPONDING

Becoming more aware of how I was behaving when faced with certain situations, particularly challenging ones, and learning to become less reactive to the events and people who pushed my buttons was one of those little things that had a lasting positive impact on my daily life.

Prior to becoming a counsellor, I didn't really pay a great deal of attention to how I was going about my business, how I was behaving towards or interacting with others, it was just something I did. It never crossed my mind that there was any difference between a reaction and a response, and certainly no awareness of how it might be affecting my wellbeing. I had just assumed they were one and the same; words that were interchangeable. However, during my training, I discovered that in practice they are not alike at all.

Before I tell you why learning this difference between a reaction and response was important to me and this journey and just in case you, like me, didn't realise there was actually a difference between the two states, let me just drop in this brief overview:

Reaction: When we react to a situation we are acting with little conscious thought, it's that instinctive "knee jerk" thing we all know about. These are those instinctive physical reactions (think touching something hot or cold, reacting to an emergency, trauma, etc.) There's not much we can do to change those types of reactions, and to be honest, in a dangerous situation we wouldn't want to anyway because they're useful.

Now I'm going to pop in with a different type of reaction - emotionally driven reactions. These can be driven by our subconscious and can also take place with no real thought of the impact or consequences. Again, often knee-jerk in nature. These reactions can be explosive and act as a type of automatic defence mechanism designed to protect us from a perceived "threat" (there goes our brain again). These perceived threats can be anything that causes us to feel things like provocation: criticism, anger, hurt, etc. - remember the brain can't tell what is real or imagined, or at what level the "threat" is.

When an emotional reaction to a situation or interaction takes place, we can often find ourselves acting before we've considered our behaviour or the outcome. These are the times when we can get those undesirable type of reactions. You know the sort, those moments when you throw an almighty hissy fit, out pops your inner a bitch or you act like someone who's undergone a complete personality transplant.

These reactions are often the result of stressors, although, speaking from personal experience, fluctuations in hormones are a definite factor too! The more stressed (hormonal) or under "threat" we feel, the more likely we are to turn a little feral, let slip those unfiltered thoughts, or to put it politely behave in a less than endearing manner.

Response: When we respond to a situation our conscious thought is much more engaged in the process. We can create a tiny window of space that gives us a brief opportunity (all that's needed) to interpret the situation and respond in a more measured and considered way. Although the unconscious mind can still drive responses, we have an opportunity to make a choice; a point where we can make a conscious decision. If you like, assess which way we are going jump. This has the advantage of allowing us to take a mental step back to consider the implications of our words and actions before deciding which would be our best course of action. On the whole, this is a much healthier state for us to be in. It helps to do away with those emotional hangovers; the sinking feeling, the guilt, embarrassment, etc., we get when we realise we've reacted too rashly or harshly to a situation or irrationally completely lost our shit.

When I look back on my pre-counselling life, I can see that much of the time I lived in reactive mode. I had no thoughts of where my reactions were coming from and I had plenty of those emotional hangovers. This is not to say that I now glide through life responding in a measured and controlled way in every interaction or situation I find myself in. Believe me, I can still lose my shit with the best of them. I know this method isn't fool proof. There have been many "post-training" moments where I've had to back-track, eat humble pie, or apologise for my words or actions. However, I can tell you that I have noticed that when we learn a different way of being, if we then cultivate it, it has a habit of naturally infiltrating our actions and is a much healthier place to live from.

Learning to respond rather than just reacting has meant that I feel much more in control of myself. Now I'm no longer permenantly knee-jerking through life like a can-can dancer. I feel like I'm less likely to get caught up in those unhelpful reactive emotions or personal dramas. Through really taking note of myself and how I was reacting, I have become much more aware of the impact my words and behaviour can have on others and myself.

Trying to come at situations from a more responsive perspective has meant that I have become less emotionally invested in certain situations and people. When I do remember to take that mental step back instead of automatically reacting, the end result is always much more beneficial to my wellbeing. By considering my response rather than jumping in with both feet, I find I don't get triggered by other people's stuff in quite the same way as I used to, which makes my life much calmer - I also expend way less energy

Choosing to take the less reactive path has helped me to deal better with other people, particularly those who previously used to rub me up the wrong way. It has meant I am more able to respond to provocation, unhelpful suggestions, opinions, etc., in a more emotionally controlled way instead of getting all emotionally wobbly or tearing strips off people with the searing, arse-stinging replies - something I used as my weapon of choice in my more reactive days.

While it can be said that sometimes it's good to vent and let off steam, over time I have come to the conclusion that when venting is directed at another person, it rarely has a positive outcome. In fact, most of the time it ends up rebounding on us. Hasty reactions, rants, and the like often end up harming the person who's doling it out just as much as the person who's on the receiving end. I have personally found that switching from always being in reaction mode to a more considered response has saved me many a time from emotional overwhelm or getting into unnecessary stressful altercations and metaphorically speaking ripping other people's heads off.

There is no doubt that emotional stressors drive physical symptoms, and often that stress can come from places that we aren't even aware of. The areas we don't give much thought to, the reactive traps and behaviours we have got caught up in with out realising. The ones that create invisible layers of tension that can make our physical symptoms worse.

Again, this is where I hop up on my self-aware soapbox for a moment and say that by getting to know ourselves inside and out, we can identify which of our behaviours and actions are having the greatest impact on our wellbeing. Once we know how what we are doing, thinking, etc., is affecting us we can make the shift towards making changes that will benefit our health. Just as I realised that instead of being a totally reactive person, it would make my life calmer and less stressful if I just wound my neck in more.

What I'm getting around to saying here is why create unnecessary emotional stress if there are more mind and body friendly ways we can go about things? If we can create a greater level of inner calm and therefore a greater level of wellbeing by learning to be more responsive and less reactive, then what have we got to lose by taking a closer look at how we behave, particularly when we are being challenged or put under pressure?

When I realised that being too reactive wasn't helping me in life, I set about trying to change this old pattern of behaviour. Like I have said, I don't always succeed in mastering my knee jerk reactions, but I'm much better than I was at managing to hit the pause button on them. Sometimes I have to mentally visualise a pause button to stop me from those immediate reactions and open a window so I can consider which option would lead to a better outcome. Illness has definitely influenced how much I use my mental pause button. When I started taking the holistic approach to health and realised that I needed to re-evaluate all areas of my life, I was surprised how much of the background stuff in my life was pulling my emotional strings. There were things going on at a level that I wasn't aware of that were creating small pockets of tension here and there. I realised that making quite simple adjustments to the way I was acting and interacting with people reduced some tension and just made life that little bit easier. It helped to make some difficult relationships much more comfortable.

When trying to heal from serious illness, reducing the negative emotional impact other people can have can help on us helps tremendously on both a physical and mental level. Of course, sometimes it is not always possible to fully remove someone we have a difficult relationship with from our lives, but we can work on managing our interactions with them and reduce the tension, upset, or conflict by monitoring our own reactions.

Over the years I have got caught up in quite a few personal dramas and emotionally charged situations, and most, if not all of them, have been stressful, completely pointless, and unnecessary. I should think there is also a high percentage of them which could have been avoided altogether if I had been less reactive to the situation. Like virtually every person on this planet, I have lost my cool or jumped in with both feet. I've had plenty of "in the heat of the moment" feelings when I've felt those immediate flares of anger, hurt, or defensiveness, but becoming more aware of how I am triggered by certain situations has made it easier for me to make that switch from an automatic reactive mode to responsive mode - I'm not 100% successful, if I was I wouldn't be human, but these days the scales lean more towards responsive than reactive mode when I am feeling challenged or provoked.

As we all know, life is unpredictable, and people are even more so. There are always going to be potential emotional triggers springing up in our interactions with others. We can't go through life trying to pre-empt situations or avoid emotional confrontations, but we can develop self-help tools that can help us to neutralise potentially explosive situations, cope better with those type of confrontation, and reduce our stress levels, all of which can support a better level of health.

Below is the handy little self-help sequence that I have learnt to use to help me to be less reactive and therefore less stressed. I don't always use all the sequence. Sometimes counting and taking a deep breath is enough, other times if I'm not in a direct situation, i.e., face to face with someone, I take longer to go through the whole process.

- **Hitting the button** - I tell myself I'm hitting the pause button, then mentally count backwards from 5 (the 5-Second Rule) to create a little space to assess where I'm at and shift the brain to the prefrontal cortex where I can consciously take in what's happening.

- **Options** - I remind myself that I always have a choice in how I'm going to handle the situation.

- **Check-in** - I take a deep breath and check where am I reacting from. What emotions I'm feeling. Then I ask myself one of the following: Is this the best place for me to react from? Is now a good time to react? Do I really want to say/do this?

- **Time check** - I question how I will feel about my reaction in 5 minutes, later today, tomorrow, a week, etc. This helps me to gauge just whether something is really worth it.

- **The bigger picture** - What will be the outcome of my reaction? Is it going to help or hinder me, my relationship, my health, my wellbeing, etc.?

- **Apply a filter** - Is my - or any - response necessary? Is it a true reflection of what I'm really thinking, or just an automatic heat of the moment emotional reaction? or one that is being drivien by other things? Is it helpful to me or to others?

This might sound like a lot of work or one of those things that you think you can't be arsed to do, but it does only take a few seconds to apply. I won't lie, it takes a bit of time and practice to get the hang of it and to remember to apply any of it in the "moment!" At the beginning, like me, you might only remember this tactic after you have lost your rag and got all stressed, but I think it's worth persevering with because it's one of those things that I genuinely believe is of benefit. If being less reactive in life creates less emotional stress and therefore has less of a physical impact, then that can only be a good thing for our health.

Body

PART 3: CHAPTER 10

BODY

The human body and mind never fail to amaze me. Both are incredibly adept at overcoming and adapting to traumatic life events and stress. Just like the mind, our body is hugely complex. It is an incredible machine that has an amazing capability to repair and fix itself. Every day it carries out millions of functions designed to keep us alive and in a healthy state; even when overwhelmed, it will do its level best to keep on functioning. If we were to stop and think about all the processes and functions the body carries out every second of the day, we would realise that even during sickness it is amazing - it may not be functioning properly, but it still keeps on trying to right itself!

I feel that we sometimes take our bodies for granted. It's often not until something goes wrong and symptoms appear that we really start to take note. Our body is the most valuable thing we own, yet a lot of the time we are not aware of just how well we need to take care of it until we reach a crisis point. Much of the time we often miss the subtle signs that something is amiss, not realising just how long our bodies have been under duress. Many of us have an expectation that it will just continue to do what it's meant to do despite not always giving it tho best of attention or the level of care it requires to function efficiently. Of course, everybody knows somebody who has managed to live to a ripe old age despite smoking, drinking excess alcohol, and eating every processed food known to man, etc. But the fact is, for the vast majority of us, we need to take better care of our bodies if we're to stand even a cat in hell's chance of being within sniffing distance of that 100th birthday telegram from the Queen.

Our body is like a vast network that connects one part to another, from our largest organ to the smallest of blood vessels. Therefore, if one thing isn't functioning sufficiently then there will be other things that are struggling or are out of balance too. This is why a holistic approach is a sound one - it takes the body as a whole, looks to bring all aspects, all parts, back in connection and balance with one another. Conventional medicine, on the other hand, mostly focuses on addressing and dealing with the symptoms at hand (what is being presented). Much of the time it fails to look at the causative factors/root causes, which are often not immediately apparent.

If we are experiencing health issues to the point that they are having a debilitating effect on our daily life, then it is absolutely essential that we address our whole lifestyle and re-establish a healthier relationship and connection with our body.

There is no doubt that true healing, the holistic approach, takes time; time to fully investigate, time to observe the body and its responses, and time to figure out the connections and pathways to ill health in order for a comprehensive recovery plan to be worked out. In my opinion, time is something that is limited in conventional medicine, particularly here in the UK. When it comes to patients who are presenting with multiple issues and symptoms that are often vague or transient, a series of 10-minute appointments with a GP or being rushed through a consult will never be enough to A) establish a person's individual pathway to illness, or B) create a personalised plan to restore health.

As I have said before, conventional medicine has its place, and sometimes, we still need to take certain medications in conjunction with or while we are waiting for other healing treatments to do their work. I feel the problem with the conventional approach is that it often takes the presenting symptoms as stand-alone issues and treats them as such. For example, it will treat reflux/heartburn without considering how a person's stress or bile production in the liver is impacting on it or treat depression without thoroughly assessing gut health or lifestyle. If a conventional doctor does not see that a bunch of symptoms are connected, they will often work out a diagnosis based on what they are being presented with and work out the treatment from there. Now that might seem like the sensible route, but it falls down when it comes to complex health issues, people's individual biochemistry, lifestyle, and past experiences, etc., because the prescribed treatment does not take these factors into account and therefore is not always tailored towards the individual. We are usually just encouraged to pop the standardised pills for symptoms, cross our fingers that it works as well for us as the person before us, and move along the bus.

As you can probably tell, I could go on and on with this topic, but the main point I am making is that the body needs and must be treated as a whole. If you picture the body like a machine and imagine all its working parts as cogs, when something gets jammed, rusted, or a spanner gets thrown in the works, then the whole machine is prevented from running smoothly. It may be able to run on a little longer, but eventually, it will seize up and grind to a halt one way or another. Treating the body as a whole, taking a holistic approach to health, is a way to get all our cogs turning and working in unison once more.

We have already taken a look at the mind-body connection and its impact on the body. In following pages, I am going to focus attention on the body itself and the ways and methods I have used to bring my body back into balance. As with most topics in this book, there will be that crossover with the other two elements, Mind and Soul, because they are intrinsically linked.

Before I get into the more physical healing aspects of my journey, I first want to mention root causes. When we get a fibro diagnosis, we are given the impression that this is the reason behind all our ills, the cause of all those random and bizarre symptoms so many of us experience. I have already called into question the validity of this diagnosis and how I feel that it is often a label that is given to us without looking deeper into underlying issues. As I worked on healing, I have been able to peel back the layers and discover the root causes (what's really wrong) behind my diagnosis, and that is the reason I have been able to reverse symptoms. Now I am even more convinced that this is something we should all consider doing.

My main root causes were emotional trauma (this root cause was basically what fucked up most things), chronic stress, overuse of antibiotics, and mineral imbalances, which led to a culmination of things that came together to create one big shit storm: thyroid issues (levels in range but not optimal and symptomatic of hypothyroid), Adrenal dysfunction, digestion and gut issues (gastritis ,reflux and leaky gut), sluggish liver, hormonal imbalances, an overgrowth of yeast (candida).

Other contributory factors I have also wondered about but have not been able to address are possible underlying infections. These are Lyme disease and EBV (Epstein-Barr Virus). Testing for Lyme disease is expensive, it is not uncommon for the NHS ELISA test to produce a false negative, and once you have that negative result, best of luck pushing for further testing. EBV is a common virus that is known to cause mono/glandular fever, and other illness and over 90% of the population has been infected at some point in their lives. After the initial illness, EBV usually stays in a dormant state, but it is possible for it to reactivate in some people with weakened immune systems. Reactivated EBV can become chronic and has been linked to chronic fatigue and produces symptoms such as sore throat, neurological issues, fatigue, achiness, and more.

As I have progressed along this healing journey of mine, I have gotten to know my body well and learned how it important it is to have everything working as one and in sync. I am sure as more time passes there will still be things for me to uncover and improve on. For now, the following pages are the areas I have worked on to date, the things I have researched and educated myself on.

This is the part of the book where I do make some recommendations, although I have been very mindful of not being too directive or encouraging you to do exactly as I have done. While reading these pages I'd like you to be mindful that this is how my progress has been achieved, and that creating a carbon copy of the things I have done will not necessarily produce the same results or create a personal route to wellness for you because, as I have written in the introduction, my story will not be yours, my root causes will not be your root causes. However, I do believe that it is highly likely there will be some shared causative factors, and I know that working on the areas of the body I write about will be of benefit to you because there isn't a single person in the world who wouldn't benefit from improving their gut health or diet, balancing minerals, or boosting their liver function, etc. These are the areas where I am directive and give you tips on how to go about it. There are also recommendations in the "Useful Websites & Stuff" section to help you move forward with your health journey.

When reading the following pages, it is especially important to be mindful that we all come into healing from a different level. Therefore, we need to do our own research, take things slowly, monitor our progress, and at times seek professional advice. Although by healing through alternative methods we are often stepping into taking responsibility for our own recovery, it does not solely need to be a DIY project. We can do an awful lot to help ourselves, but at times it is also wise to get other people on board, i.e., herbalist, naturopath, functional medicine pratitioner, hair test analysis specialist, etc. It should also be noted that if you are currently being treated by a healthcare provider, then you may need to discuss any planned changes in treatment with them. Note that you may meet with some scepticism or a lack of support for these changes. How you choose to manage that is up to you and how far you wish to push the envelope.

As before, in this section of the book, through sharing my experience of healing the body and the knowledge I have gained over the years, I hope that it gives you a starting point, a rough guide, and above all, fires up the desire to start work on healing yourself.

CHAPTER 11

RELATIONSHIP WITH MY BODY

Our relationship with our body is something that you are more likely to find being talked about in the alternative healing world rather than the conventional. I think I can safely say that in all likelihood, it is not a subject that our average healthcare provider mentions during those 10-minute appointments, yet it can have a profound effect on healing.

When we become sick, especially if it is a long-term illness, our perspective and attitude towards our body can undergo a change. I know that in the beginning, I was very critical of my body. I felt that it had betrayed me, let me down in the worst way possible by ceasing to function properly. I would say stuff like "this useless body," or "I hate my body" (and more unrepeatable things). Overall, I just wasn't very nice to myself. It wasn't until I realised that part of my healing required me to be kinder to myself and make nice with my body that I began to change my attitude.

When I became too ill to function properly my body became public enemy number 1, bearing the brunt of my anger and frustration at what I saw as its betrayal, imitations and failures. Now I know I was going about things in the wrong way. I actually needed to thank my body, thank it for getting me as far as it had despite the adverse conditions and all the shit that had been thrown at it. Instead of all body bashing and berating, I needed to tune into my body and listen to what it was trying to tell me and learn how it was communicating with me.

While I was holding that pity party of mine, I thought my body had failed me. I was convinced that it had turned against me and was trying to bring me down with ill health. The truth was my body didn't want to be sick, the symptoms I was experiencing were its way of communicating to me. It was my body's compass trying to guide me towards a better level of health. In the early days, all I could take from my situation was that everything was going wrong and my body was to blame. When I look back now, I can't believe I had that attitude. How could my body be to blame? I was its gatekeeper and guardian, and if the truth be told, I was responsible for providing it with a healthy environment. Don't get me wrong, I realise that some of the causative factors of illness were out of my control, but I did have a level of personal responsibility to my body and there were definitely times that I could have done much better by it.

I spent years being disconnected from my body. It was as if I saw it as something separate from myself, that it was somehow acting autonomously and that I had little influence on how things were unfolding. I now realise that perspective was a cop-out, a way of being able to shift responsibility, because it's never easy to look at our own role in something that hasn't turned out well. It's especially difficult to acknowledge the ways in which we may have contributed to our own downfall. By blaming my body, it made it very easy for me to absolve myself of having any part in how I came to be ill. I eventually came to realise that part of my recovery was dependent on my taking some of the responsibility and befriending my body instead of waging a war against it.

Once I finally acknowledged that my body wasn't in fact rebelling against me, I realised that it was doing its utmost to draw my attention to things that needed addressing and it had been for many years. It wasn't until much later when I started to connect the dots and dig into my route to illness that I realised that my body had been waving those red flags for a very long time before it reached a breaking point - we do not become ill overnight.

Today I see myself and my body as one. We are in a collaborative relationship and presenting a united front. It is trying to do its best by me, and I am trying to do my best by it. I am doing all I can to provide it with an environment from which it can go through the natural healing process, and it will continue to do its best to heal. Like any relationship, it has its ups and downs. Sometimes we fall out, sometimes I expect too much from it, sometimes I shame it by telling it, it looks crap in a swimsuit, sometimes I need a reminder to be more self-compassionate, but on the whole, these days we jog along quite nicely together because we're in this together.

CHAPTER 12

DIET

There is no question that food is medicine. It can help us to heal, but inadequate nutrition is one of the biggest factors that can interfere with the body's natural healing process. In today's world, our supermarket shelves are packed with every type of food we could imagine, and many of them are processed.

A diet that is high in processed foods has all the elements for ill health: refined sugar, trans fats, low fibre, preservatives, and shit that just doesn't belong in the body. At the same time, the world has never been so full of advice on how to eat right. You only need to go on the Internet to see a ton of advice being given on how to eat healthily.

We are bombarded by so-called experts who promise to give us the "answers" to how to eat our way to health and stay healthy because that is what they have experienced. Depending on who you talk to on what day, you will be advised to go vegan, go keto, go paleo, go FODMAPS, try the alkaline diet, try macro, try carb cycling, try AIP, and don't forget to count those calories! These are just a few of the diets and plans that are available to us. And trying to decipher which is our best option when we're feeling at our worst and our judgement is clouded by brain fog is nigh on impossible and delving into them is like falling down a dietary rabbit hole.

The sole reason that I do not recommend my own diet to anyone else is because of our individual biochemistry - what's good for one person might turn out to be the worst thing for another. We might have a friend who raves about how fabulous she feels on her low carb, high protein diet, but if we happened to be suffering from a weak adrenal function we might not be able to tolerate a high protein diet at that stage and eating like that could potentially make us feel worse.

There are always going to be people who do well on certain diets. I know many thrive on a vegan diet because their bodies can easily convert beta-carotene and other precursors from veggies into vitamin A (retinol). If a person can't do that due to their individual body chemistry (approximately 45% of the population) then they will at some point, when their liver is depleted of its vitamin A stores, become deficient or experience imbalances. I have read of some ex-vegans who say that they thrived for up to 10 years before finding their health began deteriorating. Now, I'm not vegan bashing here, I love and include plenty of plant-based recipes in my diet and have meat-free days. This is purely as an example of how eliminating whole food groups isn't the best fit for everyone - one size doesn't fit all.

However, one thing that I am going to bash is when calorie counting forces nutritious food off the menu. Quite honestly, it irritates the fuck out of me when someone mentions that they avoid avocados because of their high fat, high-calorie content, but they'll happily chow down on a 0% fat, low-calorie "lite" yoghurt that has, as far as I'm concerned, about as much nutritional benefit to the body as eating the cardboard packaging it comes in. Don't get me wrong, I'm not debunking the calories in and calories out equation that aids weight loss. The issue I have is when calorie counting leads to people avoiding foods that are good for the body just because they're seen as too calorie-laden, or when high-calorie nutritious food is swapped out in favour of something lower in calories but far less nutritious.

The thing is, not all calories are created equal in terms of the effect they have on the body; e.g., if we take a 99-calorie biscuit and a small avocado, both have virtually the same calorie content, but the refined sugar content of the biscuit is something that will be of zero benefit to our body. It will create sugar spikes and inflammation in the body, whereas the avocado has anti-inflammatory properties. I don't think I need to say anything more other than which is going to be better for the body. Why did I go off on that little calorie rant? Because questioning which food is going to be more beneficial for our health is the kind of mindset we need to get into when working on healing our body. While trying to heal we need to stop demonising things like healthy fats just because they may have higher calories.

Even though I am hesitant in recommend my own specific diet to anyone, I would suggest that some people might consider as part of an elimination diet temporarily removing three things that can commonly cause issues – refined sugar, gluten, and dairy. When trying to heal refined sugar is not our friend. It causes spikes in blood sugar which subsequently leads to crashes and can increase inflammation levels. Although it is said by some that inflammation is not a factor in fibromyalgia, many people with this diagnosis do have high inflammation and conditions such as arthritis. And many report a reduction in aches and pains when they remove sugar from their diet. I think the fact that refined sugar offers no health benefits and is said to contribute to disease, in general, is a good enough reason for anyone to ditch it or at least dramatically reduce it.

As you may have seen, removing gluten from our diet does almost seem to be something of a trend these days, with many people opting to go gluten-free despite having no major health issues. If you are experiencing symptoms such as gas, bloating, brain fog, muscle aches, joint pains, digestive problems, and headaches (sound familiar?) then it might be an idea to remove gluten from your diet to see if it makes a difference. Now, you might be going down that "I've been tested for gluten intolerance and I'm in the clear" road, so I'd like to point out that we do not need to be intolerant to foods to have issues. A sensitivity to a particular food can be enough to create health problems, and these sensitivities do not show up through standard testing - intolerance or allergies, yes. Sensitivities, no.

In our modern-day diet, we eat way more gluten than our ancestors ever did. It is available to us all year round, day in and day out, and the gluten of today is very different from the gluten of the past. I personally think that perhaps our bodies have not adapted sufficiently to cope with the more modern gluten in excess. I don't necessarily think it is something we need to give up forever, but taking a break to see if it's a trigger or aggravating symptoms is not such a bad idea - like I say throughout this book, what do you have to lose? When I first started healing I had issues occur within 24 hours of eating gluten; that increased to days, then months, and now I can eat gluten when I choose to without problems. Although I still restrict consumption because it suits my particular diet and habits.

Dairy is another food source that can cause problems for some people, such as digestive issues, skin conditions, bloating, nausea, inflammation, and excessive mucus. I didn't think that I had an issue with dairy until I came to add it back in after my elimination diet and realised that it was responsible for increased mucus in my sinuses and throat. As I have healed, I do now have some dairy back in my diet. I eat some cheese and grass-fed butter, but the majority of the time I still tend to steer clear of cow's milk and yoghurt simply because I no longer feel I need to consume it. I know of people who say us humans can tolerate raw milk much better and enjoy its health benefits, but it is not something I have tried due to the fact it is not readily available in the UK.

Before I round up on the matter of diet there are a couple of things I would be happy recommending for all when it comes to making changes to diet. Firstly, where possible, try and up the number of veggies being consumed, although again, this is a personal thing that folks need to work out for themselves because some vegetables such as nightshade family (potatoes, aubergine, peppers, tomatoes, and more) can aggravate symptoms particularily in people with inflammatory conditions such as arthritis, and some people can't tolerate things like garlic and onions. Secondly, is to go organic where you can. I appreciate it's not always possible due to cost, but there can be ways to bring more organic into your diet - I talk more about this in the "Questions I've Been Asked, and Things I've Heard" section.

When I first started to address my physical health issues, making changes to my diet was high on the list. My overhaul began with a programme for treating candida. I came across Dr. Jeff McCombs and the "candidaplan.com" during one of my Internet trawls. Although, in hindsight, it is perhaps now not where I would immediately start with my healing, it was still hugely beneficial from a health perspective as well as in a personal achievement sense.

The plan was what first introduced me to the power of natural healing and demonstrated the commitment and generosity of some practitioners. Part of the plan was an elimination diet, and when I say elimination, I mean elimination; a 17-week plan that jettisoned dairy, all sugars, grains, legumes, seeds, nuts, alcohol, wheat, and all processed foods. For someone who ate a daily chocolate bar as a "pick me up" and who on rough days ate white toast and marmite, this baby was hardcore! To this day I'm not sure how I did it the first time, let alone had a second go at it. I even did it over Christmas - I guess that's what desperation does to a gal!

Despite the plan being one of the hardest tasks I've encountered, I stuck with this because even early on it was clear that I was starting to feel better. Aches and pains reduced, brain fog lifted, and my energy levels picked up, which was incredible after feeling so fatigued for so long. For me, this is was the first hands-on action I took for my physical healing, and while it may not have been the full answer to ill health, it was a great first step. Therefore, I will always be immeasurably grateful to Dr. McCombs for providing me with this first steppingstone towards better health. (He also deserves a big shout out because of his generosity in advising me on UK supplements when I couldn't afford to ship his products from the US - this guy did not make a cent out of me!)

As I noted above, there is a huge number of plans, programmes, and diets out there that promise to "fix" us, and many that suggest we cut out entire food groups or detox the hell out of our bodies. From raw diets to juice fasts to Palaeolithic man's modern-day equivalent of the woolly mammoth diet, the list is endless. As I touched on earlier, about the only thing I suggest that people do when looking to change their diet for healing is to consider an elimination diet. However, I believe that once a much higher level of health has been achieved, a balanced, clean, whole food diet is a good bet. I feel that while an elimination diet is useful in helping us to identify triggers and sensitivities, it is not something we necessarily need to stick to for life once we have resolved health issues. After all, if you are having to avoid something forevermore (unless you are allergic) then it is still a form of managing symptoms rather than healing.

When I first started trying to re-introduce gluten, sugar, and dairy into my diet they all had a negative effect on me within a day or so of consuming them. Now, there are some foods that were previously no-goes for me that are regularly back on the menu. There are some foods that I don't think I will ever go back to consuming, and there are a couple of "unhealthy" foods that, given half a chance, I would still happily face plant. These are the things I choose to eat occasionally and only since I have managed to establish a stronger health foundation.

I can't say that changing my diet has been easy, over the years there have been many food-related meltdowns that would have put a tantrum-throwing toddler to shame. These usually involved the absence of pizza in my life. In fact, when I first started out, I had to physically remove myself from the room during my family's weekly pizza and movie night. I'm not ashamed to say this was one of the times that I actually cried over not being able to eat something - pizza was and always will be one of my "face plant" foods.

As time went on, things did get easier. After I stopped sulking about feeling deprived and realised that a lot of what I was feeling (crying over pizza drama) was my emotional attachment to food-related events and a FOMO (fear of missing out) on sharing stuff with my family such our Saturday night ritual, I found ways to work around it. Once I started to physically feel the progress, I reached the point where I could eat something different from other people without experiencing serious food envy or wanting to stab them with my fork. I also channelled my desire for pizza into something productive by eventually, over many weeks, perfecting an alternative pizza - a totally pizza-less life was always going to be one of my non-negotiables!

Food is a big thing for me, I have always been a foodie. It's a standing joke that when any member of my family visits somewhere my first questions are always, "What is the food like?", "What did you eat?" Now food has become a major foundational block for my healing and is my medicine. In the past, I have used synthetic supplements, but I found that although the initial results were good, they didn't suit me on a long-term basis. While I do still use some supplementation to support my diet, this is now done through natural whole foods and herbs.

To create this nutritional foundational block, I had to completely overhaul my diet and change my mindset towards it. There have been times when I'd have rather stuck pins in my eyes than consumed some of the things I have, but in the end, it came back around to that commitment I made to myself and how much I wanted to heal.

I have learned over time that diet, like everything on a healing journey, is a very individualised thing. Yes, there are lots of crossovers that are good for the majority, but ultimately this is one of those areas where we really need to work out what's right for us either by ourselves or with the help of a alternative practitioner or nutritionist.

If you are used to eating a diet that is heavy on the processed food, or like me, you're a chocoholic, this overhaul is not likely to be a walk in the park, but I can guarantee that it will be worth it. I know radically switching up your diet can be overwhelming and confusing at the best of times. I know that sometimes too much information and advice can put you into a state of inaction rather than action. So, with that in mind, although I cannot recommend any specific diet, below is what I would consider to be a good starting point.

- Keep a food diary so you can clearly establish what you are eating and the quality of your diet.
- Ditch all processed foods and consider following an elimination diet just so you can determine what foods may be causing you problems (taking note of how you feel when certain foods are re-introduced in a food diary will help to show what you are currently sensitive to). There is more information in the "Useful Websites and Stuff" for how to use an elimination diet.
- Depending on what type of person you are, you may need to make adjustments one meal at a time and build up to implementing a full elimination diet, or just jump in with both feet. Note that while an elimination diet may reveal that you are currently sensitive to certain foods, this doesn't necessarily mean it's a forever situation. As the gut heals then so does the body's ability to tolerate things.
- Learn to read the labels on everything, get to know what's in stuff - it's amazing how many hidden sugars, etc., are in our food.

My last note on this particular subject is to say that while it may at first seem like a big mountain to climb, diet is an area of our lives where we can learn to exercise a healthy level of influence. Chronic illness often leaves us feeling out of control and powerless, but diet is one area that we can be in the driver's seat of our lives and get one over on illness - give it a two-fingered dietary salute!

CHAPTER 13

GUT HEALTH

This is a big Kahuna when we are trying to heal. If our gut isn't in a healthy state, then neither is the rest of us. With poor gut health we will never be able to reap the full health benefits of good nutrition or supplementation because an unhealthy gut means we aren't able to fully absorb the goodness. Before I started healing, I never gave a second thought to what was going on with my gut. In fact, the candida plan that I first started my journey with was the first time I had even heard about the gut's function and the impact it can have on our whole body and mind.

Every day of our lives our bodies are invaded by potential threats to our health: foreign substances, bacteria, viruses, parasites, and more. Our immune system has the important job of removing these threats while still retaining all the good stuff that helps to keep us healthy and well nourished. There are certain immune cells within our intestines that are called into action to protect us from anything the body perceives as foreign. Their job is to produce the correct immune response, either zapping it to death (killer cells) or producing antibodies.

Science has proved that up to 80% of the cells that make up our immune system are found in the gut, so you can see why it is so important for our gut to be operating at full service. It is absolutely vital to our overall health that we keep our gastrointestinal health in balance and functioning on all cylinders.

In our intestines we have billions upon billions of helpful bacteria, various strains and species that work behind the scenes to keep us in good health. These are what is called our gut flora or gut microbiota. It is thought that imbalances to this flora are a factor in ill health, especially in some chronic and auto-immune conditions.

There are many things that can create imbalances within our digestive and immune system – poor diet, contraceptives, environmental pollution, stress, certain medications. In today's world, we are obsessed with wiping out germs. We use antibacterial soaps, hand sanitisers, sprays and wipes, etc., which, although they zap the nasties, they also contribute to a reduction in the levels of our good bacteria. The fact is we need to be exposed to some bacteria so that our immune system can develop properly and learn to respond in the appropriate way (recognise the good from the bad). We also need exposure to some germs to help us maintain good levels of our helpful bacteria. Our good bacteria are essential for producing a certain protective antibody that helps us to fight off foreign bodies and are necessary for helping the body to produce the short-chain fatty acids that keep our digestive tract happy and healthy. These friendly bacteria play an important part in helping the body to break down the many toxins that we are exposed to on a daily basis.

One of the major causes of my own gut imbalances came from years of antibiotics. From my early childhood up until approximately the age of 30 years old I took antibiotics once or twice a year to combat the bouts of tonsillitis I was prone to. Now that I know that one dose of antibiotics is enough to upset the delicate balance of our gut flora, and if I factor in the huge amount of emotional stress I was exposed to in my early adulthood, it's no wonder I experienced some kind of intestinal Armageddon. If I add to that that the damage done to my gut from years of taking anti-inflammatory medication (NSAIDs) for migraine it is little wonder that my digestive and immune system ended up in such bad shape - I think it's possible that my only saving grace has been that I was brought up on all-day outdoors play, digging in the dirt and making good bacteria boosting "mud pies."

Our gut is responsible for keeping levels of harmful bacteria, yeast, and parasites at bay. Without a good level of gut health, these things can run unchecked, leading to all kinds of issues such as candida overgrowth (a condition that can produce many fibro-type symptom).

There are many things that can go wrong with our gut that can influence our health and wellbeing. It would take me way too long to go into detail on each one, but because poor gut health is a common issue with people with a chronic illness, I'm providing a brief description which might possibly help you to connect some dots when mapping out your own route to illness.

- The Stomach - digestion plays a big part in the balance of our gut flora. The stomach is where we need adequate levels of enzymes, pepsins, and acid to break down the food we have consumed, or else it just sits there causing issues such as heartburn and reflux. If we visit the doctor complaining of heartburn or reflux, we can often come away with a prescription for proton-pump inhibitor medication (PPI's) like omeprazole to suppress acid production. However, in the long run, this might actually make matters worse, as unfortunately, what a lot of doctors don't seem to be aware of is that many people are actually suffering from low stomach acid rather than too high - a condition called hypochlorhydria. Our stomach acid needs to be at the correct level so we can absorb the vitamins and minerals, digest protein effectively to be able to provide the body with the right level of amino acids, and to active the digestive enzymes. It is also needed to support our immune system by killing off germs and preventing bacteria from migrating up from the intestines. The amount of stomach acid we produce is also affected by how robust our stomach lining is. Many things such as stress, too much alcohol, medication, and a bacteria called H. pylori can damage the lining of the stomach, therefore affecting the amount of acid we produce – surely then part of the answer must lie in focusing on healing the stomach lining not reducing the acid. Sometimes it is possible for people to experience reflux without pain or heartburn. Symptoms that are linked to reflux include breathlessness, hoarseness, feeling of a lump in the throat, chest pain, nausea, dry cough you can see there are some symptoms on this list we often just write off as fibro shit.

- Dysbiosis (microbial disturbance or imbalances) - This is a condition that can arise when that friendly bacteria of ours gets too low and/or the normal balance is disrupted. There are several types of dysbiosis but to keep things short and sweet, in this family we have the type where there's just not enough of the good bacteria. The one where there is an overgrowth of bacteria in the small intestine (SIBO). The one where there is overgrowth in the large intestine, the one that can cause our body to have an over-the-top response to the bacterial imbalance (inflammation), and finally the ones that cause yeast and parasites to run amok giving off shitty toxins that negatively impact on our gut lining and general health. Without getting too bogged down in the science, what this means to folks with a fibro diagnosis is that dysbiosis can cause a whole heap of issues which are familiar, such as hives, IBS symptoms, food sensitivities, joint pain, chronic fatigue, weakness, and more.

- Leaky gut - This is a condition that is not truly recognised in mainstream medicine. In fact, if you were to pop along to your local GP with this suggestion there is a high chance it would be met with fair amount scepticism. While conventional medicine does recognise that the lining of the gut can become compromised, they call it "intestinal permeability." Many in this field of medicine remain unconvinced that it can be the cause of serious health issues. While it's true there are many unscrupulous folks out there trying to make a quick buck out of selling diets, supplements, and "cures" for this issue, and there's no question further research is needed to ascertain the connection between this and ill health, I believe that it is not something that should be totally dismissed out of hand.

When taking the alternative path, we can come up against a lot of dismissals with an insistence that we should stick with what is considered the "norm" and treat it according to what conventional means suggest is best. The only responses I have to that school of thought are:

A) Opinions on health and what is the best course of treatment have changed over time and will change again. The "health" tonic laudanum prescribed in the Victorian era and touted as pain relief resulted in many women spending their days completely off their faces and addicted to morphine. Once upon a time, smoking was considered good for you too and even endorsed in adverts by doctors!

B) If I had stuck with the standard way and only considered things from the conventional perspective I would not have made as much progress as I have in regaining my health.

Okay, now I've got that off my chest, let me rewind back to leaky gut and give you a brief overview of what it is.

Normally our intestines have cells that are fixed tightly together to form a protective barrier that controls what gets absorbed into the bloodstream. When the gut health becomes compromised, gaps can form that are large enough to allow tiny particles of partially digested food, germs, parasites, yeast, and toxins to penetrate the tissues beneath the barrier. If this situation isn't remedied, then this can have a negative impact on the immune system, creating inflammation throughout the whole body, and can be linked to issues such as brain fog, depression, mood disorders, aches and pains, as well as skin disorders like psoriasis, acne, and eczema.

Although there is controversy as to whether leaky gut causes illness, studies show that it may be associated with fibromyalgia or some of the conditions that often go hand in hand with it such as IBS. That alone, in my book, makes it worth investigating further.

How are you doing so far with the body stuff? If my little science nerd moment and overview of gut issues made you glaze over, I'm just giving you the heads up that from this point onwards there's going to be more of the same. It may seem a little boring, but I promise you there are good reasons for me popping in with a spot of biology now and then. If we are going to heal, it is important to understand how our body works and what happens when it's not functioning right.

For me, gaining an understanding of how important the gut is for regaining health helped me to pinpoint what I could work on, helped me to stay focused, and gave me a purpose. When I thought about throwing a hissy about not being able to eat pizza and cake, I would remind myself that I was doing it for my gut health. By knowing how things should work I could recognise where my body was underperforming and focus my attention there.

Maybe you're the "I don't need to know" type - that's cool, you can speed read, scan, or flip past these science-y bits (although I don't reccommend it), but one thing I'd like for you to take from this section of the book is that the symptoms that can be a result of issues with the gut and the other stuff I write about are often symptoms that are attributed to fibro. They are things that crop up again and again when people list their fibro symptoms. Therefore, what I would like you to consider is that if you were to focus on areas such as improving gut health, you may be able to remove some symptoms from your own list.

While I am not suggesting that gut health is the sum total of the symptoms that are attributed to a fibro diagnosis. I do feel it is a primary factor and something that needs to be addressed when starting to heal. It is important that we understand why our gut health is so vital to our overall health – the bottom line is, without a healthy gut, we cannot have a healthy system, period.

Many alternative treatments for working on the gut, particularly leaky gut, will recommend eliminating certain foods, and again, I think this is a sticking point for some practitioners as they see eliminating whole food groups as potentially dangerous to our health. On a long-term basis, yes I can there is the chance of potentially missing out on certain nutrients. But I do believe that it can at times be beneficial for our bodies to have a temporary break from certain foods to allow a window for healing and repairing or to help us to discover what foods may be making us feel worse. Then as we heal, we increase the chances of being able to re-introduce foods without adverse side effects. I personally feel that the aim should be, where possible, to get back to eating a clean whole food diet that contains a wide variety of foods.

If you still need a little more convincing about the importance of gut health and how it may be behind some of your health issues, then let's take a quick overview to highlight its roles and why getting this area into back into good shape and tip-top condition makes sense.

- Our gut communicates with our brain and this complex system of communication is called the "gut-brain axis." The gut is sometimes referred to as our second brain because millions of neurotransmitters are hanging out down there. Research has shown that changes in gut microbiome (the collection of genes that live inside our gut flora/ microbiota) can have a profound effect on the brain and can be linked to anxiety and depression - the digestive tract produces much more serotonin (the happy hormone) than the brain. The Vagus nerve which you will read about later is vital part of this communication system.

- Our gut works with our immune system. The microbiome and the immune system constantly talk to one another - we have more immune cells in our gut then anywhere else in the body, up to 80% of our immune system is located in the gut.
- Gut health influences our appetite, food cravings, energy, metabolism, and what we absorb from our food such as calories and nutrients.
- Imbalances in gut health is also linked to skin conditions such as acne, eczema, rosacea, and psoriasis.
- Other issues that can be linked to a compromised gut health are headaches, chronic fatigue, thyroid levels, digestive issues/acid reflux, food sensitivities/allergies, joint pain, and autoimmune diseases.

As you can see, it is quite clear just what an important role the gut plays in our overall health and why healing and maintaining a good balance is a huge benefit. Just how we go about healing this area can once again depend on an individual's situation.

In general, the first point of call is usually focused on improving stomach acid levels, healing the lining of the gut, and replenishing that helpful good bacteria. This can involve bringing in natural supplementation in the form of apple cider vinegar, bone broths, collagen, probiotics, and the likes of fermented food. Oh, and sorting out other areas of your diet - ditching the processed crap, etc. Because of our individuality, I can't jump in here with a one-size-fits-all suggestion, but I can say that a good first step for healing the gut would be to take a look at stomach acid levels and note where your body is with this first stage of the digestion process.

Its also a good idea to take a look at what may be having an impact on gut health- stress levels and environment we live in can have an effect on our gut flora.

This is one of those times where I can't give you a definitive "to do" list. But the information written above is there to give you a rough guide and encourage you to look into your own gut health. This is one of the things that is stamped as a SR (self-responsibility) moment where I recommend you check out the "Useful Websites and Stuff" section and encourage you to saddle up your healing horse and trot off into the sunset to do more of your own investigating and research.

CHAPTER 14

THE LIVER

This organ of ours is truly amazing and absolutely vital for good health. It's like the workhorse of the body, slogging away day in and day out to perform essential and critical functions - over 500 of them! It is our largest, most complex organ and something that needs to be one of our main focuses when trying to heal.

The liver plays a major role in our digestion, the production of bile, absorption of nutrients, the breaking down and removal of excess hormones, removal of toxins, regulation of copper and iron, thyroid and adrenal health, immunity, blood sugar regulation, maintaining weight, heart health and cholesterol regulation, and more. As you can see, it's a Kingpin when it comes to bodily functions. The fact that we need this hard-working organ for such important functions leaves no question that we need to take very good care of it in order to stay healthy. Yet until I took a more natural approach to health, I never heard so much as a whisper that some of my symptoms could be alleviated by making improvements in this area – sadly, the liver and its vital connection to our level of health often goes unnoticed in conventional medicine unless something specifically relating to this organ shows up in tests. So, how exactly does our liver impact on our health and wellbeing? And what has it got to do with fibro? Firstly, we need to take a look at how the liver can become overburdened.

If all is as it should be, then the liver goes about its daily business of keeping our system in balance and happy without a glitch. Unfortunately, the problem is that these days the world we live in is not much of a liver lover. On a daily basis, we are bombarded with toxins from our environment. Although when we think about environmental toxins, we tend to think of air pollution, exposure to fumes, etc., but this is the shit we don't even think about, from the things we eat, the stuff we clean our homes with, the products we slather ourselves in, even the sofas we plonk our bums on every day! Yes, household furniture and furnishings, in general, give off toxins.

Now, don't panic, no waving your hands in the air thinking the end is nigh or "my furniture is killing me." The liver's job is to deal with this stuff and often does a sterling job of it. However, there are times when the liver can find it harder to do what it's meant to do. It can begin to struggle to keep up with all its daily detoxing tasks, becoming overburdened and sluggish.

Want to know how that feels for your liver when this is the case? Imagine if every day you had a whole heap of set tasks but not enough time to do them in, and then somebody keeps adding more and more newer tasks. Stressed? Freaking out? Overwhelmed? Tired? Do you think over time things would start to slide and build up? Uh-huh, *exactly!*

If you are sick there is no question that your liver is feeling the strain, so you need to make like your best supportive friend. Pep it up and give it a hand to get back on track because it's amazing just how many health issues, from haemorrhoids to hormone imbalances, can be linked to a reduction of or sluggish liver function.

If you're not sure how this relates to fibro, then cast your eyes on the points below - I've written a list of symptoms that can arise when your liver is not happy, which are a match for common fibro symptoms.

- Fatigue
- Skin issues (acne, itching, rashes, hives, eczema, psoriasis)
- Constipation
- Mood swings
- Bloating and gas after eating
- Sleep issues (insomnia, night sweats)
- Heart palpitations
- Pain the shoulders
- Memory problems
- Allergies
- Eyesight issues (poor night vision, blurred vision)
- Headaches
- Menstrual issues (heavy or irregular periods, fibroid, hot flushes)
- Dizziness
- Nausea

- Weakness

Other stuff that can cause the liver to feel less than stellar are drinking more than 4 servings of alcohol per week, processed foods, not eating enough veggies, dehydration, stress and not enough sleep, some medications (e.g oral contraceptives and steroids), and lack of exercise.

Psst...when our liver gets bogged down with crap, when it's overwhelmed by toxins, it starts to store them as fat – hello, weight gain - not necessarily on that fibro list but something many people struggle with, so I'm just going to give that a shout out.

How do we go about fixing this shit?

A very important point to remember here is that because you are ill and probably new to all of this, you need to be kind to your liver, so that means no beating the crap out of it with harsh detoxes and cleanses - you wouldn't try and force a struggling friend into action by slapping them in the face, so don't do it to your liver!

What is needed here is gentle support. There are many ways to do this. I'm personally a big fan of using herbs as a support system. I use tinctures, teas, and infusions (you can read more about this in "Herbal Help"). Something that I have used from time to time is castor oil packs. (I confess, it is something that is on my list to do more regularly) See the link on how to do a castor oil pack in the "Useful Websites and Stuff" section.

I'm not going to list everything that I have done to give my liver a boost, this is another SR moment, where I encourage you to delve deeper with some of the links I've provided or for you to find an alternative practitioner to help guide you based on your individual circumstances. Having said that, there are some things that you can start right now to help yourself, and that is to address your diet and reduce the toxins that you expose yourself to (more about this in "Cleaning Up").

Obviously, it's not great that folks who are ill are walking about with sluggish livers, but if we look at it from a different perspective, it means there is an area that can be worked on. As you can see on the symptoms listed above, there are many issues that can be linked to having an overburdened liver that correlates with the symptoms that come under the fibromyalgia umbrella. This means working on boosting liver function can be another step towards reducing or overcoming symptoms, I don't know about you, but from where I'm standing, that looks like one in the eye for fibro.

CHAPTER 15

THE LYMPHATIC SYSTEM

Our lymph system is kind of best buds with the liver, a friendship formed out of their shared interest in detoxification and the fact that both the liver and lymph are vital for removing the toxins from our body that we encounter in our daily lives. The lymph is one big old drainage system designed to remove any extra fluid, infections, toxins, waste, and other bits and bobs from our system. It does this through a complex pathway of vessels, valves, and nodes - this pathway is mapped out all over the body. The tonsils, adenoids, bone marrow, spleen, and thymus are also part of the system.

To prevent you from dropping out through boredom or information overload, I'll be brief in saying that the lymphatic system is a critical element of the immune system, shielding us from rogue cells, bacteria and infections - just call it Mr. Protective. A healthy lymphatic system is needed for good health, so just like the liver, we need to be watching out for this guy, have his back and be supportive.

When our lymphatic system is under strain, we can experience symptoms that are common in a fibro diagnosis such as muscle and joint aches and pains, chronic fatigue, sore throats, along with frequent infections and colds. Some research shows a compromised lymphatic plays a role in the development of arthritis and cancer.

Giving our lymphatic system some support can be achieved through taking some of the simple measures listed below. Once again there is more info on how to do some of this in the "Helpful Websites and Stuff' section.

- Diet - eating clean, healthy, non-processed food.
- Reducing stress.
- Improving sleep.
- Exercise - yoga, swimming, and walking are all great for the lymph.

- Rebounding - this is a basically jumping up and down on a mini trampoline for 10 minutes a day. That may sound too energetic for some, but it can be done very gently while gradually increasing the time. It can even be done sitting down or on one of those big exercise balls (swiss ball)
- Legs up the wall yoga pose - The Lymph loves this one, again this can be modified by using a chair.
- Dry brushing - this is something that I now do on a daily basis. I had to wait to do this until I was some way into my healing before I could tolerate the brushing action on my skin.
- Massage (lymphatic drainage) and using a foam roller.
- Infrared Sauna - I use a Far-infrared heating mat. This is something that I only acquired in the last year, but it has been hugely beneficial. Family members have also reported a reduction in aches and pains after a session on the mat.

All of the above are helpful and supportive measures for the lymphatic system, but they are also great all-rounder for helping to heal in general - like everything in this book, what's good for one thing is good for many others.

CHAPTER 16

WHAT GOES IN MUST COME OUT

Let's talk about poo. Gross, I know, but it's something we need to mention because firstly it's important for good health. What goes in must come out! Secondly, if it's not doing that in a timely fashion or regularly enough then we can get a little backed up - literally! Our colon is a gateway to getting the stuff out of our bodies that we don't want, it is an essential part of the digestive tract, and part of its role is to gather and eliminate toxins from our system. When it can't do this, toxins can build up and get reabsorbed, leading to problems such as headaches, skin issues, brain fog, and fatigue. Conversely, some folks find themselves going the other way with too many visits to the loo. For good health, we are looking for the middle ground.

Ideally, to maintain a good balance, we should be visiting the throne room 2-3 times a day. Many natural health practitioners take the "you eat, you poo" stance, so every time you've eaten you should be eliminating shortly afterwards. I've not exactly discussed this subject with many people, but I would think it's fair to say that most people probably aren't hitting this mark. It's something to consider and aim for (poo goals!) when thinking about health and the healing process.

Eating clean, non-processed, high-fibre foods, exercise, and keeping hydrated are all excellent for colon health – water (I like lemon in mine) first thing in the morning is beneficial, and some herbal teas such as dandelion root are also colon friendly. Some people use digestive enzymes to help things along, but it's not something I personally would recommend that should be relied on long-term as the body gets lazy in making its own. Mineral balancing, working on gut health, liver, and lymphatic system will all also help to improve colon function - I have found rebounding works a treat in this department!

CHAPTER 17

MINERAL BALANCING

I cannot stress how important this area has been to my recovery. It has been one of those elements that had a massive impact on my healing. For me, this element of health is how I feel about personal therapy - everyone needs it!

My introduction to mineral balancing first came from someone commenting on one of my social media posts - this is a perfect example of when I wrote earlier about how it only takes "one phrase, one pointer, one idea, to set you on the right path." For me, this was one of those moments; a person mentioning the benefits of magnesium. That one comment opened up a whole avenue for me to explore and led to one of the biggest discoveries of my healing journey.

Mineral balancing as a whole is a rather complex topic simply because our wonderful body and all of its functions are complex - to keep our system up and running is a delicate balancing act involving many elements. One of these elements is the balance (correct ratios) between all of our vital minerals, electrolytes, and vitamins. If I was to cover everything about this topic I would probably be here forever, or once again risk boring you to death, so I will keep it simple and give you the lowdown on the basics.

Why is mineral balance important?

The short answer to this question is, we need minerals, electrolytes, and vitamins to do life. We need them to be able to function and create energy on a cellular level. Magnesium, for example, is needed for over 300 cellular functions and is one of the key nutrients that is often lacking in our modern diet. Another essential mineral and electrolyte needed for our cells is potassium. We need a whopping 3500- 4700 mg of potassium per day to keep everything in tip-top condition. When you consider the average banana has approximately 400 mg, you can see why many people who eat a standard diet high in processed foods are not getting enough. Now if we add into the mix the likes of sodium, calcium, copper, iron, and all the other minerals and trace elements we need to keep our "plates spinning," then you can see why it's a complex business.

Minerals are what keeps our body going. They are the very foundation for our physical health are involved in every single process, and when we are in a state of imbalance or depleted, we can start to experience a myriad of symptoms. If we take just two of the essential minerals and electrolytes we need – Magnesium and Potassium - and look at some of the symptoms imbalanced levels can cause, we can see that once again they mirror "fibro" symptoms.

Low Magnesium symptoms: restless legs, muscle twitches, muscle pain, cramps, mood swings, anxiety, depression, poor concentration, fatigue, irregular heartbeat, insomnia, high blood pressure, headaches, osteoporosis.

Low Potassium symptoms: High blood pressure, memory issues, palpitations, muscle cramps, breathlessness or feeling as if you can't get enough air, fatigue, muscle weakness, constipation, numbness or tingling, dizziness, thirst.

At this point I want to be clear in saying that I am not claiming that mineral imbalances are the cause of all of your symptoms. Like I have previously highlighted in the other topics in this body section, I am noting the potential connection between symptoms that are a result of imbalances and symptoms that are often top of the list for people with a fibro diagnosis. The reason I do this is so you can start that process of questioning just where your issues may be stemming from - root causes.

Although I honestly believe that many of the things I write about will benefit others, I can only speak for myself and what I have personally achieved by addressing my own imbalances. The decision as to whether you explore this avenue is like everything in this book: a choice you alone need to make. I do, however, stand by the opinion that minerals a foundation of health, they are what it takes for us to function properly, and if these are out of whack then it can only stand to reason that ill health will occur. I cannot think of a single reason why anyone wouldn't benefit from working on this area of health.

What upsets the balance?

There are many things that can upset the balance of our minerals. Stress levels play a big part in throwing things off kilter - stress depletes our vitamin and minerals stores, it burns through the likes of magnesium and potassium like there's no tomorrow. Pretty much everything I have written about in his book can have an impact on our levels, from diet to medications to emotional trauma to our gut health to spending too much time in front of a screen. There are so many things that can create imbalances, but I feel the main point to focus on is that despite all the things that are working against us, it is possible to re-balance our bodies and in doing so regain a greater level of health.

How do we correct these imbalances?

Now, you might be thinking, "Simples. I'll go get me some supplements or multivitamins from my local chemist and fix it." Well, sorry, guys, I'm going to rain on your parade and tell you it doesn't work that way (I know it's a shitter). You see, the thing is, first you need to know what you are dealing with, and second, taking isolated synthetic supplements is not the answer.

If you don't know what your unique mineral profile is then you won't know what to address. Without testing it's like shooting in the dark - you might hit the mark, or you might just take down an innocent bystander. If you just start addressing what you think are your imbalances, then unfortunately, you risk throwing other things out of balance in the process. I say this from personal experience. The same goes for synthetic supplements. Taking isolated supplements such as potassium, magnesium, zinc, calcium, etc., isn't going to work because a delicate balance is required so as not to throw other things off. There is also the added fact that we often need what is called co-factors to help us to absorb stuff anyway. While it could be said that the majority of people could do just fine taking something like a 200 mg daily dose of magnesium, off-the-shelf supplements are just too standardised for the delicate balance our bodies need. What I have learnt from personal experience there are more natural ways to get magnesium into our bodies and if we really want to get down to doing it properly, we need to know what we are looking for and if what we are doing is right for us as an individual.

The complex thing about getting the minerals back into balance is that it is a delicate dance that involves synergy and work on other areas (hello, holistic health). We need to be able to utilise our essential minerals and vitamins, which means working on other areas of the body such as the gut and liver and resolving any stress that may be chomping its way through our vitamin and mineral stores. Otherwise we are just fire fighting or playing catch up.

Other issues that are related to incorrect mineral balance also include imbalances in our copper and iron levels. Health issues often arise with this duo when our bodies are not able to utilise them properly - when they are not what is called bioavailable. A good example of this is my own case, where a standard iron blood test (ferritin levels) showed me as having low iron, yet further in-depth testing revealed that I was storing iron in high levels in other places (in my tissues). If I had gone with conventional treatment, I would have been taking iron supplements and unknowingly making matters worse. What I really needed to do was work on reducing inflammation and help my body to be able to move my minerals into the right places by working on areas such as my liver function, healing my gut, supporting my detox pathways (lymphatic system, colon), and adrenals.

The same goes for copper. Many people, including me, have issues with copper, and it again often comes down to the body's ability to keep it in balance and make it bioavailable. In our liver, we produce an extremely important copper-binding protein called ceruloplasmin. This is a powerful antioxidant needed to regulate copper and iron throughout the body. Low levels of this crucial protein can lead to imbalances and many health issues - something to note here is that when I requested a ceruloplasmin test from my GP they didn't know much about it nor was it on their list of tests available. Yet this protein is vital for transporting iron and copper around the body. Once again, I feel this highlights just how little is understood in conventional medicine about what the body needs to be able to function as a whole.

By focussing on our supporting our liver, other organs, pathways and our systems as a whole it is possible for us to balance our levels and increase copper and iron bioavailability. This, in turn, enables us to regulate other minerals much more effectively. One of the reasons mineral balance is so important is because once there a greater balance in this area, the body can begin to heal from other underlying issues such as infections and can tolerate other healing methods such as detoxing.

When I first started the balancing process, I followed a protocol that among many natural components involved supplementing with magnesium. My initial results were fantastic, I felt like I was back on track with my health. However, after about 3 years, I began to feel as if things were slipping a little and I went on to discover that my potassium was tanked despite taking all the measures to keep levels up. In hindsight, I think I was a little too gung-ho in my approach to this particular branch of healing. I didn't fully understand the mechanism behind it, or the care needed to maintain the delicate balance between the individual minerals. Our body is like a finely tuned machine. We need all of our minerals to be at the correct level and at the correct ratio with one another for it to function at optimal health.

The protocol I originally followed appears to have undergone some changes in the last year or so, and the regime has been refined somewhat to make it a steadier, slower process, but I still feel it is not something that I would go back to because it is still too standardised to be a good fit for me.

Like everything I have encountered while healing, I am still grateful for the protocol; without it I would not have gotten to where I am today. I learned a tremendous amount from their research and files, and while it turns out that it wasn't the perfect fit for me, it did go a long way towards increasing my understanding of the body, its functions, and what is needed for optimum health. No experience is ever wasted- there is always a learning curve.

After learning once again through the school of trial and error, I went on to research and educate myself further on this subject, and although that initial protocol I followed had many natural elements to it, I have discovered that I respond much better to an even more natural approach of using herbs and whole foods to support my healing. And leaving off the manufactured oral supplements (chelated products).

Now that I have explained why mineral balancing is such a complex matter, let me make things easier by explaining how I got on board with this branch of healing.

As I have written above, trying to second-guess what imbalances we might have and wanging in the supplements in hope that it will correct things is not the best way forward. What we need to do when trying to re-balance is to obtain a clear picture of how our body is functioning. This best done through an HTMA test (Hair Tissue Mineral Analysis). This involves sending a sample of hair to a specialised lab that will then test and analysis the hair. A hair analysis test can track the last three months of our tissue activity and can reveal a great deal about our body including:

- Mineral deficiencies and imbalances
- Our metabolic type (whether we are a fast or slow oxidiser)
- Adrenal function
- Thyroid function
- Inflammation
- Energy and vitality levels
- Heavy metals toxicity
- Sugar and carbohydrate tolerance

- How well our nervous system is functioning

There has been much debate regarding the accuracy of HTMA tests, with some in the health profession dismissing its effectiveness. Some of the controversy surrounding its legitimacy seems to come from is the fact that some labs wash the hair samples before testing, which can skew the results. It also needs to be noted that the interpretation of the results needs to be done by someone who has clear knowledge and fully understands the interactions of minerals - there's a lot of "experts" out there who quite frankly don't know their arse from their elbow when it comes to interpreting results.

I feel that what this debate boils down to is that HTMA is one of those areas where you need to decide if you are getting on board the alternative train and if you are willing to be open to stepping outside of the norms of conventional medicine. Hair testing is not something that is practised in the conventional world. It is very common for GP's is to dismiss its validity and put the kibosh on it. Considering this branch of healing is one of those moments where you need to decide if you're willing to suspend your scepticism and put your faith into something you have never experienced before. I personally have found it to be incredibly insightful. The results of the analysis have without doubt led me to take actions that have resulted in lasting progress and reversal of health issues.

In my further wanderings in the natural health world, I have been fortunate to discover a fantastic natural healing website called Sassy Holistics (founded by Kristin Merizalde). I think for the first time in all the years I have been working on healing, the process, the approach Sassy Holistic takes towards healing is the only one that I have found is truly aligned with my own approach. Kristin's perspective has all of the elements that I have researched and discovered to be the most important aspects of the healing process. Therefore, I have no hesitation in recommending that anyone who wants to take this alternative path should head on over to her site and FB group. Her blogs and posts will definitely help you to gain a further understanding of everything I write about in this book and her services include HTMA and more. I also recommend one of her ebooks on foundational healing as I feel it is an excellent follow to what you have read here. This book goes into much more detail about healing the body. Kristin's information is in, yes, you've guessed it, the "Useful Websites and Stuff" section.

VITAMINS AND MINERALS

Over the years of healing, I have come to the belief that the best way for me to get my vitamins and minerals is through diet, natural supplementation, and transdermal (through the skin) methods. What vitamins we need and can take is again an individual thing. I personally take things to keep my B vitamin levels up, support the immune system, support my adrenals and thyroid, and give my gut a helping hand. I now regard these supplementations as part of my self-care and health maintenance rather than part of a healing protocol.

Below is a list of the main things that I regularly take that work for me. Please note that this is my personal regime. Everybody reacts differently to things (allergies, tolerance levels, etc) and you need to be mindful in researching what will work best for you, seek advice if you need to, and go slowly when introducing new things. I am listing this stuff because I want to demonstrate the type of things that helped me to heal in the first instance, now help me maintain a good level of health, and are helping me to prepare for any future challenges (at 45 years old I'm dipping my toes into the perimenopause pool).

- Bee pollen - these golden granules have nearly all the B vitamins (except B12).
- Grass-fed beef liver - This is the "rather stick pins in my eyes than consume" supplementation I mentioned earlier on in the book. It is something I tolerate (barely) because it really is one of those nutrient-dense super healing foods. Alongside its many other benefits, it's an excellent source of B12. I know people who take beef liver capsules to combat that "blergh" feeling, but I've found it too expensive for me to source a high-quality brand in the UK and you have to take quite a few capsules to achieve the benefits.
- Cod liver oil - I use this as a natural source of vitamin A and D and all-round joint oiler.
- Herbal infusions and tinctures - more about that later.
- Dead Sea salts and Magnesium chloride flakes - I use these in foot soaks or the bath to boost my mineral levels, mainly magnesium and potassium. The Dead Sea salts are higher in potassium. Using this method (transdermally) is a gentle and effective way of getting minerals into our system. In the past, I have also used magnesium spray for the same reason and to relieve pain.

- Multi-strain probiotic.
- Collagen powder - for supporting gut health, and, well, boosting collagen levels as I age.
- Whole food Vitamin C (Cherry-C) - this is different from the synthetic ascorbic acid version you see in most health shops and supermarkets (those can deplete other levels). This is made from the whole fruit and contains other goodies like bioflavonoids and phytonutrients.
- Elderberry syrup - Once a year I go all Mother Earth, gather elderberries, and make my own syrup. High in vitamin C, this baby has been the bomb for my immune system, but I hear that some people cannot tolerate it.

Other things that I have also used for my healing, but I am not currently taking on a daily basis, are; aloe vera, potassium broth/bone broth, and adrenal cocktails. They are things that I keep in my health toolbox and revisit from time to time when the need has arises.

CHAPTER 18

ADRENALS, THYROID AND HPA-AXIS

Our adrenals are two glands (approximately 5 cm long) that sit on top of our kidneys. These little fellas may be small, but they are big players when it comes to our health. They are part of our endocrine system and part of a trio known as the HPA Axis (the other two are our Hypothalamus and Pituitary gland, which are found in the brain). This trio works together to regulate our digestion, immune response, energy levels, stress response, libido, and mood - you can see how important they are!

Adrenal dysfunction is something that was highlighted on my HTMA test. Again, it is something that is not always recognised in mainstream medicine. In the UK the NHS tends to only focus on the extreme end of adrenal issues such Addison's disease or cortisol deficiency. As the adrenals are responsible for cortisol regulation, a cortisol test is often carried out when a patient complains of prolonged fatigue. However, the blood test that is offered can only measure the level of cortisol at the exact point of extraction and is unable to pick up fluctuations throughout the day.

My case was an example of this. My cortisol test was taken mid-morning, the results came back as in range, yet further investigation revealed that my night-time cortisol levels were too high, were contributing to insomnia and therefore fatigue. Like many dysfunctions, there can be a wide spectrum of symptoms, and sadly, it seems that conventional medicine is only looking at two scenarios. Your adrenals are either considered to be fine or totally fucked, it does not recognise that can be a lot going on in-between where symptoms may arise because the adrenals are under stress and are no longer functioning well.

The adrenals have an important role in controlling the stress-related "fight or flight" response. Following years of chronic emotional stress, my body's response to stress was completely off the wall. My system became stuck on high alert and I would respond in full stress mode to the slightest of stressors – loud noises would be enough to send me into orbit. I can remember one particular day when I was driving somewhere, and someone beeped their car horn. It took me a full 30 minutes to calm down: racing heart, flushed face, and the shakes. I used to thank my lucky stars I lived in the countryside; I think city life might have killed me!

The adrenals are also responsible for the production of aldosterone (helps control blood pressure, sodium levels, and the amount of fluid the body holds onto) and androgens and oestrogen (sex hormones). When they are not fully functioning, health issues can include tiredness (particularly afternoon slumps in energy), hormone imbalances, headaches, fluid retention, depression, irritability and moodiness, salt cravings, hair loss, dizziness/ light headed, decreased sex drive, sleep disturbances, blood sugar issues, weight gain, heightened stress response, and chronic fatigue.

Many of these symptoms can also be seen with thyroid imbalances too. Despite a family history of thyroid issues and being symptomatic of hypothyroidism, I have had little success in getting it recognised by going through conventional channels. A private (still conventional) full thyroid panel test resulted in my being declared within range, but through my own investigations and research I was not functioning at the optimal range and an HTMA test flagged up hypothyroidism. Whatever the test results have been from either camp, what is important was the fact I was symptomatic. Focussing on supporting my thyroid has led to improvements in my health.

Supporting my adrenal and thyroid function has been a focus of my healing. Initially, taking adrenal cocktails (a drink that supports electrolyte balance) before moving onto herbs (see "Herbal Help"), reducing stress, reducing inflammation, diet (non-processed, good fats, plenty of greens, etc.), getting the B vitamins in, mineral balancing, heat pad, low impact exercise (yoga and walking), getting out in nature, meditation, and improving gut health have all featured heavily in my improving this area of my health.

The HPA -axis refers to a complex interaction between three separate parts of the body: the hypothalamus gland, the pituitary gland, and the adrenal glands. The Hypothalamus gland (H) and the Pituitary gland (P) are found in the brain and the Adrenal glands (A), as you will have already read, sit at the top of the kidneys.

Now these guys are all on the same team. They form a network that plays a part in regulating certain functions such as our mood, temperature control, immune system, stress response, metabolism, energy levels, blood sugar, and libido.

This HPA-axis is one of the most important aspects of our overall health because our stress response is primarily governed by it. Stress is what activates this axis and starts a whole cascade that leads to the release of certain chemicals and hormones in our body – remember, stress can come from numerous sources and our brains can't differentiate between a real and a perceived threat.

When our body is placed under stress from whatever source, it kickstarts a process (stress response) that starts with the sympathetic nervous system and goes on to trigger the HPA-axis. The hypothalamus is the first to respond to an increase of stress chemicals in the blood stream by releasing corticotrophin-releasing hormone (CRH). The hypothalamus communicates with the pituitary gland to do its part of the process, which is to release the adrenocorticotrophin hormone (ACTH). The pituitary releases ACTH into the bloodstream, which then travels down to adrenal glands and stimulates the production of cortisol and other substances.

Now this whole process should be a temporary response, but if a person is placed under constant stress on a daily basis then the HPA-axis becomes overstimulated, which can lead to dysregulation in its function, which can lead to physical and psychological symptoms such as the ones I have listed in the passage on adrenals. As part of the stress response process, the liver releases glucose and other functions such as digestion and immune systems are suppressed, so you can see this is another reason why being in this state long term is not good for our health.

The HPA-axis is complex in its function. What I've given you is the simplified description (I know right!). The HPA-axis is involved in the secretion of other hormones and is the link between our nervous system and our endocrine system. It plays an important role in the mind-body connection and is closely linked with the thyroid function.

The easiest way to look at the HPA- axis response is to think that when the body is continually producing a stress response and releasing stress hormones it becomes less sensitive and can't re-balance as it used to.

There has been some research into the potential connection between the HPA-axis and fibro. Decreased HPA-axis activity results in a lowered cortisol response, which is linked to chronic fatigue. Some studies have suggested that early life trauma can lead to an over-active HPA- axis later in a person's life, which may lead to an increase in anxiety and Central Sensitivity Syndromes, which chronic pain and hypersensitivity are part of.

Note that when the HPA-axis is out of whack and overstimulated it is called HPA-axis dysregulation (HPA-D). It is often referred to as "adrenal fatigue," but HPA-D is a much more accurate description because, as you will have probably gathered by now, where there's one imbalance there's another! Fatigued adrenals are an indication all is not well in other areas, i.e., the

HPA-axis.

So how do we show our HPA-axis some love and get it responding correctly?

- Rest: get a good sleep routine and be consistent – See "sleep" page.
- Get some sunshine - natural light is a must for resetting the body's natural sleep-wake cycle. Morning sunshine is great for this.
- Gentle exercise, and I mean gentle. Going in too hard with exercise will raise cortisol and trigger stress responses - think gentle stretching, some restorative yoga poses, and gentle walks.
- Diet - eat easy-to-digest foods that are warming and nutrient dense. Eating warming foods in this case is better for the body than raw or cold foods. Plenty of healthy fats, we need cholesterol for healthy hormones.
- Address inflammation levels in the body. Holistically this can be done through diet, managing stress, using herbal support and other alternative therapies.
- Reduce stress - All of the above will help reduce overall stress on the body, but it's important to remember that we need to tackle stress on all levels - psychological, emotional, and physical.

Adrenal, thyroid, and HPA-axis function can all be assessed through HTMA testing.

CHAPTER 19

HEAVY METAL, CANDIDA, AND PARASITES

Heavy metals, parasites, and overgrowth of yeast (candida) can be an underlying contributory factor in illness. As you have read, I started my healing with a protocol to deal with an overgrowth of candida, and partway through my journey I also did an herbal parasite cleanse.

Although I found both to be helpful in my healing, as I wrote earlier, it's not necessarily where I would start the second time around. Following more research and being further along in the healing process, I believe that it is better to strengthen the body before embarking on detoxes and cleanses so that it is able to tolerate the process better. Some people however may feel that these issues are so bad that they need to address them first, again this is personal choice and individual needs.

Our gut, liver, and lymph are heavily involved in the detoxing process, so to me it makes sense to strengthen these areas first before subjecting them to taxing detoxification protocols, etc. As I've said some people prefer to go straight in for the kill with detoxes and the like, but if our system is weak, we can end up tanking our adrenals and feeling a damn sight worse with what is called "die off" symptoms. I was fortunate with the candida protocol because the process involved supporting the body through various supplements, but even with that support, I still spent the first two weeks with the common reaction of feeling like I had the flu.

I have not personally experienced health issues due to heavy metals, but I am including it in the book because I see them mentioned a lot in natural health groups and know that they can have a significant impact on health, with many symptoms being a match for the symptoms attributed to fibro. Therefore, I feel it's useful to be aware of them when looking for factors that may be contributing to ill health.

Some people find heavy metal cleanses, detoxes, or chelating beneficial. Again, if or when people choose to go down this path is entirely a personal choice and should be based on the individual's underlying causes of symptoms and the many other factors that make up their personal health puzzle.

Heavy metals - we encounter heavy metals every day of our life just through living: the air we breathe, our water supply, the food we eat, what we cook with, and even the fillings in our teeth. Part of the body's function is to remove these from our system. However, for some people, heavy metals can reach excessive levels, leading to illness and what is known as heavy metal toxicity. This happens either because their exposure has been excessive, or their body is too overburdened to be able to effectively eliminate heavy metals.

Depression, anxiety, insomnia, cognitive problems, fatigue, digestive issues, and poor recovery from exercise are some of the symptoms associated with heavy metal overload. Diseases such as Alzheimer's, MS, and Parkinson's have also been linked to toxicity.

If you do a search on heavy metal toxicity you will see many detox protocols/ chelation therapies, but once again, if your system is not strong enough, jumping into this kind of action will only result in you feeling doubly shit when a whole heap of toxins gets dumped into a system that doesn't have the ability to deal with it effectively. I feel the key, once again, is to strengthen the body, then tackle this issue if necessary.

As I have mentioned, I did not have an issue with heavy metals so have not had a need to explore further. For anyone wanting to know their levels and explore any potential links too ill health, I do know that the level of heavy metals in our body can be detected through the Hair Tissue Mineral Analysis test (HTMA) mentioned in "Mineral Balancing."

Candida - As you know by now, my journey started out by dealing with an overgrowth of candida due to the overuse of antibiotics. Using antibiotics time and time again to rid my body of tonsillitis-causing bad bacteria, unfortunately, obliterated millions of the good guys too, inadvertently creating a desert landscape of what was once a much lusher intestinal flora, and causing the candida to move into overdrive.

Like most of the stuff that starts to run amok in our systems, our body, when functioning correctly, is able to maintain enough of a balance so that it doesn't cause us any problems. When we experience imbalances within the body, it's like leaving a door wide open for things that shouldn't be let in - like a bunch of gate crashers at a teenage house party. As time goes on things escalate out of control and stuff becomes compromised, and we end up with a load of weird shit happening to our body.

Candida can live naturally in our gut quite happily without causing us any harm, but under certain conditions, it can become rampant and set up camp in other areas of the body. Symptoms associated with a systemic overgrowth of candida include chronic fatigue, muscle pain, mood swings, brain fog, joint pain, digestive problems, IBS, and sinus infections.

Although there is no doubt that the candida protocol I did was successful, if I was to rewind back to that point of my healing, I would probably opt for working on balancing my minerals first then possibly the protocol. Copper balance can play an important role in curbing the overgrowth of candida. It is a natural anti-fungal and yeast fighter, but if it's not bioavailable in the body then it can't do its job of controlling the likes of candida. Mineral balancing can play a significant role in the body's ability to keep candida under control. Supporting and improving our liver function is also key for keeping nasties like candida in check. If the liver is sluggish, then it affects our ability to make bile, which is another bacterium-zapping fella we need on our intestinal health team.

Parasites – This is something else we need to talk about but is a topic that freaks many people out. Perhaps it's because we associate parasites with being unclean, or maybe it's because we simply don't want to think that we might be harbouring other life forms - the thought of things wiggling around inside of is enough to send most folks into a spin. (Hands up: who's imagining that scene from "Alien" right now?)

As undesirable as it is the fact is, almost every one of us is playing host to some unwelcome guests, the reason being that we can't really avoid coming into contact with parasites during everyday life. Eating undercooked food, raw veggies, sushi, people not washing their hands, stroking pets, walking barefoot, contaminated soil, and swimming in natural water are some of the most common places we can encounter parasites. While some people can live alongside them without any problem (some scientists theorise that some parasites at a certain level can be beneficial), for others it can be a real health concern. As with heavy metals and candida, issues can arise with parasites when these fellas get out of hand and think they can start running the show.

Parasites levels getting out of control can happen for a number of reasons. If our health is already compromised through illness, stress, poor diet, etc., it makes it much easier for these foreign invaders to take up residence in increasing numbers - poor health weakens the immune system, giving these guys the green light to set up camp. Once this happens, they can weaken the system even further.

On a little side note, if you're still wondering whether you need to address your diet, parasites love to dine out on junk food. Like many of us, they are particularly fond of sugar so a diet high in processed and sugary foods is a bit like open season at the buffet cart for them - I found this little thought does wonders for curbing chocolate consumption!

Symptoms that can be caused or exacerbated by parasites include: skin problems (itching, hives, rashes, etc.), anaemia, joint and muscle pain, fatigue, constantly feeling hungry even after eating, teeth grinding, anxiety, yeast infections, loss of appetite, itchy bits down below, digestive problems, brain fog, and mood swings.

As you can see, these symptoms could also be attributed to many of the other things I have written about in this body section, so you're probably wondering, "How do we know for sure if we have any of these nasties lurking in our system?" There are a few tests that can be run to confirm the presence of parasites:

1. Stool test
2. Endoscopy and colonoscopy
3. Blood tests.

If you're in the UK and hoping the NHS will step up to the task of establishing the presence of parasites, then as they say, "Best of British" in achieving that. You may strike lucky in getting these tests performed. Otherwise, if this is an avenue you wish to explore, then you are looking at private testing or opting for "the try a cleanse and see what comes out" method - not very technical but certainly interesting!

Remember, as always, when embarking on something different, bear in mind how capable your body would be in handling the changes. The elimination process with parasites can be unpleasant. They get really pissed off when you start attacking them, and as they die off they release toxins into the body, which is why it's a good idea to work on strengthening the parts of the body that deals with this, i.e., gut, liver, lymph, and colon.

Boosting our immune system, reducing stress, healing our gut, and eating a clean diet can go a long way to keeping these nasties at bay. Dealing with potential unwanted guests is a "decide for yourself" thing. Some people feel the need to go for a parasite cleanse. For others this is not a priority. It all depends on how much of an issue you think it could be.

I opted to do a cleanse about halfway into my healing, and only after I had done a considerable amount of work on my gut health. I did feel as if it moved my healing on another step, but in hindsight, I'm not sure it was necessary at that point. Doing a parasite cleanse is one of those moments where, as an individual, we need to assess where we are with our health and whether the body is strong enough to go through the process.

CHAPTER 20

THE AUTONOMIC NERVOUS SYSTEM

The Sympathetic Nervous System (SNS) and Parasympathetic Nervous System (PNS) is something that I have only researched and worked on in the last year or so as an extension to supporting my adrenals. Both are elements of the body's Autonomic Nervous System (ANS) and help the body respond to stress. The SNS is what prepares us for action when faced with stress, such as a threat or injury. It triggers the "fight or flight" response - blood pressure, heart and breathing rates rise, adrenaline and other chemicals are released into the bloodstream. The PNS does the opposite. Its job is to act as a brake and help the body to return to a normal relaxed state after stress. It triggers what is known as the "rest and digest" response.

When we experience prolonged levels of stress (remember one person's stress is another's walk in the park), we can get stuck in the sympathetic state. Obviously, the sympathetic response is great if you need to dive out of the way of a speeding car or win the parent's sports day race, but not so great when it gets all bent out of shape and fires up when you're watching a movie or someone shouts "Happy birthday."

Getting stuck in sympathetic response mode is also known as having sympathetic dominance. It was only about 8 months ago, after a period of stress and a shift in hormones that lead to some sleep issues, that I learned about sympathetic dominance. Although my body wasn't overreacting to everyday stuff as I had in the past, I had begun to experience some really weird shit at night-time. I would get this strange swooping sensation in my chest, a bit like that sinking sensation you get in that moment when you think you've really fucked something up! This sensation would come and go in waves, and every time I'd get to the point of drifting off into sleep, I would suddenly jump as if someone had crept up behind me with an airhorn. It got so bad that I would dread getting into bed at night, which I'm sure just added more stress to the situation.

It was my herbalist who first drew my attention to sympathetic dominance. After researching it further, I was able to make the connections with some of the reactions I had experienced in the past. It was clear that this issue with my nervous system was responsible for how my body had previously been reacting wildly to everyday events such as sirens, loud voices, certain music, tense movie scenes etc. (I had just chalked it up to more weird fibro stuff). Following this discovery, I could see that years of chronic stress had resulted in an overwhelmed nervous system and sympathetic dominance, which meant my PNS wasn't able to fully put on the brakes and return me to a calm baseline after what my mind perceived as a stressful event.

For years my startle reflex was ridiculous. I would react to the slightest of things, even someone starting up a conversation after a period of silence could have me jumping a mile high and throwing a cup of tea all over myself. Dogs barking, someone beeping their car horn, rushing to be somewhere; you name it, I reacted like a cat on a hot tin roof. Not only was it annoying, it was exhausting. It triggered my mind to race with random and sometimes bizarre thoughts that I couldn't seem to switch off no matter how hard I tried - it was like I was on strung out drugs without the drugs. This side of things was part of what prevented me from sleeping at night, which of course contributed to the fatigue.

As I'm sure you can imagine, or know yourself, being in the heightened state is not good news for the body. It depletes vital nutrients such as potassium, magnesium, and zinc, creates tension in the muscles, causes imbalances in posture, tightens ligaments, affects digestion, and adds to fatigue. "Feeling wired but tired" is an expression that fits perfectly with this state of being.

Making the connection between having issues with my nervous system and the symptoms I experienced over the years reaffirms in my mind that there are so many elements that we can work on to over come symptoms and help raise our level of health. For years, I just assumed that all this jumping and reacting to the slightest thing was something that was part of the condition and something I just had to resign myself to. If I had known sooner that there were things I could do to calm down my nervous system, I think I could have alleviated some of my symptoms way back.

In more recent times, when I hit a stressful patch combined with entering the perimenopause and found myself in a heightened state once more, I went back to what I know, which is pretty much everything I have written down in this book. I re-assessed my life, identified the things that I had let slide, I made sure my diet was still on a healthy track. I upped the self-care, researched techniques that focused on the parasympathetic nervous system (breathing techniques), cranked up the relaxation/meditation, employed the help of my herbalist, and within a matter of weeks, my nervous system resumed its normal service.

I think my nervous system and my adrenal function are always going to be areas that I need to be very mindful of. Both have taken a beating over the years, and I am aware that certain situations, stressors, have the potential to send my body back into a spin. I am aware that years of chronic stress have impaired my HPA-axis function too which play an important part in regulating the body's stress response. I accept that for now, this is one of my weaker points. Although I'm not thrilled about the situation, I find that having this knowledge about weaker areas of my body is helpful. It reminds me to be mindful of taking good care of myself and prevents me from putting myself into health compromising situations. Because of it, I don't let people take advantage of me as I have done before. I put myself first and prioritise my wellbeing above giving too much of myself to others, and I feel that is a much healthier state for me to live in.

THE VAGUS NERVE

The vagus nerve is not something that I intentionally focused on, but my work on my SNS and PNS and other healing practices have indirectly boosted my vagus nerve function.

The reason I have chosen to mention it is that I have come across a fair bit of discussion during my Internet wanderings, I know of people finding health benefits from focussing on this area and my recent research shows it to be an important player in our overall health.

Therefore, I am going to give you a quick lowdown on what it is and what it does and leave you to decide if it's something you'd like to investigate further and focus on when planning your route back to health.

The vagus nerve contributes to the autonomic nervous system. It sends messages to our brain and every major organ in our body through a network of meandering "branches" that run off larger stems. It travels all the way through the body (left and right side) from the brainstem to way down in the abdomen, touching base with our organs on the way down. Its functions include sensory activities, regulating heart rate, blood pressure, sweating, digestion, sending anti-inflammatory signals,aiding communication between the gut and the brain, and it even helps us to speak, influences our eye movements and facial expressions It also plays a significant role in helping the parasympathetic nervous system to calm the body and is a key part of the mind-body connection.

How people cope with stress can also, in part, be dependent on how strong their vagus nerve function is, whether they have what is called high vagal tone or low vagal tone - high is the better end of the spectrum when it comes to this part of the nervous system.

The vagus nerve doesn't seem to attract much attention in the conventional medical world, but seeing as it has a fairly sizable role in keeping us alive and plays a part in our overall wellbeing and health, you'd think it would get more of a look in.

When the vagus nerve isn't functioning properly it can contribute to many health issues such as IBS, depression, anxiety, food sensitivities, chronic fatigue, high or low heart rate, heartburn, palpitations, chronic inflammation, gut issues, tinnitus, and more.

Raising the vagus nerve function (vagal tone) has been shown to have a positive impact on many aspects of our health and general wellbeing. Some research shows that treating the vagus nerve via an implant that electrically stimulates the nerve can have a positive impact on reducing chronic inflammation.

Some ways to improve vagal tone:

- Yoga
- Tal Chi
- Singing/humming/chanting
- Laughing
- Gargling
- Cold shower or washing face in cold water
- Massage
- Diaphragmatic breathing
- Improving gut health
- Meditation

As you can see from this list, many topics that are written about throughout this book can have a positive impact on our vagus nerve, so whether you chose to make this a focus or not, by implementing and working on stuff from the book you will be indirectly working on your vagus nerve anyway. Another high five to… yes, you've guessed it. The whole-body approach!

CHAPTER 21

SLEEP

I think I am probably right in stating that for many people with a fibro diagnosis, sleep is one big fucking problem. Nearly every health article you read bangs on about the importance of getting a good night's sleep, how the body repairs itself at night, how we're doomed if we don't clock up 8 hours, yadda, yadda, yadda. Yet, like some kind of cruel universal joke, the very thing we need the most to heal is the thing that for many is the most elusive – oh, the irony!

I don't know which side of the fence you are sitting on when it comes to this sleeping business; I know people with fibro who can sleep until the cows come home yet remain unrefreshed. I was of the non-sleeping variety, and as you have read, at one stage I was in contention for a gold medal in sleeplessness. As I can only speak from my own experience, I'm sorry to say that I haven't done much research or learned much that might help the folks who can sleep, and sleep, and sleep, yet still feel like shit - apologies! Although I would imagine that once the body becomes more balanced, then it's likely that their quality of sleep would also improve. That they would start to enter into more restorative sleep cycles.

There is a kind of double-edged sword situation going on with sleep and illness. Symptoms often make it hard to sleep, and lack of sleep makes everything, and I mean everything, feel worse. Now that I am back on track with my sleeping, I often wonder how I even survived, or at the very least didn't commit murder. I worked out once that I spent nearly 20 years without a full night's sleep (something that no doubt contributed to illness). Even now, with much improvement, I fail to make that golden 8 hours. A good night for me is 5-6 hours, yet after years of only snatching sleep here and there, my body thinks this is absolute bliss. I see it reflected in my ability to function much better on a daily basis. On a pleasing note I have read recently that the 8 hours may not be something that everybody needs, some people can do just as well on less.

I think the jury is out on what exactly is the cause of the sleep disturbances, and I am sure it varies from person to person. Pain is a big issue for some. For me, now I know all that I do, I think having nervous system issues was a biggie. I was unable to relax enough to get off to sleep, and because my system was always on high alert, too much stimulation from external sources kept me too "wired" at night. Mineral imbalances meant restless legs and tingling extremities - if you've experienced restless legs you will know that it's enough to drive a person crazy, let alone interfere with their sleep.

When we think of going to sleep it's easy to think that our body kind of shuts up shop for the night, but in fact, our body works extremely hard at night, processing memories, detoxing, working on hormones, repairing cells and more. According to Chinese medicine, our organs work to a schedule (body clock) that has a set time for when each of our organs is most active (see that "Useful Websites and Stuff" section for more info). According to this branch of alternative medicine, if you find yourself awake at the same time every night it may be an indication that a certain organ is not happy or is overburdened in some way. If sleep issues are a case of being awake most of the night, then it might be an indication that the body is overwhelmed and imbalanced as a whole - another reason to take a holistic approach!

Although it is a fairly daunting prospect to think that our whole system could be in trouble, it does stand to reason. If something is out of balance in our body, then other things will be too, simply because everything within us is interconnected; our organs, nerves, vessels, etc., aren't standalone elements, they are part of a system and therefore one impacts on another. Therefore, that's why treating the body as a whole, working on all levels, make complete sense.

Sleep issues are deeper than just not being able to sleep, they are a signal that something is amiss and a call to action. It is another way of our body communicating with us, drawing our attention to stuff that isn't working properly.

I can't say there was one definitive thing that improved my sleep, as my nocturnal wakings just got better as I worked on bringing my body back into balance. However, the first noticeable difference was when I started on the elimination diet as part of the candida protocol. The change in my diet reduced pain levels and gave me more energy, which in turn enabled me to work on building up my exercise tolerance levels. This combination had a positive effect on my sleep patterns.

One thing that I have found to be of great importance to getting a better night's sleep is to have a good and consistent sleep routine. While there are times when it has been hard for me to fully stick to my own sleep routine, I do, on the whole try, my best to be consistent.

Below are a few things that I have found useful in getting a better night's sleep.

Environment - an environment that promotes sleep is half the battle, trying to sleep in a room that's cluttered or messy, too stuffy, too cold or too overstimulating (I'm talking TV's, phones, bright lights, not sex) is not great. Think "Goldilocks and The Three Bears," we're looking for something that it is "just right," and that means a room that helps us to relax and set the tone for a restful night's sleep. To set a calm tone I keep the lighting low and use a diffuser in the bedroom to waft relaxing blends of essential oils about the place. I also do my best to keep the room clutter free. If there are piles of laundry and other crap stacked in the room, then it's harder for my mind to switch off.

Reducing blue light - when I first used to find myself awake at all hours I would get up and watch back-to-back episodes of "Criminal Minds." I would often watch 3-4 hours of TV in the early hours or scroll endlessly on my phone. It wasn't until I discovered that the blue light that is emitted by devices such as mobile phones, TV's, and laptops can disrupt sleep patterns that I realised that my nocturnal viewing habit was just making matters worse. Exposing myself to blue light at the time when I was supposed to be sleeping was the worst thing I could do because it was suppressing my body's melatonin production – melatonin is a hormone released by the pineal gland in our brain that plays an important role in helping us to maintain a healthy sleep cycle. Melatonin levels in the bloodstream are meant to rise in the evening when the pineal gland kicks into action. The production of melatonin is governed by the amount of light that is present. We need the dark, or at least a dimly lit room, for the body to be able to start producing it, so blasting our eyes with endless hours of blue light, especially late into the night, does not promote a good night's sleep.

I have often heard people say that they watch TV in bed before going off to sleep and that they actually find it helps them to get off to sleep (although not maybe fibro folk?). To that I say, if it works and you can stay sound asleep all night afterwards, then that's cool, but for me it's a no-go. I suspect the majority of people with fibro would benefit from reducing their exposure to it too.

I am so sensitive to blue light that too much screen time in the daytime can have a negative impact on my ability to get off to sleep at night. I now have a blue light filter on my laptop and phone, and I stop looking at screens of any sort by 9 p.m at the latest. This kind of sucks because, let's face it most of the good TV programmes start around this time, but unfortunately, it's something that I must forgo for the sake of my health. At least with the wonders of today's technology, there's always the record button! Instead of nightly screen time, part of my routine is to read a book (good old-fashioned paperback) in bed with the lights down – if I'm honest, I prefer to do this anyway.

As a little add on to this it's also good to be mindful of what type of things we are viewing too, I've no doubt my "Criminal Minds" habit did little to help keep my nervous system in a calm state!

Winding down - Winding down is a big part of my sleep routine. I start the process at least an hour before bedtime (my regular settle down to sleep time is 10 p.m. - I know, what a party girl, huh!). Taking a relaxing bath before turning in for the night is something I do regularly. I often dissolve approximately 2 cups of Epsom salts or magnesium flakes to help my muscles to relax. Although I have never experienced any issues, to give you a heads up, I have heard some people can't tolerate putting magnesium into their baths, so if you do try this take it slowly.

Some nights I do a few yoga stretches to release any muscle tension, other times I focus on my breathing (see "Breathing Techniques"). Every night I go to bed listening to a guided meditation or some kind of relaxing music. I like the ones that use specific sound frequencies. I download all my meditations, etc., from the Insight Timer app so that I can switch my phone to airplane mode and avoid any EMF (Electromagnetic Frequencies) during the night.

Herbal teas are also part of my wind-down process (see "Herbal Help"). Before I start my meditation, I have a quick re-cap of my day. Sometimes I write stuff down in my journal to stop thoughts whizzing around and clear my headspace, and no matter what kind of day I have I had, I try to bring things to a close by thinking of three things I am grateful for.

I know that this might sound like a lot; you might be thinking, "Really?! Does she really do all this shit?" The answer is yes, on the whole, I do. Why? Because it works for me, it is a process that I have honed over the years that helps me to get the best night's sleep I can. While it may seem dull to some, maybe a tad excessive or a bit picture perfect to others, I just see it as part of my daily routine and something I do to take good care of myself - a vital part of my self-care. When it comes to my sleep, I am unapologetically routine!

CHAPTER 22

EXERCISE

Regaining exercise tolerance is something that needs to be a gradual process. I cannot tell you how many times I've gone, "Yay, I'm feeling great!" and then pushed my body into an exercise routine that proved too much. Every time that I have made that mistake, I've found it hard to deal with mentally. I would get overwhelmed by my feelings of frustration and I have had to be very mindful of halting that downward spiral into beating myself up over it.

My lack of ability to tolerate higher levels of exercise is one aspect of healing that I still find so frustrating that I struggle to keep myself in the right mindset with it, mainly because muscle wise I have always wanted to be one of life's super toned people. I feel that if I didn't have the physical limitations I have I would be achieving this goal.

In fact, it was only a few months ago during a city break with my family that I had a "moment." On the last day of our trip, we hired bicycles and I found myself struggling with not having the muscle strength to get myself up a hill. When I say "moment," what I really mean is I had a tearful hissy fit at not being able to physically do what I wanted to do. Despite all the work I've done on mindset and the physical progress I've made, being able to reconcile myself with my current fitness level and being accepting of the fact that I am still not where I want to be is something that I have to regularly work on. This recent exercise-related meltdown is obviously a testament to that!

My husband has been the one to teach me how to deal with my feelings about not being as fit as I would like. Whenever I have found myself getting caught up in disappointment, when I've been feeling despondent and frustrated, he has reminded me to take a mental step back and review my overall progress. As he mopped up my latest bout of tears and helped me up that hill, he reminded me that 5 years ago we took the same trip. I was exhausted on day one, spent 10 days in a flare up on our return, and never so much as looked at a bicycle. When I look at my current situation from that perspective, I can see that while I might not have biked up that hill the way I wanted to, while I may not have progressed with my fitness as fast as I would have liked, I have made progress, and I will continue to do so.

When I first started out on my healing journey, I couldn't walk upstairs without my muscles feeling like they'd run a marathon, and simple tasks like getting myself dressed felt like they required a superhuman effort. I couldn't even begin to contemplate an exercise routine because my idea of a routine wasn't a match for my new reality of poor physical health.

When I thought about exercise it was classes and hour-long sessions, not simple actions that would just get me moving and bring relief to my body. Therefore, I stopped the activity, I gave up trying to keep any sort of routine, and consequently I found myself on a kind of boom or bust path, leaping into action when I felt better and then setting myself back through doing too much.

Just like sleep, we know that exercise is a must for maintaining good health, yet it can be one of the first things to go out the window when ill health strikes. When it's a struggle to get out of bed, when we're in pain or we feel completely depleted just taking a shower, exercising is the last thing on our minds. Unfortunately, as I discovered, exercise is one of those "use it or lose it" situations. Once our ability to tolerate exercise is lost it becomes that bit harder to get ourselves back on track, which can create a kind of exercise apathy. Although this might be the case, it is also true that establishing a very gentle regular routine can help us to build exercise tolerance back up and lead on to greater strength and increased energy, so it really is a must that we try on some level to get moving more.

Once I began addressing my diet and working on some of the other elements I have written about, I began to see a significant drop in pain levels and a rise in energy, which meant I felt more able to work on rebuilding my fitness. As I have mentioned, I have a habit I went into things too hard and too fast. I didn't want to admit it at the time, but my exercise tolerance level was flatter than a pancake and needed a "slowly, slowly catchy monkey" approach. When I finally got my head around the fact that I wouldn't be joining energetic exercise classes anytime soon I focussed on starting small.

My 4 step "slowly, slowing catchy monkey" method

#1 Stretches & movement - in the beginning, morning muscle stiffness was a big problem for me, and stopping activity was the worst thing I could have done. I found that gentle stretches in bed before my feet even hit the floor helped to get me started. I initially did stretches sitting down before progressing on to bringing in more movement. As my flexibility improved, I started a beginner's class in Pilates. This helped to strengthen my core, and after approximately 2 years I made the shift to yoga (something I had previously practised before I became really sick).

Stretching and movement can bring so much relief to tense and taut muscles. When we are in pain, we tend to shy away from anything that we think might make it worse. Unfortunately, it then becomes one of those cyclic situations where the pain gets worse because we're not moving, and our muscles get increasingly tighter. As much as we may fear pain, movement and stretching is vital because it increases circulation and helps us to heal. Gentle daily stretching is a must for releasing tension and helping muscles to relax.

#2 Walking - when I first started out, 10 minutes of walking and I was out of puff and feeling as if I was wading through mud, so I cut it to 5 minutes in total (there and back). Although on the one hand, I felt ridiculous setting out for a couple of minutes before heading back home, it's what I needed to do to be able to retain energy so I could avoid setbacks and build on my time. Surprisingly, doing it this way, within a matter of months I was up to a 40-minute walk 2-3 times per week. I know walking isn't going to be a good fit for everyone because of their type of pain (swimming or hydrotherapy might be a good call for these people) but I have found with walking that it not only strengthens my body, it helps me to relax and boosts my mood. Gentle walking also helps to lower cortisol.

#3 Gentle resistance training - as I have mentioned, once I began to regain more flexibility through my daily stretching, I joined a Pilates class. This helped me to really strengthen my muscles and increase my core strength. The class often involved using one of those stretchy bands, which helps support you while you gain a greater range of movement and flexibility. I had an excellent instructor who tailored certain exercises to suit my needs and limitations - this is really important when you're starting from ground zero.

#4 Yoga - practising yoga has really enhanced my recovery. I think sometimes there is a misconception around the practice (possibly due to the amount of super fit bendy people showing off their best poses on social media). Therefore, when people envisage yoga classes, they often think of super flexible people getting into all kinds of positions that someone with flexibility issues and pain can only dream of - I want to assure you this is not the case.

There are several types of yoga and it's about finding the right one for your ability. I do various types of yoga at home (YouTube is great for this), but the class I attend on a weekly basis is a very gentle practice that very much focuses on the breath while holding certain postures (Hatha yoga). Yoga is something I have practised on and off over the years and my ability has ebbed and flowed with this. When I first returned to classes I was surprised to find that at the age of 43 I was one of the youngest in the class, and even more surprised to find that some of the other elder members could hold a down-faced dog way longer than me - that was one of those life reality check moments! At first, I was more than a little downhearted at my limitations, seeing a 70+-year-old with more stamina than me was quite something! However, once again I have been blessed with an amazing teacher who helped me to work through my difficulties, adapted poses, sometimes using a chair so that I could get the most out of them, and helped me to steadily improve. She also helped to remind me that I needed to keep the focus on myself and my own progress and not to be concerned with what others were achieving in the class - not get caught in the comparison game

When writing this book, I wasn't sure which section to place yoga in because it is one of those things that has far-reaching benefits. Not only is it good for the physical body, it also helps on a psychological and spiritual level. Yoga is something that I would encourage anyone to take up. I would recommend that they suspend any awkwardness or apprehension they might feel about joining a class and give it a shot.

Below are some little tips I think might be useful if you're unsure whether this practice is for you.

- Find the right class, speak to the teacher about your circumstances, and make sure they are happy to give you instruction on how to adapt poses to suit you - jumping into a hot yoga class is not for newbies or people with limitations.
- Focus on yourself, don't concern yourself with what the person on the mat next to you is doing.
- Listen to your body, don't be afraid to rest during class or come out of a pose when you've had enough. There are no medals given for who can hold the longest.
- No one gives a shit what you look like, what you do or don't do. Occasionally people break wind in yoga classes or snore in meditation and no one bats an eyelid.
- Although I highly recommend you find an instructor, if you're not ready for a class, then give it a go on YouTube. There are some excellent instructors you can subscribe to. Just remember to make sure it's suitable for your level of movement and strength

I know as well as you do that building up exercise levels alongside illness can be a struggle. I know that it's often not as simple as just getting yourself out there. If I had a £1 for every time someone has said to me, "Maybe you'd feel better if you exercised more," I'd be turning a profit. Everybody is different, we all have different limitations, but I think one of the key elements and a good starting point is to simply bring more movement into your day, whether that means starting from ground zero or building on what you already do. There are so many ways to do this. If you're starting from scratch you might need to start small with a few gentle stretches in bed or on a chair, or you might be able to spend a few minutes a day moving your body to your fave tunes. Perhaps Tai Chi could be your thing - a study in the BMJ (British Medical Journal) showed that this practice was beneficial for people with a fibro diagnosis.

Whatever choice you make, I think the important thing to remember is that "slowly, slowly catchy monkey" is a sound approach. It took me a long time (sometimes I still struggle with this) to realise that when it comes to exercise, small steps lead to big strides. And trying to run before you can walk will only lead to setbacks, enforcing the belief that exercise is something you can't do. If you can only manage 2 minutes a day, then do just 2 minutes a day. Consistency is queen. Stick with it and build on it.

CHAPTER 23

AND BREATHE

We all know how to breathe, right? Of course, we do! After all, it's an involuntary action. But just how well are you breathing? There is a lot more to breathing than just keeping us alive, and certain techniques can be a big help when dealing with pain, anxiety, stress, and fatigue. When we are in pain or under stress, we often have the tendency to breathe shallow and from the upper chest. Certain breathing techniques that improve the quality of our breath can help with pain and stress levels by triggering the release of endorphins, slowing down the heart rate and decreasing stress levels.

The 5 basic principles behind beneficial breathing are:

- Breathe through the nose - the nose helps to filter some of the air coming into the body (think viruses and bacteria).
- Breathe using the diaphragm - belly breathing gives the liver, stomach, and intestines a kind of internal massage. It put less pressure on our heart and helps our chest to relax down, which in turn helps to relieve tension in the neck and shoulders.
- Relaxed breathing – calm, relaxed breathing basically sends a message to the rest of the body to just chill the fuck out.
- Steady rhythmic breaths - helps the whole of our body to stay in a natural rhythm that promotes optimal health.
- Silent breathing - the aim of the game is to be breathing silently. Loud breathing, snoring, etc., are a sign that we are not breathing at an optimal level and indicators of other health issues (there are exceptions to this rule, such as certain yoga breathing methods and releasing things in meditation, but this is done consciously).

When we are not breathing optimally it can create tension and stress within the body. Therefore, by learning to breathe more effectively, we can have a positive impact on our health from boosting the immune system, calming the nervous system, and boosting digestion to helping our circulation, organs, muscles, and more. Did you know that the way we breathe can even affect the way our facial features develop? Weird, huh!

Okay, let's have a quick check-in… When was the last time that you paid any attention to how you are breathing? It's surprising just how little attention we give to our breath. It wasn't until I started practising yoga and meditation that I became aware of just how beneficial it can be to be more mindful of the way I breathe. Obviously, it's pretty much impossible to be able to breathe correctly or optimally 100% of the time, but it doesn't take much more than being mindful and trying some different techniques to improve it.

The first step is to tune into how we are breathing, what pattern does it take. This can be done anytime, anywhere. The next step is to make the effort to breathe in and out through the nose and try and follow the basic principles above. This is being mindful of our breathing in the simplest of forms. I have included some more information on various breathing techniques in the "Useful Websites & Stuff" section.

Before I round up on this subject, I want to give a shout out to a certain breathing technique that I discovered about a year ago called Buteyko breathing. I include more info with a "how to guide" in the section I mentioned above, but as a quick overview this method is all about nasal breathing and using controlled pauses to help to increase the amount of carbon dioxide in our body, therefore, boosting the body's functions and healing.

I have found this to be particularly effective in helping me to relax and to calm my nervous system. The majority of us are what are called "over breathers," taking approximately 18-25 breaths per minute (8-12 breaths is best). When we take less breaths per minute, we experience a mild level of hyperventilation, which although it doesn't sound great, it can actually very beneficial for the body. The Buteyko breathing method helps to balance the oxygen and carbon dioxide ratio in our body, which leads to better oxygenation of the muscles, tissues, and organs (a good thing for fatigue), while also helping to smooth out internal muscles. It can also boost our body's immune system.

Checking in with how we are breathing is something that I think would benefit everybody regardless of whether they have an illness. It's one of those things that is very much taken for granted - if we're still breathing, then things must be okay! But it is also one of those things that if we paid it more attention to, we could potentially make significant changes to our health. Our breath is one of the most powerful self-help tools we can possess, particularly when it comes to dealing with stress, trying to control our responses, and boosting energy.

I think the best thing about learning to breathe more effectively is that it's one of those self-help things you can start immediately. At any point, anywhere, you can take a moment to check in and change your breathing for the better. In fact, as long as you promise to return to reading this book, why not give it a go right this minute? Take a break right now, tune in to how you're breathing, see how it feels to breathe from the belly (belly rises on the inhale falls on the exhale) see how it feels to slow things down with long, slow, rhythmic breathing for a minute or two.

CHAPTER 24

HERBAL HELP

When I started out healing myself, I didn't know much about the power of the plant, but as time has gone on and as my love affair with all things natural has increased, it seems a logical progression that I would eventually find myself tapping into this healing resource.

My interest in plant-based healing was first sparked about 3 years ago when I realised the amazing healing properties of plant oils while studying for a diploma in natural skincare. From there I progressed to having an interest in how plant-based medicine could boost my healing.

About 8 months ago the realisation that some radical shifts in my hormones were probably signs of the perimenopause, I set off on a hormone re-balancing mission which found me booking in for a consult with a medical herbalist. It turned out this was one of the best healing decisions I have ever made. In fact, now I have witnessed the amazing healing benefits of herbal tinctures it is an avenue that I really wish I had explored earlier.

Herbal preparations are as old as the hills and have been part of healing practices for centuries. Plants have been used for medicine for as long as there have been humans on the earth. Herbal medicine is the most incredible thing. I've had a strong belief in natural medicine for some time, but I have come to realise that plants are extra special. They have this amazing natural affinity with the human body that nourishes and supports it back to health. I swear there is a plant-based remedy for most ailments!

Although I currently consult with a medical herbalist, before I enlisted her help, I had already been using herbal infusions for some time. These are made by pouring boiling water over herbs, like making tea, only leaving it to steep for a minimum of 8 hours (I usually leave mine overnight). Infusions are a brilliant way of getting vitamins and minerals into the body. My fave infusions are nettles and oat straw. Like many other herbs, these two natural beauties are packed full of the good stuff, containing magnesium, calcium, iron, silica, phosphorus, manganese, potassium, folic acid, amino and fatty acids and vitamins A, C, E and various B vitamins. They are a kind of a one-stop health shop.

Something I want to highlight here is that if I was to rewind back to how I was at the start of all of this, before I started trying to heal, I would never have considered doing "herbs," and I mean never. In fact, I probably would have scoffed at this and many other things that have now become part of my everyday life. The reason I've chosen to pop in with that little snippet of information is because I feel I need to draw attention to the fact that when thinking about making radical changes to achieve something, we often need to let go of long-standing beliefs, scepticism, and any prejudices we might hold. We need to be open to doing an about turn, flipping 180 degrees, and considering doing things that we would never normally have been caught dead doing.

When I first started drinking this herbal help it started out as one of those, "I'm only doing this because I know it's good for me" type of situations. At first, I would pull a face every time I had to chug a glass of what in my mind was akin to drinking ditch water. However, as time went by, I became accustomed (or maybe just desensitised) to the taste and I found that my body actually craved the stuff. I have since discovered that you can "pimp" up your infusions with other garden herbs such as lemon verbena and mint and use it as a base for other drinks, juices, and smoothies, etc. This summer I'm planning on making infusion ice-lollies – if the old me could see me now. I am herb obsessed!

Although the tinctures that I am currently being prescribed by my herbalist are to deal with hormonal issues, among other things, they focus on supporting the liver, digestion, adrenals, and thyroid. I feel that if I had known earlier in my healing that herbs could be used like this, I would have opted to try them sooner. As I have already highlighted, the liver, adrenals, digestion, etc., are areas which greatly influence our overall health, and I now feel that supporting my body's functions with herbs at an earlier stage might have speeded up my recovery.

Something that I also want to draw attention to is that while infusions, teas, and the like are a great DIY introduction to herbal remedies and can help tremendously with replenishing and nourishing the body, I feel the real power lies with an experienced practitioner. On my healing journey, I have achieved a lot of my progress through my own research and administrations, but there are certain things that I believe are best left to the professionals, and this is one of those areas. Although these days I am pretty confident in my own skills and knowledge of my body, my herbalist has been able to take things to another level. Because her knowledge of herbs is so in-depth, she is able to create an individual blend of herbs that suits my needs and can be adjusted as I progress through different stages, which has led me to believe that if you really want to experience healing on a deep level using herbs, then seeking out the services of a qualified medical herbalist is your best option. It also needs to be noted that working with herbs takes time and patience, its not a magic overnight wonder cure but more of a steady supportive process where one day you just realise you feel a hell of a lot better.

ESSENTIAL OILS

My love of essential oils (EO'S) is probably on par with my love for plants-based skincare and herbal preparations. Just like herbal medicine, essential oils have been used in healing for centuries. They have many healing properties and can be used to improve physical, mental, and emotional health, or as I have found, just make your laundry smell good!

EO's are highly concentrated. Just one drop can be powerful, which is why they should be treated with as much caution as we would medicine. Essential oils, when used on the skin or in the bath, should be diluted properly in a carrier oil. Using them neat or wanging them in our bath water can cause sensitisation issues further down the line, or even burns. Some people advocate the use of ingesting oils to heal. This is something I have never done nor would advise anyone to do unless they are under the supervision of an aromatherapist trained in this practice. Popping a couple of drops of peppermint oil into a smoothie to combat IBS symptoms may feel good for now, but regardless of what some EO suppliers advise, by self-regulating doses with something as powerful as EO's there is a risk of causing issues in the future. While it's true some people may be able to tolerate ingestion for months or years, I personally don't think it's worth the risk. Imagine how painful an EO burn to the oesophagus would be!

Essential oils have the ability to work on different levels. They are great for the mind, from calming and relieving anxiety to aiding focus and boosting energy. For the body, they can help relieve muscle and joint pain, reduce inflammation, improve circulation, aid digestion, relieve nausea, boost the immune system, and more. And for the Soul, they can help us to connect with ourselves and enhance our spirituality.

I use essential oils on all levels. I sometimes use them to give my adrenals some extra support by rubbing diluted Frankincense in a carrier oil into my kidney area before bed. I diffuse different blends depending on what results I'm looking for, i.e., relaxation or rejuvenation. Sometimes I add a couple of drops to a tissue and inhale for a quick pick-me-up or to help me to relax. I also use them when cleaning the house or doing the laundry - diffusing oils beats synthetic air fresheners hands down, and it's much healthier too. I have included more information on EO's for you to check out in the "Useful Websites & Stuff" section.

CHAPTER 25

CLEANING UP

There is no doubt about it, we live in a toxic world. On a daily basis, we are exposed to environmental toxins, many of which are out of our control, but we can still make our little corner of the world less toxic by making some simple changes to our personal products and household environment that can help us on our healing journey.

About a year or so into my healing, I knew that I had to do everything I could to reduce stress on my body and give it a helping hand by providing it with the best environment I could to make the healing process easier. Through my research, I had discovered how part of our liver's function is to eliminate toxins, so I figured, why make mine work any harder than it needed to? One of the ways for me to help my body, in particular my liver, was to remove some of the synthetic chemically laden products and items around the house.

Over time, I switched all of my personal care and household cleaning products over to natural ones, buying natural brands or making my own products to avoid nasties such as parabens, SLS's, BPA's, and many more chemicals that are known to be irritants, carcinogenic, or hormone disruptors.

Steps I took to reduce toxins in my personal environment:

- Switched to all-natural brands for my make-up and personal care products, such as fondation, deodorant, shampoo, shower gel, toothpaste, sunscreen, moisturisers, body lotions etc.
- Stopped using traditional laundry detergent and softeners.
- Started using natural cleaning products such as soda crystals and white vinegar.
- Gave up gel nails - although I wasn't always a regular gel nail gal, this was a sacrifice.
- Used glass storage containers instead of plastic.

Until I looked into this aspect of healing, I had been pottering through life completely unaware of the amount of potentially harmful products I was coming into contact with from what I put on my skin or inhaled into my body every single day. I had never even given a second thought to slathering myself in synthetic chemicals via body lotions, stepping into a cloud of Chanel perfume every day, or steeping my clothes in highly fragranced detergents and softeners. I had no idea that these things were just adding unnecessary toxic stress to my already overburdened system.

Since making the switch it is amazing how differently I perceive the products I used to think I couldn't do without. My senses have become so accustomed to natural fragrances that now I can't stand the smell of synthetic fragranced products. All the stuff I used to think smelled fab now smells too overpowering and artificial. My nose has become as sensitive as a sniffer dog's - I can smell the neighbour's laundry on the line and detect other people's fabric softener at 20 paces.

I know a lot of people who are healing the alternative way that go a step further and replace things like their bedding, mattresses, carpets, sofas, and such to avoid the chemicals they have been treated with. This has not been an option for me, but it's one of those things that I feel I can't stress about; I am doing the best I can by making the changes I have made, and I figure that is good enough for now. I feel this is a good mindset to have. It can be very easy to get overwhelmed by all the options of going natural and using alternatives. I've seen a number of people healing naturally get to the point where they start to see everything as a potential health hazard. To me, that just adds an extra level of stress that could hinder the healing process. I prefer to take the stance that my focus is better directed towards getting my body to a place where it can cope better with the toxins we encounter in this modern world, i.e., work on my liver and detox pathways.

When starting out on cleaning up our home environment, there is no need for us to go crazy and start lugging our furniture out into the street. Simple small changes can help reduce the number of toxins we are exposed to and give our healing process a boost. For example, we really don't need to be puffing synthetic chemicals into our rooms via plug-in air fresheners, burning synthetically fragranced candles, or using 5 different cleaning products.

Over the years, clever advertising and marketing has led us to associate highly fragranced cleaning products, detergents, etc., with things being clean and fresh. Once I got over my fabric softener sniffing habit, I realised that all the artificial scents in my everyday products just meant I was surrounding myself with a bunch of synthetic chemicals that were potentially harming my health and making my recovery harder, so I swapped them out for less harmful products that achieved the same results.

There are so many websites, articles, and how-to guides for taking a more natural lifestyle approach that changing things up in this area really is as simple as a Google search. Pinterest is brilliant for this. Making the switch to less harmful products couldn't be easier either. There are absolutely heaps of natural products available, from household cleaners to make-up. I made the switch to more natural products to ease the stress on my body, but I know that chemical sensitivities are something that can be on the symptom list for a lot of people with a fibro diagnosis, so if this is you and you haven't delved into this side of things, it might be worth considering – anything that may reduce symptoms has got to be worth a shot.

CHAPTER 26

OSTEOPATHIC TREATMENT

Cranial and biodynamic osteopathy is something that I have used over the last few years to help recover from nerve and muscular issues and to keep my body balanced and in alignment. This form of osteopathy is a gentle yet effective therapy which makes it ideal for those with a fibro diagnosis. One area cranial biodynamic osteopathy focuses on is balancing the subtle rhythms within the whole body - stress and trauma, etc., can become "locked" within our body and disrupt these rhythms.

A biodynamic practitioner can gently manipulate and work with the body's natural rhythms to release underlying tension, allowing the body to re-engage with its natural healing mechanism. This type of therapy can also ease joints, trapped nerves, muscle spasms, and help to reduce inflammation.

When we are in pain or overwhelmed with fatigue, we tend to carry a lot of tension in our muscles. Over time this can cause further pain as well as affect our posture and spinal alignment. I have found this type of therapy to be particularly helpful in relieving pain, tension, and stiffness in the body.

Osteopathic treatments of this type also work with the fluid system within the body. CSF (cerebrospinal fluid) is what protects our brain and spinal cord. As is it flows around and through our central nervous system, it nourishes, supports, and removes waste and toxins from the body. Readjusting and realigning the body and working with the fluctuations of the CSF allows the fluid to flow freely throughout the body, therefore easing discomfort, pain, stress, etc.

By re-establishing a good flow of fluid throughout our system, a cranial biodynamic osteopath can also help us to maintain a healthy fascia. The fascia is a connective membrane that covers pretty much everything - our muscles, tissues, bones, cells, vessels, and organs. It's a super important network of connective tissue that runs throughout the body and is basically what holds us together. Without it, we'd just be a messy, leaky blob of body parts.

The fascia is also what helps our muscles to move smoothly as they contract and relax. Within this amazing connective network, there are nerve endings and receptors which communicate with our central nervous system, therefore maintaining this membrane can make a big difference in the body's alignment and our overall health and wellbeing. Having a fascia in tip-top condition can help to boost the immune system, relieve tension, stress, aches and pains and more.

My osteopath explained fascia to me by telling me to imagine it to be like cling film (plastic wrap) surrounding the body parts. Injury, inflammation, emotional trauma, or chronic stress can cause the fascia to crumple and get all bunched up - If you're anything like me you'll have no trouble imagining this by picturing that moment where you try and wrap a sandwich in cling film and it ends up all stuck together, crumpled in places and too tight in others. Well, a good biodynamic osteopath is a like champion sandwich wrapper. They use their magic hands to help the body's fluid system to flow correctly and release the bunched up clingfilm (fascia), effectively re-wrapping the muscles in a lovely smooth membrane that allows for a greater level of movement free from tension. (On a side note I no longer use cling-film as it didn't make the cut in the personal environment clean up.)

In the world of cranial biodynamic osteopathy, the fluid that flows through our system is considered to be the "Breathe of Life," delivering potent life energy to every cell in our body and therefore, the bringer of health and wellness. By working with the subtle energetic rhythms of the body and the natural fluctuations of this fluid, a practitioner working in this field of osteopathy can help to calm and rebalance the body.

Cranial biodynamic osteopathic treatments can help with many conditions, including headaches, stress, insomnia, chronic fatigue, myofascial pain, muscle pain, and plantar fasciitis.

Note that biodynamic osteoplathy is my treatment of choice but there are other techniques out there that I haven't ventured into that others might find a better fit. This is once again where self-responsibility comes in and it's up to you as an individual to research and discover what works best for you. I say this because it can be to easy sometimes to just think that alternative healing doesn't work, but often it can be the case that one particular modality/ practice isn't suited to you.

CHAPTER 27

HEALING POWER OF NATURE

If you have ever experienced that deep sense of wellbeing when you're out in nature, then it will come as no surprise to you that studies have found that taking time out in natural environments is great for our health. In fact, there is a name for it - Ecotherapy. Ecotherapy is used to improve our physical and mental wellbeing through the process of connecting with nature. The basis of this type of therapy is simple... basically, get your ass out into green spaces and let Mother Nature work her magic. Getting out in nature is good for the Mind, Body, and Soul. Spending time out in the open, in green spaces, can help to ease depression and anxiety, reduce anger, improve our mood, raise our vibe and energy levels (see Soul section), reduce inflammation levels, lower the heart rate, reduce high blood pressure, and balance cortisol levels.

Other studies have found spending regular time in nature can help to improve sleep patterns, boost the immune system, and lower stress. In Japan, there is a practice known as Shinrin-yoku or "forest bathing." In Japan the health benefits of spending time in the forest have become so well known some doctors actually prescribe it for their patients.

In the last few years, getting back to nature has been a big part of my healing process. Building up my exercise tolerance by taking walks has not only improved my physical health. It has reintroduced me to the healing benefits of being outdoors. When I am in nature, I feel more balanced and relaxed. It helps to calm my mind and focus my thoughts. Taking time out to observe the natural world around me makes me feel more grounded in the here and now. By getting back to a more natural approach to life I have rediscovered a few other simple ways for me to reconnect with my surroundings: walking barefoot in the grass, sitting with my back against a tree, listening to the birds singing; basically, just taking the time to observe nature at its best. On sunny winter days, I have gotten my dose of nature by bundling myself up and taking my lunch outside. Okay, I know this might all sound a bit like rose-tinted spectacles, but spending time in nature has really helped me to balance my body. And it's not as airy-fairy as it sounds, because here I come with another nerdy science moment.

In the alternative healing world, a practice called "grounding" or "earthing" is something that is seen as being beneficial to overall health and wellbeing. This is the practice of connecting barefoot to the earth (simply walking barefoot outside). How this works is, it allows the body to absorb the negatively charged electrons from the earth through our feet. As humans we are positively charged, so by connecting to the earth's negative charge, we can help our body to rebalance and boost our immune system. Our immune system functions at its best when it is supplied with an adequate number of electrons. A 2007 PubMed article shows that "free electrons from the earth neutralize the positively charged free radicals that are the hallmark of chronic inflammation." What this means is that the electrons which can be absorbed by the body through the simple act of walking barefoot on the ground can help to protect the body from inflammation.

Grounding can also promote physiological changes within our bodies, improve glucose regulation, and relieve stress. Research shows that by connecting with the earth's energy we can obtain antioxidants for free, synchronise our biorhythms, and balance our sympathetic and parasympathetic nervous system.

Not bad, huh? Cell rejuvenation, less stress, better sleep, just by chilling out with Mother "N," and what's more, it's totally free and accessible. The practice of grounding is like plugging ourselves into a free open-air charger. All we need to do is walk barefoot, or lie or sit on grass, sand, stone, or soil. Granted, the beach or the park is better than your veg patch, but the name of the game is to get your bare skin in contact with a natural surface wherever possible. Walking on wet, humid surfaces can amplify the effects of earthing even further.

Although I think that it's great to get outdoors to practice because we get the added bonuses of daylight and fresh air, grounding/earthing can also be done indoors using special mats, bed sheets, cords and patches. One advantage of the indoor method is that people are more likely to keep up a regular practice, especially in the UK where the weather is often unpredictable! Either, way indoors or outdoors grounding is something that has the potential to help healing along and increase wellbeing, and it is something else to add to the self-help toolbox.

DAYLIGHT HEALING

When I was first diagnosed, and for some time before that, I spent a lot of time holed up indoors. Although on "good" days I was still going out and about, there were some days (too many) where the school run was about the only time I was exposed to the fresh air and outdoor light - if going from house to car and 5 minutes into the playground counts! As I ventured further into trying to over come my symptoms, I realised that I needed to get myself outside some more, so when the weather was dry, I would take myself into the garden whether I felt like it or not. On colder days I would bundle myself up, take a cup of tea and a blanket, and spend 15 minutes catching some daylight. Sometimes I was a very reluctant participant in this activity, but regularly spending a little time outside made me feel better in general. At the time I was just doing it because fresh air is meant to be good for us. I didn't realise that there were other great health benefits to be gained.

While it's well reported that we need to be mindful of too much exposure to sunlight, getting out in daylight and catching a few rays is very beneficial for our health. Obviously, burning our skin to a crisp is not a good thing, but equally, too little exposure can create or add to health issues. It's probably one of the most well-known facts that we need sunlight to help keep up our vitamin D levels, but there are other important health benefits too, ones that can help us to deal with some of the symptoms on the fibro list.

Sunlight exposure can help the body to keep its natural waking and sleeping cycles (circadian rhythm). When we are exposed to natural light it encourages the body to recognise when it should be awake or asleep. Our circadian rhythm is also important for temperature control, hormone release, blood sugar, and more.

Natural light can have a helpful impact on our endocrine system (the body's chemical messenger system) too. Getting out in daylight helps the body to know when to produce melatonin, the hormone we need to maintain a healthy sleep cycle, something that is often messed up for people with fibro. When our eyes are exposed to sunlight it triggers an increase of serotonin in the brain, which is associated with maintaining our mood. Low levels of serotonin are linked to depression.

Getting some natural light is an inexpensive way to help boost our recovery. Some studies show that morning sunlight is the most beneficial, but I think getting out at any point in the day can only be a good thing.

Of course, being in the UK can be somewhat problematic when it comes to that big orange ball in the sky. Our climate is not renowned for extended periods of sunny weather! However, I sign up to the opinion that any daylight is better than no daylight, so we might as well just get ourselves out there regardless, and if we happen upon the sun then that's a bonus.

When I think about using fresh air and sunlight as a healing tool, I am reminded of days gone by where people were packed off to the countryside or the seaside to recover from illness. I think maybe we can take something from this in our own healing journeys. Sometimes the old ways are the good ways.

CHAPTER 28

HEATING THINGS UP

Heat can be a wonderful thing for our body. When our muscles are nice and warm, they become more relaxed and we get that kind of Loosey-Goosey feeling - you know the one, where your limbs feel all deliciously languid and you know if they could they would be letting out a big sigh of relaxation. Massage can be great for achieving that blissed out feeling, but I have also fairly recently discovered so is a heated pad. To be precise, a Far-infrared heated mat.

A Far-infrared (FIR) heated pad/mat produces a heat that can penetrate far deeper than ordinary heat pads. It's like harnessing the benefits of an infrared sauna without packing your husband off to the local wood yard to get sauna building supplies or searching the local area for someone who offers this facility.

FIR heat has the power to penetrate as deep as 2-8 inches into the body, warming up the muscles, joints, bones, nerves, and blood vessels. It raises the body's temperature, triggering an increase in blood flow, which promotes detoxification and healing.

The healing properties of these type of mats are enhanced by the addition of different crystals, such as amethyst, jade, and tourmaline. These natural crystals release what are called negative ions. We can also find these ions in concentration all around us in nature, which is one of the reasons why getting out in nature can feel so good and the practice of grounding can provide health benefits.

Negative ions can have a positive effect on our body by boosting serotonin - the "feel-good" chemical in our brain. Not only do the ions help us to feel more positive on a mental level, the serotonin helps with the production of melatonin, which is the hormone needed to regulate our natural sleep cycles, therefore promoting a better night's sleep. These ions can help our healing on many levels. They can help reduce inflammation, support the immune system, increase the flow of oxygen in the body, relieve stress, boost lymphatic function, and enhance mental energy. There are a few other health benefits too, but I think at this stage all I need to say is that the negative ions, or “happy ions” as they are sometimes called, can have a positive impact on our overall health and general wellbeing. And a great way to tap into the power of negative ion healing on a regular basis is to heat things up with a crystal enhanced Far-infrared heat pad.

CHAPTER 29

CHECK-IN

Well, now we've worked our way through the Mind part of the book and reached the end of the Body section, I'm just going to check in with you. How are you feeling? At this point you may be experiencing one of two things. You might be all fired up and ready to start work on bringing your body back into balance, or you might be in overwhelm and thinking, "Where the fuck do I start?"

If you are in the latter camp, then this is for you - I know this is a lot to take on board, especially if you have brain fog! Burying your head under a pillow or sticking your fingers in your ears and making la-la noises might feel like the best option right now, but I want you to put the pillow down, unplug your ears, and just breathe. Sit with what you have just read, over the next few days go back over it, let it sink in. When you have done that, take a moment to consider that while it is a lot to take on board, what lies underneath all this information is hope. When you picked up this book, the likelihood is that after diagnosis you were told the best you could hope for would be the management of your symptoms. It's likely you are bouncing from flare-up to flare-up. It's also likely that your hope has done a runner and left you in a state of hopelessness. This body section has been all about calling into question the opinion that managing symptoms and weathering flare-ups is your best case scenario; it is showing you that there potentially many more things that could be driving your symptoms and there is still much you can do to help yourself feel better. It is encouraging you to look for your root causes so you can begin to re-address the balance and start the climb back up.

If you can set aside the sense of overwhelm you may be feeling for a moment, you may be able to glimpse a window of opportunity, a chance for you to start taking action to help yourself get on more of an even keel. You might just feel the start of a spark, a growing sense of empowerment, nudging that overwhelm aside and a little voice telling you better health is possible.

Yes, I know that there is a lot for you to think about, but there are also a lot of simple steps you could start today that could help your body begin the recovery process. Before you do get started, I would really recommend that you first work on getting yourself into the right mindset - get your healing attitude on, start believing you can heal! Then when you've nailed that attitude, do one small thing that puts your foot on the first rung of the healing ladder; e.g.,assess your current diet, start a food diary, reflect on your life experience to date and map out your route to illness, or check out what alternative resources or practitioners are available in your local area.

Just before we leave this section, I'm going to leave you with one last snippet which would have helped me scoot along my healing road quicker.

IF I HAD KNOWN THEN WHAT I KNOW NOW.

We all know that hindsight is a wonderful thing, and this healing path I have been on has not been an exception to that rule. Over the years, following hours of research and a fair bit of chasing my tail, there are a few avenues of exploration I would not necessarily choose again and a few shortcuts I wished I had discovered earlier.

Now because I know what it is like to feel information overload and overwhelmed by choices, I'm going to try and simplify things somewhat. If your brain is in a whirl from everything you have just read and you are not sure where would be a good starting point, below are the first two major steps I would have taken for healing my physical body if I had known then what I know now.

HTMA (hair tissue analysis test) and consult to determine my mineral status and initial plan of action for re-balancing - focussing on gut health, liver, lymph, adrenals and HPA-axis.

Consult a medical herbalist or homoeopathic practitioner or functional medicine practitioner to help support my healing.

Following on from there, I would start to address all the other stuff: sleep, emotional issues, exercise, environment, etc.

Soul

PART 4: CHAPTER 30

SOUL

Depending on where you stand with things like connecting on a Soul level, spirituality, and the metaphysical stuff, this is the part of the book where you might nod along in agreement, be open to exploring this subject more, or experience a "WTF" moment. Part of this section is where the spiritual side of me gets an airing, and you either read it with a "Yeah I get this shit," or "Jeez, this woman is completely woo-woo!" Confession: yes, I am!

There are some suggestions within these next pages, but equally some of what I write about in this Soul section, like the first part of this book, is very much my own personal perspective, my connections and experiences with what I feel is an important part of healing.

**Note* in this section I use the terms Soul and Authentic-Self interchangeably.*

So, let's dive right in... what does the Soul mean to me? And what the heck has it to do with healing? The first question is one of those big ones, like what is the meaning of life? I don't think the answer to this one is completely clear cut because it can mean something to different to all of us. Although I think many of us out there would agree that when we shuffle off this mortal coil that something leaves the body - the thing that makes us who we are. For me, that's my Soul, the true unique essence of me, my Authentic-Self. It is the spark, the vital life force that exists within me, yet it is independent of my physical body.

It also that part of me that lay hidden beneath all the stuff that contributed to my route to illness - conditioning, limiting beliefs, and learned behaviour that my life experiences and events put upon me for years. My Soul is my truth, who I really am, it's the part that I became disconnected from during the years I was getting all bent out of shape and squashed by the environment I was in and trying to meet other people's expectations.

When I talk about being grateful for some of the things illness has given me, reconnecting with myself is one. When I realised that I needed to take a Mind, Body, and Soul approach to heal, it became clear that I had lost touch with who I really was. To get back to really understanding what my Authentic-Self was, I first had to look at what it wasn't. It wasn't my identity that was shaped by the roles I played in life, i.e., wife, mother, etc. It wasn't defined by other people's agendas or thoughts and opinions of me. It wasn't the changes that illness had created. Most importantly, it was the discovery that my Soul wasn't extinguished by the challenging life experiences I had faced. Buried for a time, disconnected, yes, but never fully extinguished.

My Soul is like a BFF, it calls me to attention when things need to change in my life. It's what fires me up and helps set me on the path to bettering myself. It the voice of my intuition (when I chose to listen to it), my higher self, my source of empowerment, and my innate wisdom. It encourages me to learn, to be open to the alternative perspectives, and guides me to the people, the experiences, the learning, etc., that will bring a greater sense of self, enlightenment, wellbeing, and peace into my life. It is what drives my inherent ability to reach my full potential on all levels.

So, that all sounds good (or crazy, depending on where you are at), but what has it got to do with healing? To be honest, this has the potential to be one of those rabbit hole situations I often write about, so to try and keep it nice and simple I'm going to go with the following. When we are consistently caught up in stuff that compromises our values, morals, and principles, when we are not being who we really want to be or feel we can't be who we really want to be, when we give too much of ourselves to others or we allow others to continually dictate the direction and flow of our lives, when we are continually squashed or cowed by others, when we live in fear, we become disconnected from our Authentic-Self. When we seek happiness or validation of our worth from external shit, like new cars, designer gear, holidays, money, people's opinion, etc., etc., we are disconnected. Over time this can create an imbalance within. This disconnect and imbalance may be something we are aware of or it may be out of our awareness. It may manifest itself in depression, blaming others, unhelpful patterns of behaviour, self-sabotage, anger, frustration, sadness, yearning for life to be different, self-damning, and a whole plethora of other stuff.

When we have a strong connection to our Authentic-Self we find a sense of greater peace and contentment within ourselves, and a lot of the external stuff that stresses us ceases to matter. We stop clinging on to the people, things, situations that hold us back or drain our energy. We grow more confident in speaking up for ourselves and making ourselves a priority so that our genuine needs are fulfilled. We step into action making better and healthier decisions because we are in alignment with what with who we are, what we really want. We make decisions based on our own wellbeing not what we think is the right thing to do or based on external expectations. All of this can help us to create a healthier life.

I often think that connecting with the Soul is like tuning in a radio. When we hit the right frequency everything becomes crystal clear, there's no static or interference, just clarity. To tune into our Soul radio station, we need to have a sound level of self-awareness. By being more aware of how we are functioning in the world, what is driving, influencing, and shaping our lives, we can re-assess and re-adjust where we are so it is more in tune with our Authentic-Self. This enables us to operate from a more authentic, genuine level, attract the things which will benefit us, which puts us on course for achieving a greater level of wellbeing. From a healing perspective, acting from a more authentic place, being more connected with who we truly are, helps and guides us to make healthier choices in all areas of our lives.

Now, you may or may not believe that we need a connection with our Soul to be healthier, but I personally feel that it is an aspect of ourselves that shouldn't be ignored when we are trying to achieve balance and health. When we show up in life from a place that is in alignment with our true selves we tend to let go of the masks, pretences, or behaviours that we use to fit in, protect ourselves, or conform to social norms – the very things that tend to create conflict within us, make us feel compromised, stressed, or overwhelmed. The things that can contribute to ill health. Therefore, a strong connection with our Soul can help us to resolve some of these unwelcome states of being and replace them with a greater sense of wholeness and contentment. In my eyes, this can only have a favourable effect on our physical and mental health.

CHAPTER 31

SPIRITUALITY

This is one of those parts of the book where things get really personal for me. This is something that may or may not resonate with you, who knows? Putting out a personal perspective on spirituality is like religion or politics. It's one of those subjects that either attract agreement or dismissal or gets people all fired up.

As a child, I grew up in the Church of England, attending Sunday school, and as a natural progression, I was confirmed into the faith. In my late teens, I considered myself to be an atheist before circling around and coming to rest with faith in Universal energy, One Source, consciousness, manifestation, and a belief that there is way more to our existence than the confines of our human body and its five senses.

I'm a bit of a mixed bag; on the one hand, I have a belief in divine intervention, angels, guardians/spiritual guides, on the other, I am also drawn towards science and how it connects with the Universal Laws. I 100% believe that it is possible for us to create our own reality, and the ways in which the Universe works intrigue and amuse me in equal measures (although not always the latter). Someone once said to me, "You'd believe anything that was in a fucking crystal ball, you live in a bloody parallel Universe." Obviously, it was not meant as a compliment! But hey, if I'm totally honest, I kind of think "The Force" in Star Wars is potentially achievable, so you know, maybe they had a point...

The truth is, I don't crystal ball gaze and I'm not sat around always wondering if another version of me has got their shit together in a parallel Universe (although in the interests of full disclosure, the thought has crossed my mind), but I do have an unshaken belief in the One Source - that we are all connected to one Universal energy. I consider this energy to be all-knowing, all-creative, all-powerful, and always present everywhere at the same time (omnipresent). For some that may equate to God. To me, it is just is what it is, a source of energy that encapsulates everything and has infinite power. I believe that this energy is determined by metaphysical laws and science, not by any one divine deity that takes a human form.

How does this fit into healing? Okay, so this is where I may be on slightly rocky ground with some, but this is my personal belief and it has served me well in my recovery so far, so I'm sticking by it and just letting it hang here. Because of my spirituality, I have the belief that everything we encounter, everything we go through, all the people we meet in life, are to teach us, because at the end of the day we are Souls having a human experience while on our path to enlightenment.

For the purpose of clarity and not triggering people, this is not to say that I think the awful situations we sometimes find ourselves in are deserved, or consciously asked for. Let's face it, this thing called life can be brutally unfair at times, but it is my belief and experience that within the unfairness is learning, and often the unexpected good things and the greatest learning can come out of the shittiest situations. Don't get me wrong, when I've finished with this life and get on over to the other side I'm going be like, "Really? Were you fucking kidding me with those life lessons? Jeez Louise, that one was a toughie!" But in my heart, in my Soul, I know that the life lessons I have learnt through the hardships I have encountered in this life could not have been delivered to me covered in pom-poms and glitter. They needed to be difficult and messy for me to "get it."

Whether you buy into this or not, my belief system has been a component of my recovery in the sense that it has helped me to hold fast during the worst times. My belief that every shitty situation I experienced was part of a wider learning experience made the hard days more bearable. I believed that as hard as it was, the place I was in at any given time was because I was meant to be there on a learning level. Through my faith, I was able to view my circumstances from a slightly different perspective, ask myself questions such as, "What is this showing me?" or "Who do I need to be?" And it was that different take on what I was going through that pushed me to seek the answers that led to a better level of health.

CHAPTER 32

FEEDING THE SOUL

What I'm talking about here are "the things that make you go ooh," the things you love that give you that deep sense of peace and connection, strengthen, replenish, and light you up. Feeding the Soul revolves heavily around developing a good level of self-care on all levels. When we feed our Soul, we create positive shifts and habits that enhance our wellbeing. Taking time out to connect with ourselves and do the things we love to do can have a huge impact on our health. Finding the space to reconnect with our Authentic-Self through self-care and doing the things we love means we can get to know ourselves on a deeper level. And truly understanding ourselves is one of the key factors in being able to recognise what changes we need to make to help us to feel better.

All of the things written from here on in are the things that I have found have increased my overall wellbeing through the act of nourishing my Soul.

MEDITATION

Meditation is a helpful tool on all levels and is one of those subjects that made separating this book into three distinct parts difficult. Although I have placed it in the Soul section, there's no doubt that mediation can have a powerful impact on the Body and the Mind. (see mindfulness)

A 2011 study found that if we meditate daily for a period of 8 weeks it can change the physical structure of the brain. In another 2010 study by Barbara Fredrickson and Bethany Kok, it was found that regular meditation could increase a person's vagal tone (see Vagus Nerve). It is known that meditation can help with stress, depression, and anxiety, improve concentration, aid sleep, and boost overall psychological wellbeing. As we know, the mind-body connection is a powerful one, so it goes without saying that if meditating is good for the mind then it is good for the body too.

Although I have written about mindful meditation in a previous section as a useful tool for the Mind and Body, I decided place more about mediation here in this part of the book because daily practice provides us with an opportunity to spend quality time with ourselves. It allows us to sit with who we are and just "be." And when we do this, we can connect more deeply with our Authentic-Self. Through regular meditative practice we can learn to let go of some of the external stuff: people's opinions, judgements, expectations, etc. When that happens, we can become reacquainted with who we really are, tune into our unique frequency. It can also enable us to connect with the universal energy which can aid healing on all levels.

Mediation is something that anyone can step into and start practising (you don't need to be spiritual), but like any new skill, we need to give it a bit of time to develop and find what works best for us. Because I'm not a sit in silence type I find guided meditation or listening to some kind of gentle music is a better fit for me - I can focus much better this way.

This practice is something I have dipped in and out for many years, but this year I decided to up the ante somewhat and vowed to make the time to complete a meditation every day. To date I am well over 200 consecutive days of practice, and what started as a bit of a personal challenge has now become an essential part of my day. Over the months of practice, I have tried various times of the day, but have found morning to be especially beneficial in helping to set me up for the day ahead. If I leave it until later in the day I feel as something is lacking, that I haven't quite got off to the best start.

As part of my morning routine, depending on what time I wake up, I spend anywhere from 10 to 40 minutes meditating before I get out of bed to help me get into the right mindset. Because I am a spiritual person, I enjoy this side of my meditation practice and get a lot out of it on that level. On a more physical level, my body benefits from the slowing down of my breath and it provides a mini oasis of calm before the daily hustle and bustle. At the end of the day I switch between listening to a guided meditation or soothing music in bed to help me to decompress from the day and drift off to sleep - quite often I am fast asleep before the end.

I think there is sometimes a misconception around meditation that it requires too much time, that it involves sitting for hours in the mountains or in silence somewhere trying to achieve a state of zen. While that could be an option for some, it doesn't have to be like that at all. It's really easy and quick to incorporate it into everyday life. Just closing our eyes and focusing on listening to the birds or the sounds around us while practising breathing from the diaphragm for 5-10 minutes will work. I personally like to use an app called Insight Timer because I suck at being able to sit in silence. This app allows me to download meditations that take anything from a few minutes to over an hour.

Practising meditation is a self-help tool that gets 5 stars from me, not just because of the health benefits, but also because it's free and something anyone can start today.

JOURNALLING

This is one of those self-help tools that I initially poo-pooed but have come to recognise as a very handy little helper. My first thoughts on journalling was that it all felt a bit like channelling my teenage angst of old and pouring out my Soul. Well, the clue is in that sentence - "Soul." Journalling is an excellent way of establishing a connection with our emotions and thoughts, gaining clarity, and forming a deeper connection with our Soul. It enables us to develop a solid relationship with our sense of self, increases our self-awareness and emotional intelligence. Simply put, journalling helps us get to know ourselves better, and why we do the shit we do.

What I love about this practice is that there's no right way to go about it. Some people do it daily, others every now and then. I have periods where I write regularly, and sometimes there are longer gaps in my writing, but on the whole, at some point or another, I will circle back to it because it helps me to sift through all of the stuff that life throws at me and stop my mind from whirring. I often find that once thoughts are on paper it's like a release. They take up less space in my head, create less noise, and I can see more clearly how to make decisions, making it a great stress reliever.

Writing my shit down has been especially helpful at the times when I have been depressed. I use the pages of my journal to say all the things that I need to say without running the risk of loved ones thinking I'm about to remove myself from this world. It gives me a safe space to voice my inner thoughts and all the stuff I need to get out of my head but am not particularly keen on another person hearing.

Journalling has also helped me to track my progress and encouraged me to keep going. When I look back at the pages of my old journals, I am able to recognise how far I have come. This has proved to be really useful when I've had the kind of day when I feel like I'm getting nowhere and can't seem to keep up the momentum I need to push forward. I love the freedom of writing stuff down too, and the fact it doesn't even have to make sense. It's the perfect opportunity to release pent-up feelings and thoughts without any limits or judgements. I have found that when I remember to, venting on paper is much healthier than venting out loud, taking it out on another person, or typing a comment on social media that I might later regret. I once filled a page with scrawled expletives - it was a very cathartic experience!

For me, journalling isn't just about writing about what's going wrong or what's stressing me out, it's also a tool to help me to recognise the good stuff in life and to identify what skills I have for managing situations and life. When I write about how I feel, what I think, how I've behaved, etc., I am creating a record of an event or an experience from which I can gain valuable insight. I can learn what works and what doesn't, what helps or what hinders my way through life, what makes me feel good or what makes me uncomfortable. This is an excellent way for me to build up my emotional resilience and create a road map to help me navigate any future difficult situations - it helps me to recognise my inner superpowers.

Over the years I have learned that questioning myself, practising self-enquiry within the pages of a journal, is a great way for me to increase my self-awareness. So many times, it has helped me to question what I truly want and need. It has enabled me to connect with myself in ways I might not have been able to do if I was just to sit with my thoughts. Ways such as being able to determine if the stuff I was doing and thinking were a true reflection of myself, or if were coming from someplace else - other people's expectations, conditioning, inherited beliefs, etc. All the kind of things that had the potential to impact on how I was living my life and influence my wellbeing. Over time, I have learned that when I act out of a place that is more of a reflection of my Authentic-Self I tend to have fewer stressors, conflicts, and negative emotional reactions. I also tend to make healthier choices that have a much more positive effect on my health and wellbeing. Getting stuff down on paper helps me to see to sort through everything that is going on around me and make sense of it. This has always been particularly useful in difficult and challenging times.

Lastly, journalling is just a lovely way of reminding myself that even on the shittiest of days, there are still some things that are good in life and things I am grateful for. Whenever I journal, no matter what I have been writing about, I end with three things that I am grateful for. This helps to reset my mindset to a more optimistic mode, it helps me to reconnect with the stuff that is going right in my life, and to reframe anything that isn't.

If you want to give it a go but are unsure how to get started with journalling, then enlist the help of Mr. Google and search "journalling prompts" or check out the info in "Helpful Websites and Stuff.

THAT LOVING FEELING

You've probably seen 101 quotes about self-love, and while it may seem a bit whimsical, the power of self-love is something that can be overlooked when we are endeavouring to improve our health. Loving ourselves and being compassionate towards one's self definitely has a place in the healing process.

Fostering a greater level of self-love helps with healing process simply because when we love our self, we tend to engage less in behaviour that is detrimental to our wellbeing. Self-love increases our feelings of self-worth, making us more likely to seek out experiences and make choices that are healthier for us. When we place more value on ourselves, we tend to care more about how we treat our body, and just as importantly, how we let others treat us. We become much better at creating and maintaining boundaries and recognising the things that are no longer serving us well. We also become much more comfortable and confident about putting ourselves first - something which is incredibly important when healing.

Self-love is to love oneself on a Soul level; truly love the essence of ourselves. Being kind, compassionate, and our very own cheerleader places us in a more harmonious state with our inner self and with life in general, which has a wonderful ripple effect of making us that little bit nicer to the people around us. A healthier relationship with our self tends to create less internal conflict and tension, which can see a reduction in overall stress and healthier daily interaction with others – basically, the bottom line is when we're not being such an arsehole to ourselves and others, it makes for a much more content and peaceful life!

The great thing about loving and appreciating ourselves more is that we become less critical, exhibit less judgemental behaviours, and become more open to new experiences, which again can help the healing process along. When less energy is spent in unhelpful negative behaviour it leaves space for more positive, beneficial actions, thoughts, and behaviour to enter our lives.

Although on paper it seems a relatively simple process, self-love is not always an easy thing to practice. Wouldn't it be great if we could wake up one day and decide to fully and unconditionally love ourselves? After all, we are often quick to fall in love with other people, places, or things. Sadly, for a lot of us, self-love is something that needs to be worked at rather than something that is natural or second nature. I have often wondered why, when it comes to partners, children, pets, and even our favourite holiday destinations, we seem to feel less encumbered in vocalising our love. How it seems much easier to compliment or show compassion to others than it does to ourselves. Be honest, when was the last time you looked at yourself in the mirror and said, "I love you?" I know that until I started healing, I had never once looked at myself with even half the love I felt for others. In fact, when I was really sick, I went in the opposite direction by damning myself at every opportunity.

To me, this all seems a bit fucked up. We somehow seem to have got this love thing all turned around. There this sort of unspoken acceptance that while it's okay to love everyone and everything else, it's not quite so okay to love ourselves with that same level of intensity. When you really think about it, how crazy is that notion? Surely, we should start with loving ourselves before giving it out to others. We should be our own favourite person, loving and liking ourselves in the way we do all the other stuff in our lives.

I personally didn't get off to a great start with this self-loving thing. I grew up with the notion that loving yourself too much was not really the done thing. It was deemed a somewhat conceited act, that thinking too much of yourself would lead to you becoming "too big for your boots" or getting "ideas above your station." I just knew from an early age that being described as someone who loves themselves was NOT a compliment. It was only through self-awareness work that I came to recognise that these weren't my own thoughts on the subject, but a belief I had constructed from the images, messages, and opinions received from others.

My relationship history with myself has not always been a good one. Like many people, I could be my harshest critic, quick to bring myself down or criticise what I had or hadn't done and behaving in ways towards myself that I wouldn't dream of doing towards others. In the years leading up to illness, my lack of self-love was an extension of my lack of self-worth. When I became sick, it was a simple skip, hop, and jump to blaming my body for letting me down. Sadly, it felt more natural to turn against myself than it did to start being more loving and self-compassionate. When I started to get my emotional shit together, I could see how this attitude was detrimental to my recovery. Once I began to be kinder to myself, to love myself more, to forgive myself, I saw changes on both a psychological and physical level. As I began to progress further, I came to realise showing myself a little more compassion and self-love was a key element of my healing.

My own level of self-love is still a work in progress. Sometimes I seem to have grasped it, other times feels it a little more elusive. Over time, I have learnt that some days loving myself just flows and on other days it is something I have to actively practice or remind myself to do.

Below is a list of stuff that has helped me to feel more loving towards myself over the years.

My self-love self-help list:

- Identifying and appreciating the qualities I possess.
- Forgiving myself.
- Learning to be ok with my faults and quirks.
- Knowing that I'm not always lovable and that's all right.
- Thanking my body for getting me through each day no matter what my level of health is.
- Praising myself for weathering personal crises.
- Learning to recognise what others love about me.
- Being compassionate towards myself and not just others.
- Saying no to things and experiences that don't fit in with my own values or plans.
- Seeking things and experiences that inspire and uplift me.
- Learning to trust and believe in my own courage, ideas, and intuition.
- Learning that other people's poor behaviour towards me is not a reflection of my worth - they are just being a shit.
- Creating personal mantras.
- Practising EFT- Emotional Freedom Technique
- Mirror work by Louise Hay (see "Helpful Websites and Stuff" section)

Of course, our ability to self-love is often wrapped up in and stifled by what I call our life layers, our upbringing, how we rate ourselves and the world around us, life events/experiences, and more. This is why it is crucial to liberate ourselves from the weight of our emotional baggage - we need self-love to help us to connect with our Soul and our sense of self so we can build another one of those foundational blocks which enable us to live a more emotionally balanced and healthier life.

YOGA

I have already mentioned yoga as being beneficial to my physical recovery, but I am just going to give it a few lines in this section too because the practice is as good for the Soul as it is for the Mind and Body. Yoga gives us the time and space to connect with our self on all three levels. It helps us to create a personal environment of peace and contentment that balances the interconnected energy centres (the Chakras) within the body and stills the mind. It creates a window of time where we can switch our focus from all the external demands that everyday life places on us. It turns our focus inward so we can connect more easily with our Authentic-Self. Although I practice yoga at home, it is my weekly yoga session where I see the most benefit. For an hour and a half each week I can totally switch off everything that is going on around me, tune into my body, and strengthen myself on all levels.

ENERGY HEALING AND GOOD VIBRATIONS

This subject could have easily been placed in all three sections of this book due to its far-reaching benefits on all levels. I have chosen to place it here in the Soul section because this is where I feel an important connection lies - our physical bodies cannot be in existence without our Soul acting as the connection between our physical form and Universal energy.

Energy healing spans many cultures and there are many different modalities within this area with numerous practitioners offering services ranging from reiki to rituals to cranial sacral therapy. There are far too many techniques for me to cover in this book, so I have included a link in the "Useful Websites and Stuff" section that has a list of 50 energy modalities for those wishing to delve deeper into this subject.

Although I have dipped in and out of this healing modality over the years, it has only been in the last 12 months that I have seriously explored this area to help rebalance and boost my general wellbeing. Energy healing has proved to be hugely beneficial and is added to my "wished I tried it sooner" list. It is also one of those areas that really highlights just how everything is interconnected when it comes to holistic health and how by working on one aspect of your health you can influence another. I have discovered that energetic healing has been one of those things I have inadvertently been working on while practicing other things - sometimes you're healing even when you don't know you are!

The subject of our energetic field, like a lot of subjects, can be complex and I cannot profess to understand all the different ways different cultures interpret where energy comes from and how it flows through our physical bodies. I can only base my writing on my own understanding of how I think this slightly weird but amazing aspect of our existence works.

When I talk about vibrational energy to a lot of people, they get that kind of glazed-over look, and I strongly suspect there is some inner eye rolling going on too, because for some, this is just one step too far on the woo-woo scale. But the reality is our energy field and raising our vibration is all about the science.

A 2002 study by Dr. David Hawkins is just one modern study that concluded that every human being has a personal frequency (energetic field), and it is this energy that can determine what other energies, circumstances, people, and experiences come into our lives. (Law of Attraction).

So, how this all works is that our energy field acts like one big ole magnet, attracting things, people, etc., who are operating on a similar or compatible frequency. Now, this may all sound a bit too "out there" for some, but if we change our frequency, if we raise our vibration, we can attract into our lives the things that will increase our level of wellbeing.

I know, try to resist that eye roll, hang in for a minute longer, and hear me out. I'm not saying we can totally heal ourselves (although it may be possible) just by upping our vibration, but we can use it as a self-help tool to aid the healing process. You see, our vibration frequency is not set in stone, it is something that can fluctuate, and can change according to our mindset, thoughts, actions, behaviour, and experiences. (I promise you, this is science, not all woo-woo.)

As I have touched on in other sections as human beings, we are multi-dimensional with an energy system that is made up of different frequencies. Our physical body only takes on a solid tangible form because of what frequency the energy that we are made up of is vibrating at. There's no getting away from it. It's a scientific fact that everything in our world, on our planet, is vibrating. We can't see it with the human eye, but everything from the pen on our desk to the food we eat to our own body is in a constant vibrational state. How? Because everything single thing, us included, is held together by atoms and energy. And what's more, everything is vibrating at a different level and emitting a certain frequency. In plain English, this means we and everything on this planet is vibrating and has a frequency (soundwave) that is unique.

There is so much more to us than this one solid form, we are also made up of a other subtle energies that we cannot physically see because they are vibrating at a faster frequencies – if you don't believe me on this one then check out whatshisname, you know that guy who knew a lot about this kind of stuff, small fella, white hair…Oh yeah, that's right, Albert Einstein.

Now, as humans some of us (particularly in the West) can be a bit wary or sceptical of shit we can't see. We love to see evidence that stuff exists and tend to be more comfortable with the things that we can physically see and touch. Therefore, when it comes to healing our focus is generally fixed on making the physical body better, but working on our subtle energy systems and working with Universal energy can have a profound impact on our health and wellbeing too.

As we all know, when we are sick, we are not happy bunnies, which of course is totally understandable. However, being in this state does have a big impact on our vibrational energy. Being angry, sad, frustrated, etc., places us in a low frequency where, quite frankly, all the other shit things like to live.

To give a simple demonstration: you know those days (I'm sure you do) where something goes wrong with your morning that sets the tone for the rest of your day? Those days where things just refuse to go your way on all levels, with one crappy thing piling up on top of another? Well, replace the word "tone" with "frequency." Those morning dramas, disasters, crises, complete fuckups, and such create a low vibrational frequency. When we become stuck in that frequency, we might well wear a giant magnet on our head with a sign reading "more crap things this way."

This is not to say everything bad that happens to us is our fault. Nobody asks for or wants bad stuff to happen. Sometimes it just does. I am simply pointing out the science behind the Law of Vibration and Attraction and how raising our vibration can help us to attract things into our lives that are going to make it feel a whole heap better.

Okay, if you're still with me, let's just take this a little step further. It is also known that our emotions, thoughts, or states of being can impact on our vibrational frequency. As you can imagine, joy, contentment, gratitude, love is the stuff that raises our vibe, and things like sadness, anger, frustration, grief, etc., lower it. This is a kind of extension to the mind-body connection we looked at earlier in the book, in the sense that our thoughts and emotions can not only have an impact on our physical body, but also the vibrational frequency we are operating at, therefore influencing what we attract into our lives.

Not quite signing up to this theory? Then let me just drop another little science bomb... research at the HeartMath Institute has documented exactly what gratitude looks like on an EEG. Believe it or not, gratitude can actually be seen on a machine that measures frequencies. Surely, I'm not alone in thinking it's amazing that our emotions emit frequencies! If we go back to the mind-body connection, we know how expressing gratitude can positively impact on the physical body - vibrational energy and the mind-body connection are like two cogs in the same wellbeing machine. Expressing gratitude helps to up our vibe too – I told you all this was connected!

While our thoughts and emotions can alter our vibe, there are also many external experiences and things that can shift our vibrational frequency to the higher end of the scale too. Certain types of music, being out in nature, doing things that bring us joy, being creative, surrounding ourselves with positive, uplifting people, and amazingly, even the food we eat can raise or lower our vibration.

The thing that I find so cool thing about this whole vibe and energy stuff is that we have control over it. We can actively choose to raise our vibe, change our energy, and when used as part of a holistic approach to wellbeing, it can make a difference to our health. I do know that when you're feeling sick day in and day out that it can be so hard to feel upbeat. I know how easy it is to slip into an illness apathy and feel as if you can't be fucked to do anything. Believe me, I've been there and got the t-shirt. The trick with this vibe stuff is like everything in the book: start off slowly. Do one thing each day, every day, that will help raise your vibe. You might not feel like it but do it anyway. The "fake it until you feel it" rule applies here. Make it a daily habit, part of your new routine, and eventually, that brain of yours will start looking forward to it and responding and those vibes will be on the up and your energetic life force will begin to flow more freely.

As I mentioned I've been unknowingly reaping the benefits of energy healing through some of my other practices, but in the last year my intentional area of focus has been to work on raising my energetic frequency, increasing the flow of energy through my being on all levels and ramping up my connection with Universal energy.

Energy healing is something that I plan on delving much deeper into as I am intrigued by the possibilities this has to offer from a healing perspective as well as the impact it could have on my life in general. I don't have a huge amount of experience in this area to report, but from the few techniques and practices I have applied the result has been significant, therefore it thoroughly deserves a shout out. To date, from my own personal experience, it has worked really well for anxiety, calming my nervous system, and making me feel strengthening and rebalance in general. It's hard to explain, but I do feel as if my brain has been rewired, I don't have some of the same thought patterns as I did previously (REBT helped tremendously with this too). I also feel physically different, much more energised and warmer - for someone who's always had cold hands and feet this is a blessing. If I focus my mind, I can actually feel the energy within my body and detect which areas it feels the strongest - who knows, maybe I'll make a Jedi yet!

Below are just a few of the things that can help raise our vibrational energy. As you can see, a lot of things on this list of cross over with things throughout the rest of the book - these are all things I have personally used or worked on.

- Practice gratitude.
- Doing what you love.
- Eat more unprocessed organic stuff & stay hydrated - limit caffeine and alcohol.
- Meditate/visualisation.
- Use essential oils - each oil has its own frequency!
- Take an Epsom salt or Dead Sea salt bath.
- Digital detox - have a day or at least a few hours unplugged from technology.
- Grounding.
- Sing.
- Listen to music that you feel connected to and resonates with your Soul.
- Dance.
- Use positive affirmations/mantras.
- Upping the self-care on all levels
- Decluttering your environment.
- Where possible, stay away from the shit, people, environments that bring you down or drain your energy.
- Getting out in nature.

- Qi Gong & Tai Chi.

ME SPACE

In the alternative world, you will see articles and hear talk of how to create sacred space. This a practice that focuses on enhancing spirituality and connection, the creation of a space where we can connect with our Soul; the idea being that when we have a designated calm space, away from distractions for contemplation, meditation, and such, it is easier to connect with who we really are - our Authentic-Self.

I think that the term "sacred space" can feel a little too New Age for some, evoking images of joss sticks, sage burning, altars, and crystals. That can certainly be a part of it, but if a person isn't into that side of things it can be a bit off-putting, which is a shame because so much can be gained from creating a personal space. Therefore, I prefer to think of it as creating a "Me Space."

Having personal space is about all about connection with self. It is a space where we can shut off from all the expectations and demands of others and be our true selves: a place to relax in, meditate, read, listen to music, create stuff, journal, do the stuff we love, or simply take time out to reflect on how we are feeling - all the things that enable us to connect with who we are.

In today's world, we can be so busy, so involved with our day to day, giving a lot of ourselves to external stuff, that it's good for us to have a place to come back home to. When I say "home," I do mean from a soul perspective. If the connection with your Soul doesn't float your boat, then just go with the notion that creating a space that is just for us can have a really positive effect on our general well-being. It can be a place of comfort; a mood and vibe booster. It can provide a sanctuary within our own home, a little oasis of calm where we can go to deal with stress or overwhelm and practice all the techniques that can help strengthen our Mind and Body too.

A "Me Space" sends a healing message. If we make a conscious effort to ensure that space we create is a place of self-care, a space for doing things that boost our wellbeing (not somewhere we go to sit and think how crap we feel), then in our minds it becomes synonymous with healing - the place we go to feel better. This helps to reinforce a healthy mindset and a positive mind-body connection.

Creating a personal space is a fairly easy process, yet it is one of those things that can be empowering and instantly mood boosting. If a person has a whole spare room they can convert, then they've hit the jackpot. There's nothing like shutting the door on the demands of the outside world for a while! However, if like many people's houses, there just isn't the extra room, then a little space of our own can still be achieved by simply commandeering a corner of a room and declaring it our "Me space."

Our personal space doesn't necessarily need to be confined to indoors, either. We can create an outdoor space too, or both! Wherever our space ends up, the key is to make it solely for us and make that non-negotiable. Nobody else gets to hang out in the space unless invited to do so. It will not have the same vibe or effect on our wellbeing if we come home to find kids lolling around in it or someone chowing biscuits and spraying crumbs everywhere.

Below are a few tips for creating a "Me Space"

- **Seating** - Buy a chair you really love, re-cover an existing one, or just use a gorgeous throw to refresh a current piece of furniture. Buying new or refreshing items brings in a whole new vibe. You don't want to be sitting in a chair where you wept yourself senseless when the cat died. If you like to sit or lie on the floor, then choose a special cushion with a design that reflects your personality. Even a yoga mat will do, just make sure you can sit comfortably.

- **Just You** - Own the space, use it as a place to read, relax, journal, meditate, or reflect. Think of your space as a place of good vibes and intentions, a place you can go to refresh your energy. Place objects in there that bring you joy and inspiration, like a treasured photo, your favourite books, a beautiful decorative item. Make sure that every object, colour, and scent reflects you and is based on what you love. Remember this space is just for you. Tell other family members to "do one" and make it clear that you don't want to find them lounging around in your space.

- **Nature** - Plants and fresh flowers can also make a great addition. Plants help oxygen levels, and flowers bring a splash of colour and fragrance to a space. Images of nature can also help to raise the vibe. Collect shells, stones, etc., and make a creative display. The key is to go with whatever resonates with your personality and brings happy thoughts to mind.

- **Lighting** - A "Me Space" is all about creating the right vibe, so consider what kind of lighting you'd like to create the right atmosphere. Think low-level lamps and candles to give off a beautiful soft glow. You might even choose some fairy lights or create your space by a window for natural light. Just to note: a red light and a window is probably not a great combo!

- **Scent** - A lovely fragrant space can make all the difference to your mood and energy levels. Place an essential oil diffuser or a naturally scented candle in your space and reap the benefits of aromatherapy by choosing scents to either energise, uplift, or relax you – make sure you stay away from synthetic fragrances, air fresheners, etc.

- **Keep it cosy** - Having a cosy environment can be super restful and comforting. Consider the furnishings that will best add to the general loveliness of your space – soft, tactile blankets and squishy cushions. Try to keep fabrics natural and pick different sorts of textures… you're looking for that "ah bliss" factor when you enter your space.

- **Keep it clean & tidy** - Keep your space clutter-free and clean to keep the positive energy flowing. Clutter, dirt, and dust lowers vibrational energy. If you are using the space for crafting or creating, have boxes or a cupboard to pop all your bits and pieces in to help keep an open feel.

PART 5: CHAPTER 33

QUESTIONS I'VE BEEN ASKED, AND THINGS I'VE HEARD

In this last section of the book are the things that people have asked me, said to me, or I've heard on the subject of healing over the years. Some of my responses to this stuff might raise a few eyebrows or sound a little bit on the harsh side, but if you haven't caught on by now, I'm a straight-talking kind of gal.

You're so lucky that you've been able to heal...

Honestly, this one is an absolute corker; I've had a few people say this to me, and every time I've had to curb my immediate reaction and refrain from suggesting they get their coat and fuck right off. Luck has nothing to do with it. I didn't miraculously stumble across a magic cure. Last time I looked I hadn't been paid a visit from the good health fairy, nor have I ever been granted three wishes.

Lucky is winning the lottery, surviving your parachute not opening, or narrowly avoiding being hit by a speeding car. Healing is not lucky, it's self-responsibility, taking the bull by the horns, and fucking hard work. Sure, I have been blessed to have encountered some amazing people that have helped steer me in the right direction, but it has been me hauling my arse off of the sofa and taking action that has opened up space for these people to come into my life.

This statement appears first on the list of this section because I want to dispel a myth that I just got lucky or health was gifted to me. I want to dismiss any notion that regaining a sound level of health was just a fluke and not something that could happen for others. Healing cannot happen without work, period. That is as simple as it gets. We don't get results through luck; we get results through action.

You mustn't have had it that bad...

I think that everyone is unique in their experience of illness, so it seems pointless to try to gauge where I was at on the scale of symptoms, level of pain and such compared to other people. All I can say on this subject is that at times I found symptoms debilitating and after mapping my personal route to illness I can now see that I was experiencing ill health many years before I reached the point of diagnosis.

Below is the list of symptoms that I experienced prior and after diagnosis.

- Weakened immune system
- Chronic fatigue
- Over sensitivity to smells, noises and medication
- Food sensitivities
- Gastritis
- Silent reflux
- Bloating
- Chronic dry cough
- Sore throat
- Blurred vision and watering eyes.
- Eye pain and twitches
- Constipation
- Migraines
- Chronic headaches
- Dizziness
- Unsteady on feet
- Nausea
- Painful scalp, sore skin
- Insomnia
- Muscle pain and joint pain
- Stiffness
- Weakness
- Shooting, stabbing pains in jaw, joints and extremities
- Muscle twitching and spasms
- Restless legs
- Frequent urination
- Vibrating, tingling and buzzing sensations on random parts of the body
- Crawling sensation over skin
- Numbness, pins and needles, feeling of something crawling under the skin
- Itching
- Hives
- Feeling like I was tremoring inside, jerky movements
- Poor temperature control, cold hands and feet
- Depression
- Anxiety
- Panic attacks
- Mood swings
- Brain fog- problems recalling words, poor concentration, not able to think clearly, forgetting train of thought mid-sentence. Walking around in a daze
- Painful and heavy menstruation
- Painful glands
- Poor exercise tolerance
- Poor stress response

Isn't it expensive? / I can't afford to get well...

The answer to this question is yes and no. Not having the money to do the stuff that you know will help you to heal totally sucks. There is no doubt in my mind that I would have been able to take a few shortcuts on the road to health had I had more funds to throw at the cause. However, I also think that sometimes the more money you have for this stuff, the easier it is to get caught up with trying this and that and to fall down healing rabbit holes.

In the past my funding limitations meant that I had to spend wisely, I had to research and make sure that what I was spending my money on was really going to be of benefit. I believe this helped me to sort some of the wheat from the chaff. I couldn't afford to be blasé with my spending so I didn't get hooked into the quick-fix type of protocols or spend money on the huge amounts of supplements I see some people taking by using the "I'll just see if it might help" approach.

Of course, there are many things I would have liked to have tried that I know would have benefited me: stuff like regular massages, reflexology, and acupuncture, etc., or being able to afford more regular testing to track my progress, but you know, sometimes in life you have to go with and work with what you've got available to you.

With healing, you have to make sacrifices. I have often heard people say that they can't afford to get well. While yes, I am absolutely sure there are people out there who literally have no spare cash at all to divert to their health care, there are also a lot of people who don't have it because they're spending out on other shit. These are the people who I address this to. Are you ready for some straight-talking, people? If you are spending money on clothes, on holidays, on tattoos, on takeaways, on eating out, on days out, on visits to the coffee shop, on alcohol, on the cinema, then you have money to heal. The uncomfortable truth is you're just not keen on diverting your money to pay for the less nice stuff in life.

You know, I get it, all that stuff is way nicer than getting tested, having an osteopathic treatment, or buying monthly probiotics, but at the end of the day, all of that stuff might make you temporarily feel better, but it won't make you well. This may sound harsh, but when that enjoyable double mocha latte with cream on the top moment is over, you will still be sick. I hate to break it to you, but as crap as it is, this healing thing comes down to priorities - ditch the mocha and buy something that will help you to heal.

At one point while I was healing, I didn't buy new clothes for a year (cue the violins). I also had blood tests in lieu of birthday and Christmas gifts... That was not fun or sexy, but it was a must. I needed to heal, healing was my priority, so for a while, days out, holidays, new clothes, etc., were put on hold because at the time these were the places that I could divert the cash from.

I also hear a lot of how it's too expensive to eat healthily. Yes, to some degree I go along with that school of thought. Processed and convenience food is often much cheaper than a lot of the fresh and organic food. I, for one, haven't always been able to afford to eat as much organic food as I would like, so my way around this was to decide what I prioritised from a health perspective. For me, it was important to eat organic meat, eggs, butter, and certain fruits and vegetables. To be able to afford this I ate less meat and made cheaper vegetable-based meals. I added to my store cupboard one item at a time until I had a stock of healthier basics. I went without those more enjoyable things in life to fund the stuff that was going to get me well. Again, not fun, but it was something that needed to be done in order for me to regain my health.

Although when trying to heal organic is the best option, I do also believe that a switch to eating any fresh unprocessed food is going to be better for a person's health than sticking with convenience processed food.

One tip for getting into the right mindset and budgeting for buying products/ services for healing is to work out how much it would cost you daily. E.g when you work out visiting the osteopath twice a month would initially cost £3.20 per day (less once visits get further apart) .This helps you to compare it to some of the other things you may be buying on a daily basis and consider whether you can adjust your priorities.

I don't have the time/energy to heal...

Hear that noise? That is my BS meter going off. Yes siree, I'm calling BS on no time to heal. We all have the same number of hours in the day. What we choose to do with that time outside of our non-negotiable tasks and responsibilities is what counts.

Now, I totally appreciate when people are working and struggling with fatigue, taking on something else is time and energy consuming, but again, this comes down to priorities. If we were to rephrase and change that statement to "It's not a priority for me to heal," then that puts a whole different slant on things, doesn't it? Saying that doesn't feel quite so comfortable. Often saying, "I don't have the time" is a cop-out. (I'm sorry, another tough love moment coming up.) If you watch Netflix, spend time on social media, socialise, etc., then you have time to assign to healing. No, cooking a healthy meal isn't as entertaining as "Game of Thrones," but it's going to be better for you in the long run (psst try watching programmes AND cooking or prepping).

When I first started out healing, I had chronic fatigue so my energy levels were somewhere down in my boots. Did I feel like preparing healthy meals? Fuck no, I wanted to wang a piece of white bread in the toaster, smother it with marmite, drag myself back to the sofa and watch "Criminal Minds." But when I realised I needed to do this shit, I made it my priority. I sat down to chop my veggies, I enlisted help, and I cooked in bulk, so I didn't have to do it all the time and had a stock of 'go to' foods. And I ate a lot of the same food! - boring but effective.

A lot of healing comes back around to being willing to ask for help, setting boundaries, and prioritising. It's surprising what people will do to help you if you just ask. Saying no to other people and having firm boundaries as to what you are prepared to give can help free up valuable time and energy that you can use to focus on yourself. Unfortunately, sometimes we also need to place our healing above doing some of the stuff we find more enjoyable. The way I used to get my mindset on board with this was that I would tell myself how much more I would enjoy doing things when I was healthier.

I've tried EVERYTHING and I'm still not well…

My answer to people who say this to me is a blunt, "No. No, you haven't." Nobody has tried EVERYTHING, and there is always something else to try - a different avenue to explore. What this usually means when people say this is it FEELS like they have tried everything. More often than not, when trying to fix ourselves we dabble, we try a bit of this and a bit of that, and we don't give stuff long enough to work before moving on to the next thing. Why? Because we're so fucking desperate for it all to go away. In our haste we search for the latest miracle cure, we emulate what others have done to heal, and we get frustrated when it doesn't work in the same way for us. What this all really means is that we haven't found the right pieces for our individual health puzzle… yet.

Healing is really frustrating, sometimes. It can feel like we're going around in circles, but it's important to stay consistent, work from the whole-body perspective, and learn what works for us as an individual. Yes, this does, unfortunately, mean a trial and error process - sometimes we need to know what doesn't work for us so we can discover what does.

I tried that natural alternative stuff and it didn't work...

This one of the most common things I've heard while taking the alternative path. While it's true not everything works for everyone and things work differently for different people, most of the time when people say this it's not the full picture. On closer inspection, a lot of the time it turns out that folks are trying to use alternative/natural stuff as standalone treatments, taking just one or two things to address a symptom. Holistic/alternative healing does not work this way.

When I've had these conversations with people, I have often found that when I dig a little deeper, I discover that they have often not incorporated it into their life for long enough, are not taking a whole person approach (addressing all areas) or are constantly flitting between stuff; e.g., I hear a lot of women say, that they have tried the natural route to deal with menopausal symptoms. When you explore the subject further you discover that they bunged in a bit of maca powder here and there, dabbled in black cohosh with red raspberry leaf, or tried an off-the-shelf supplement from their local Boots. Although there are some who are fortunate to see a lessening of symptoms, doing things this way often doesn't work long term. Healing properly requires monitoring and adjustments to meet our individual needs as we go along the process. Sometimes we need to bring in the experts because taking standardised doses from off-the-shelf products or self-regulation just doesn't cut it.

When it comes to alternative healing, patience and commitment are the words of the day. It takes a whole lot of time to rebalance things that have been off kilter for many years or maybe even a lifetime. A thing many people overlook when dismissing the alternative approach is the little signs that the body is starting to heal. When we are sick, we want it fixed and we want it fixed now. More often than not we focus on the big things, the issues that are causing us the most pain or are in the foreground - the symptoms shouting the loudest. With alternative healing, sometimes it's the very things you are desperate to see the back of that are the last to leave the party. The health issues with the biggest voices tend to drown out the other 101 little voices that are signalling that the body is working hard behind the scenes and that things are improving. It is often these little things that get fixed first, and if somebody is not paying attention, not tuning in to the subtleties of what's going on with their Body, Mind, and Soul, they can miss the signposts that things are beginning to heal - a shout out to self-awareness

The very first thing that showed my body was healing was my eyebrows! I kid you not, here I was fatigued beyond fatigue, stomach issues, pains, brain fog, the whole kit and kaboodle, and the first sign that a shift towards better health was being made was the outer edges of my eyebrows grew in. For as long as I could remember the outer edges of my eyebrows were non-existent. I just thought I was a person who had short, thin eyebrows, so you can imagine my surprise at finding myself sporting a set of full-length, rather luxurious brows in my late 30's. Were magnificent brows on my list? Of course not, but that's what I got, and what it meant for me was that my thyroid function and my hormonal balance was improving.

What I'm trying to demonstrate with my little eyebrow story is that healing alternatively can be full of surprises. It's not always immediately obvious there has been a shift towards better health, which is why it is important to be self-aware and really get to know our body so that we can track progress, celebrate the small things, and as they say, "keep the faith."

I feel worse since I started on alternative healing...

Yep, there's no getting away from it, this shit can happen. I always think healing is a bit like unpacking a suitcase on arrival home from holiday; piles of shit everywhere, it's messy, it's chaotic, it can feel like an overwhelming task, but as we methodically work through it, stuff finds its place and everything settles. You see, the thing is, healing is not a linear process. There is no straight line to wellness. Some people find the road to health is reasonably smooth, but for others it can be bumpy or a rollercoaster of a ride. Sometimes we can feel worse as we begin to peel back the layers and address years of issues and imbalances. At times, it can feel like we are doubling back on ourselves or taking one step forward and two back as issues we thought we'd resolved circle back around.

In natural healing, it is expected that the body will experience some turbulence or other. There can be flare-ups or an initial worsening of symptoms as the body releases and clears toxins. You will often hear these stages referred to as a healing crisis, aggravation, or reaction. As scary as it can sound or feel, it doesn't mean things are not working. Sometimes it's a signal that we need to back off a little, that maybe we've gone in too hard or fast with certain things. Other times, we just need to buckle up, sit tight, up our self-care, and take extra measures to support ourselves during this time. There's no doubt that peeling back the layers and re-aligning ourselves can throw up some weird shit, so sometimes it's good to go with the notion of "expect the unexpected" because healing can also have this uncanny ability to highlight other areas in our lives that need attention or re-evaluating.

In alternative healing, there is also something called "retracing." The jury is out as to whether this is a thing, but having personally experienced it, and having heard many other accounts, I'm putting it out there as a possibility. Retracing is where the body can revisit old imbalances, infections, viruses, emotional issues, and injuries. It is believed to be the body's way of fully healing by revisiting things in order to properly heal them. I feel that it's important when dealing with what feels like a "setback" to remember that it can be a normal part of the healing process. A process where we need to pull everything out and deal with it before we can settle into a new, healthier state. It does, however, need to be said that common sense should be applied when healing and care should be taken not to allow reactions to get out of hand – remember, slowly does it is the best and safest route.

Healing reactions are probably one of the major reasons that people give up on alternative healing. If we have been used to following the conventional path, healing this way requires us to take a different perspective. When thinking in the conventional way we tend to have the expectation that if we take some form of action/treatment we'll feel better. When this doesn't immediately happen, as is often the case on the alternative path, we can leap to the conclusion that it's not working or that it's too hard to continue. The key to keeping on track is to know that reactions, crises, etc., are temporary and we do eventually pop out the other side. This might take anything from a few hours to a few days, a few weeks, or a few months - a large dose of patience and consistency is required for this journey.

If you are finding the thought of going through something like this too daunting, then let me remind you that this can also be the case with conventional treatment. Many medications or courses of treatments produce side effects that can cause all manner of reactions that can take months or longer to adjust to. Thyroid medication, for example, can sometimes take a couple of years to find the right balance.

The truth is, there's no escaping the fact that healing is a commitment. It will not work if you do not fully commit to the process. Good health is not something that will come knocking on your door. It requires the right mindset, action, consistency, and patience. There will, without doubt, be times where you feel you can't go on, when you will want to throw your toys out the pram and lament the skies. There will be times when you might have to dig deeper than maybe you've ever done before, but I assure you that something better awaits you on the other side, something better than the hamster wheel of symptoms you are currently on.

As a final note, as you move through the healing it's likely that you will experience shifts in other many other areas of your life. Some of them may be profound, some may be a little scary, and some may be utterly, groundbreakingly fabulous!

How long does it take to heal?

Ah, now this question is one of those impossible-to-answer questions. What we have on our hands here is one of those "how long is a piece of string" type of situations. I know, this is probably not what you are wanting to hear, but the outcome depends on so many variables - how long a person has been sick, what their particular issues are, how far they are willing to go, and what level of effort they are prepared to put into their healing.

As you have just read, healing is not a linear process, and it is also a very individual thing. Some people take longer to heal than others, some issues are quickly resolved, and others take longer or may need revisiting further along the process. For me personally, now that I know what I know, I think I could have probably halved the time I have spent on this journey, simply because when I first started out, I had nothing to guide me. Having said that, I am a firm believer in the process, experiences, and being at the place you're in at the time you were meant to be there, so although I could have made some shortcuts, I think there were other things for me to learn from this experience that were bigger than just my physical health.

I cannot say for sure what you will get from your own health journey should you decide to embark on this path, but I stand firm in my belief that whatever is meant for you will unfold in its own good time. If you commit to the process, stick with it, you will gain a greater level of health.

CHAPTER 34

GATHER ROUND

Okay, people, gather round, huddle up, let's have a quick little pep talk before we leave off.

I'm optimistically going with the notion that you found the information in this book useful and I'm also going to take a guess that you may be in one of two places... You might be thinking, "Let's do this," or you might be feeling overwhelmed by the thought of working on everything and not even know where to start. Whichever space you're in, just stick a pin in those thoughts, take a deep breath, and relax - you've got this.

Here's the thing, you do not have to do everything at once. Remember that this book is the culmination of everything that I have been learning and have been working on for years. I hope by now that you have received the memo that this thing is a process and that the "slowly, slowly catchee monkey" approach is what will get you there.

You don't need to immediately book yourself a therapy appointment for any emotional baggage you've been hauling around. In fact, it's a good idea to strengthen the body first with the basics before unearthing some of that deep-sealed stuff. To repeat my earlier advice, give yourself some time to let what you've read sink in, revisit some of the sections, or all of it, until you feel that you have a good understanding, then do what you need to do to get yourself in the right mindset to embark on your first step towards better health.

As humans we often like to complicate stuff. We also have this super annoying hang-over from our ancestral days that makes our brains naturally veer towards the negative side of things (negativity bias). Now is not the time for any of that shit. I admit you've just been handed a ton of info, but don't let overwhelm get in the way of action. I promise you this thing is not as complicated as it seems. Break your intended action into a small, manageable framework, and believe me when I say you are more than capable of making this work for you. Revisit the "If I knew then what I know now" section for a starting point and use the information in the "Useful Websites & Stuff" it's there to guide you and help you to learn.

It's also worth noting that while I have shared how I have healed there are still many other alternative treatments and modalities out there. It's possible that something I haven't explored will be a good fit for you.

One thing I have learnt over the years is that as humans we are totally amazing, and we can achieve totally amazing things. This healing journey could easily be your amazing thing. Remember, it only takes one small action to set something bigger in motion. Be brave enough to take this on, have faith in yourself, and know that you have the ability to heal.

Before I go, I want to leave you with this last thought: Our Mind, Body, and Soul are an intrinsically connected system. We are not just a collection of parts that have nothing to do with each other. This is why taking a Mind, Body, and Soul approach to balancing our lives is the foundation of health, wellness, and fulfilment.

Wishing happy, healthy days.

Marie

x

RESOURCES & NOTES

MIND

Muehsam D. (2014) Life Rhythm as a Symphony of Oscillatory Patterns: Electromagnetic Energy and Sound Vibration Modulates Gene Expression for Biological Signaling and Healing - www.ncbi.nlm.nih.gov/pmc/articles/PMC4010966/

Wilson C. (2011) - www.newscientist.com/article/dn20347-mind-controls-good-vibrations-reach-deep-in-the-brain/ (accessed 08 April 2019)

https://psychcentral.com/blog/words-can-change-your-brain-2/ (accessed 08 April 2019)

Britta K.(2010) Mindfulness practice leads to increases in regional brain gray matter density - www.ncbi.nlm.nih.gov/pmc/articles/PMC3004979/

Franco F. (2018). Childhood Abuse, Complex Trauma and Epigenetics (accessed 08 April 2019) - https://psychcentral.com/lib/childhood-abuse-complex-trauma-and-epigenetics/

Ennis C. (2014) - www.theguardian.com/science/occams-corner/2014/apr/25/epigenetics-beginners-guide-to-everything (accessed 09 April 2019)

Alegia- Torres JA. (20110 Epigenetics and lifestyle. - www.ncbi.nlm.nih.gov/pubmed/22122337

Dube SR. (2009) Cumulative Childhood Stress and Autoimmune Diseases in Adults. - www.ncbi.nlm.nih.gov/pmc/articles/PMC3318917/

Stojanovich L. (2008) stress as a trigger of autoimmune disease. - https://www.ncbi.nlm.nih.gov/pubmed/18190880

www.health.harvard.edu/disease-and-conditions/the-gut-brain-connection (accessed 08 April 2019)

Resnik N. (2018). 5 Scientific Reasons Decluttering Your Home Will Make You Happier. - https://thriveglobal.com/stories/5-scientific-reasons-decluttering-your-home-will-make-you-happier/

Baumeister D. (2016). Childhood trauma and adulthood inflammation: a meta-analysis of peripheral C-reactive protein, interleukin-6 and tumour necrosis factor-α. - www.ncbi.nlm.nih.gov/pmc/articles/PMC4564950/

Liu YZ (2017). Inflammation: The Common Pathway of Stress-Related Diseases. - www.ncbi.nlm.nih.gov/pmc/articles/PMC5476783/

Debbané M. (2017). Brain activity underlying negative self- and other-perception in adolescents: The role of attachment-derived self-representations. - www.ncbi.nlm.nih.gov/pmc/articles/PMC5403860/

Bhattacharya S (2003). Brain study links negative emotions and lowered immunity. - www.newscientist.com/article/dn4116-brain-study-links-negative-emotions-and-lowered-immunity/ (accessed 08 April 2019)

Hampton D (2017). How Your Thoughts Change Your Brain, Cells and Genes. - www.huffpost.com/entry/how-your-thoughts-change-your-brain-cells-and-genes_b_9516176 (accessed 08 April 2019)

Lipton B. (2014) What do you want to learn about the subconscious mind? - www.brucelipton.com/blog/what-do-you-want-learn-about-the-subconscious-mind

Westland F. (2017) Here's How Colours Really Affect Our Brain And Body, According to Science. - www.sciencealert.com/does-colour-really-affect-our-brain-and-body-a-professor-of-colour-science-explains (accessed 08 April 2019)

Coloureffects.co.uk - www.colour-affects.co.uk/psychological-properties-of-colours (accessed 08 April 2019)

Greenberg M. (2015) How Mindfulness Improves Your Brain and Relationships. - www.psychologytoday.com/us/blog/the-mindful-self-express/201509/how-mindfulness-improves-your-brain-and-relationships (accessed 08 April 2019)

Jacobs T. (2015) Evidence Mounts That Mindfulness Breeds Resilience. - https://greatergood.berkeley.edu/article/item/evidence_mounts_that_mindfulness_breeds_resilience (accessed 08 April 2019)

Mcceevey S. 2011 - https://news.harvard.edu/gazette/story/2011/01/eight-weeks-to-a-better-brain/ (accessed o8 April 2019)

BODY

Fields H. (2015). The Gut: Where Bacteria and Immune System Meet. - www.hopkinsmedicine.org/research/advancements-in-research/fundamentals/in-depth/the-gut-where-bacteria-and-immune-system-meet (accessed 20 May 2019).

Elysium health.com The Human Microbiome: Why Scientists Are Searching Your Gut for Cures. https://endpoints.elysiumhealth.com/microbiome-explainer-e345658db2c (accessed 20 May 2019)

Furness JB. (1999). II. The intestine as a sensory organ: neural, endocrine, and immune responses. - www.physiology.org/doi/full/10.1152/ajpgi.1999.277.5.G922

Mcquillan Susan Ms RDN. (2018). https://www.psycom.net/the-gut-brain-connection (accessed 20 May 2019)

Fasarno A. (2011.) Leaky gut and autoimmune disease - https://www.ncbi.nlm.nih.gov/pubmed/22109896

Tlasllova H. (2004) Commensal bacteria (normal microflora), mucosal immunity and chronic. inflammatory and autoimmune diseases - www.ncbi.nlm.nih.gov/pubmed/15158604

Mullan-Muller S. (2008). The Gut Microbiome and Mental Health: Implications for Anxiety- and Trauma-Related Disorders. - www.ncbi.nlm.nih.gov/pubmed/28767318

Sekirov I.(2018). Gut Microbiota in Health and Disease. - https://doi.org/10.1152/physrev.00045.2009

Acheson DW. (2004). Microbial-gut interactions in health and disease. Mucosal immune responses. - www.ncbi.nlm.nih.gov/pubmed/15123077

Marcelo Campos MD (2017). - www.health.harvard.edu/blog/leaky-gut-what-is-it-and-what-does-it-mean-for-you-2017092212451

Goebel A. (2008) Altered intestinal permeability in patients with primary fibromyalgia and in patients with complex regional pain syndrome. - www.ncbi.nlm.nih.gov/pubmed/18540025

Health.harvard.edu - www.health.harvard.edu/diseases-and-conditions/the-gut-brain-connection (accessed 20 May 2019)

https://www.blumhealthmd.com/ (accessed May 2019)

http://www.sassyholistics.com (accessed 20 May 2019)

http://drbrucelipton.com (accessed 20 May 2019)

Blum Susan. M.D M.P.H (2013). The Immune System Recovery Plan 2013) Published by Orion Spring. - https://badgut.org/information-centre/a-z-digestive-topics/the-liver-an-amazing-organ/ (accessed 20 May 2019)

Kesler CT. (2013). Lymphatic vessels in health and disease. - www.ncbi.nlm.nih.gov/pubmed/23209022

Liao S. (2013). Lymphatic function and immune regulation in health. - www.ncbi.nlm.nih.gov/pubmed/24024577

Padera TP. (2016). The Lymphatic System in Disease Processes and Cancer Progression. - www.ncbi.nlm.nih.gov/pmc/articles/PMC4946986/#__ffn_sectitle

Rawls B. (2017) - https://rawlsmd.com/health-article/epstein-barr-virus-a-key-player-in-chronic-illness (accessed 20 May 2019)

'Mono' virus linked to seven serious diseases: Epstein-Barr virus may affect health in more ways than known. (2019). - www.sciencedaily.com/releases/2018/04/180416121606.htm (accessed 20 May 2019)

Jovanović I (1995). The Epstein-Barr virus and chronic fatigue syndrome.- www.ncbi.nlm.nih.gov/pubmed/8643052

Delingpole J. (2019). - www.spectator.co.uk/2019/02/arthritis-nerve-pain-and-chronic-fatigue-my-life-with-lyme-disease/ (accessed 20 May 2019)

www.drlwilson.com/articles/SYMPATHETIC%20DOMINANCE.htm (accessed 20th May 2019)

Vince G (2015) One nerve connects our vital organs, sensing and shaping your health. If we learn to control it, the future of medicine will be electric. https://mosaicscience.com/story/hacking-nervous-system/ (accessed 20May2019)

National Institute of General Medical Sciences (2017). Circadian Rhythms - www.nigms.nih.gov/Education/Pages/Factsheet_CircadianRhythms.aspx (accessed 20 May 2019)

www.fromevalleyosteopaths.com (accessed 20 May 2019)

The beneficial Effects of Negatively Charged Ions on Sleep - www.slumberslumner.com/product_pdf.php?id=653 (accessed 20 May 2019)

Vatansever F. (2012). Far infrared radiation (FIR): its biological effects and medical applications **-** www.ncbi.nlm.nih.gov/pmc/articles/PMC3699878/

Youssef NA. (2018) The Effects of Trauma, with or without PTSD, on the Transgenerational DNA Methylation Alterations in Human Offsprings. www.ncbi.nlm.nih.gov/pmc/articles/PMC5977074/

Babbel S. (2010) The Connections Between Emotional Stress, Trauma and Physical Pain. **-** www.psychologytoday.com/gb/blog/somatic-psychology/201004/the-connections-between-emotional-stress-trauma-and-physical-pain

Oschman JL (2015). The effects of grounding (earthing) on inflammation, the immune response, wound healing, and prevention and treatment of chronic inflammatory and autoimmune diseases. - www.ncbi.nlm.nih.gov/pubmed/25848315

Oschman JL. (2004.) Our place in nature: reconnecting with the Earth for better sleep. - www.ncbi.nlm.nih.gov/pubmed/15650460

Schmid AA. (2019). Yoga improves occupational performance, depression, and daily activities for people with chronic pain. **-** www.ncbi.nlm.nih.gov/pubmed/31156199

Wang C. (2018). Effect of tai chi versus aerobic exercise for fibromyalgia: comparative effectiveness randomized controlled trial. - www.bmj.com/content/360/bmj.k851

Soul

www.heartmathinsitute.com (accessed 29 May2019)

www.thetahealing.com/about-thetahealing/thetahealing-theta-state.html (accessed 29 May 2019)

www.cosmicpineapple.co.uk/wisdom/your-cells-are-listening/(accessed 29 May 2019)

What Does Life Force and Energy Body Mean? - www.gateways-to-inner-peace.com/life-force.html (accessed 29 May 2019)

USEFUL WEBSITE AND STUFF

Below is a list of things that may help you on your healing journey.

WEBSITES

sassyholistics.com -My favourite site. They offer a HTMA test and consult and have some fantastic articles on everything to do with healing naturally. You can also join their FB health group (Mineral Mavens). I recommend the Foundational Care ebook as a good follow on to get you started on healing. (see link in "books")

Dr.Axe.com - Information and articles on healing, nutrition fitness, remedies and natural lifestyle.

Brucelipton.com - stem cell biologist who makes understanding epigenetics and healing easy. Tons of information on energetic healing, how our emotions effect our health, all backed up by science. Plenty of free resources to get you started- guides, podcasts and meditations, YouTube videos

wellnessmama.com - lots of fab tips, recipes, articles, podcasts on living a natural lifestyle and natural health.

Candidaplan.com - articles, resources and info for anyone wanted to delve deeper into candida. https://www.candidaplan.com

APPS

Insight Timer App – downloadable guided meditations, music, talks and courses.

VIDEOS

YouTube videos to help you to delve deeper into some of the topics discussed in this book. YouTube is also an excellent resource for guided meditations, relaxation techniques and visualisations.

How to make an herbal infusion - https://youtu.be/Mj9pO1PNHuI

The Science of Yoga - https://youtu.be/ClbR7odQklk

The Science of Meditation - https://youtu.be/JAJ87Dwmx2E

How Qi Gong can help fibromyalgia - https://youtu.be/8ajznAzYkoE

Rebounding Tutorial - https://youtu.be/U8Blm2irGQE

YouTube is also an excellent resource for guided meditations, relaxation techniques and visualisations

ARTICLES

Further reading to help you to research and plan your return to health- some useful "how to's" for some of the topics discussed in this book.

Elimination diet part 1 **-** https://health.clevelandclinic.org/switch-elimination-diet-fight-chronic-pain/

Elimination diet part 2 - https://www.verywellhealth.com/the-elimination-diet-for-fibromyalgia-cfs-715721

Mineral Balancing - https://nutritionalbalancing.org/center/htma/science/articles/htma-science-disease-prevention

Chinese Body Clock - https://foreverconscious.com/traditional-chinese-organ-body-clock

Dry Brushing How To - https://wellnessmama.com/26717/dry-brushing-skin/

Buteyko Breathing Guide - https://innovativemedicine.com/short-guide-breathing-right-buteyko-breathing-method

Emotional Freedom Technique (EFT) - https://www.eftuniverse.com/tutorial/eft-tapping-tutorial-center

Yoga Types for Chronic Illness - http://arogayoga.com/the-ultimate-cheat-sheet-on-yoga-for-chronic-illness/

Restorative Yoga Poses - https://www.sleepysantosha.com/blog/restorative-yoga-chronic-illness-warriors

Benefits of Tai Chi for Fibromyalgia -https://www.futuremedicine.com/doi/full/10.2217/pmt-2018-0021

Essential Oils Guide - https://theherbalacademy.com/a-guide-to-essential-oil-safety/

Benefits of Grounding - https://www.earthinginstitute.net/wp-content/uploads/2018/11/rx-earth-the-original-painkiller.pdf

Benefits of Infrared Heat - https://www.lifeextension.com/Magazine/2009/6/Far-Infrared-Therapy/Page-01

The Human Energy Sources (a guide to Chakras) - https://www.crystalherbs.com/chakras-subtle-bodies.asp

The Ultimate Guide To The Best Types Of Energy Healing - https://spiritradical.com/2017-08-30-50-energy-healing-modalities/

A guide to journalling - https://medium.com/find-focus/my-guide-to-journaling-4-techniques-i-practice-regularly-25d67217524c

BOOKS

Books that I recommend or have found helpful on my healing journey.

Sassy Holistics Foundational Care by Kristin Merizalde https://www.sassyholistics.com/foundational-care-ebook/

How to Liberate Yourself from Pain by Dr Grahame Brown with Denise Winn

Fibro Fix by Dr.David Brady

The Mindbody Prescription by John E Sarnos

The meaning of Pain by Nick Potter

The Power of Your Breath by Anders Olsson

Happy by Ferne Cotton

Using Positive Psychology every day by Ernest Bohlmeijer and Monique Hulsbergen

The 5-Second Rule by Mel Robbins

Mirror Work by Louise Hay

You Can Heal by Louise Hay

The Law of Divine Compensation by Marianne Williamson

Intergenerational Trauma: The Ghosts of Times Past by Thomas Hodge

ACKNOWLEDGEMENTS

This is the part of the book where I get to imagine myself up on stage, at some star-studded event, delivering a thank-you speech which starts with the words "this would not have been possible without..."

My "would not be possible without" list starts with my HE - Husband Extraordinaire. Without his unfailing support and encouragement, I wouldn't have got to the point of writing a book because I would have fuck all to write about. This man picked me up off the floor more times than I can count, he gave me the time and space to work through my healing process. Every time I hit a brick wall, he helped me to climb over it with a level of patience that would be a lesson to us all - I love you; I thank you.

I also thank my children for keeping me going, for reminding me that I was more than just an illness, for believing in my ability to write this book and championing me along the way. To my firstborn Alex, for the older-than-his-years wisdom and inspiring phone calls - just when I thought I was the parent. To the amazing Ellie, who is the epitome of having the courage to seek a brighter future- you are an inspiration my wonderful girl. And to Ethan, my still-at-homer who did his level best to keep his wants to a minimum when Mum was writing, saved me from a few technological meltdowns and ate more than his fair share of hastily prepared meals.

Much love and thanks to all the other lovely people in my life that have encouraged and supported me, not only in bringing this book to life but during the darker days- you know who you are. Special thanks to Michelle, my thrice-cooked chips and tea partner who has been drumming up business since the halfway line and to Charanjeet- because I can!

A huge shout out to the wonderful Naudia Lorraine. When we met 3 years ago, little did I know how much value you would add to my life. Friend, accountability partner to end all accountability partners, cheerleader, and BS caller- this book could not have progressed without you.

A big high five to all the amazing people I have met on my healing journey and whose wisdom I have learnt from; without them, this would be a very short book.

Finally, thank you to my editor, Elaine Roughton, who has helped shaped this book into my first literary achievement.

NOTES TO SELF

NOTES TO SELF

NOTES TO SELF

NOTES TO SELF

Printed in Poland
by Amazon Fulfillment
Poland Sp. z o.o., Wrocław

52891529R00139